CONTENTS

ACKNOWLEDGEMENTS

Photo credits

All photos supplied by Getty Images, apart from the following:

- p.17 Stromotion photo from Dartfish.
- p.18, p.40, p.55, p.60 (top), p.247 (top) Photodisc 10 (NT)
- p.37, p.43 (top), p.54, p.65, p.66, p.121 Photodisc 51 (NT)
- p.2 (top), p.8, p.23 (right), p.25, p.47, p.50, p.56, p.67, p.69, p.80, p.91, p.108, p.110, p.111, p.112, p.113, p.114, p.163, p.184 (bottom), p.196, p.232, p.261, p.262 photographed by Simon Punter.

Dear Student,

Welcome to the world of sport. We are very pleased that you have decided to study physical education and sport. Over the next two years you will acquire a wealth of knowledge about your own body and how it stands up to the stresses and strains of modern sport. We are sure that you are already aware that sport makes many physical demands. However, our bodies are extremely adaptable. With a well planned and sustained training programme you will certainly improve your sporting performance.

A thorough and wide-ranging knowledge of the workings of the body is essential for an understanding of sporting performance. Nevertheless your own performance will not improve merely by reading books about sport or by watching sport on television. It is on the games field, in the gym or in the swimming pool that your sporting knowledge is applied and becomes of real value.

We know that you will get a great deal of fun and enjoyment from your course as you improve your sporting skills. You will also have the opportunity to gain a valuable GCSE in Physical Education. For us and for thousands of people around the world, sport is a daily inspiration and a challenge. We hope that you too will continue to enjoy sport for the rest of your life, and we wish you every success on this course.

Paul Beashel
Andy Sibson
John Taylor

SYLLABUS STRUCTURE

This book has been written to match precisely the requirements of the Edexcel GCSE Physical Education syllabus. At the start of each chapter we have set out the necessary key words, together with a summary of the syllabus requirements. At the end of each chapter there is a set of Edexcel examination-style questions.

Sporting activities and analysis of performance

The ability to observe and accurately analyse sporting performance is at the heart of this course. This section helps you develop these skills. You will also learn how to take training sessions and improve your leadership skills. You will be expected to demonstrate all of these skills as part of your GCSE assessment.

Exercise and training

In this section you will learn about the many factors which affect participation and performance. You will develop your understanding of the reasons for taking part in sport, the various types of fitness, the principles and different methods of training, your diet, health and hygiene. You will also be given clear guidance and support to enable you to produce your six-week Personal Exercise Plan (PEP).

Safety aspects and risk assessment in sport and physical activity

Sport is not only exciting it is also potentially dangerous. You will need to know how to assess the risks in a wide range of sporting activities in order to prevent accidents and injuries. You must also be able to recognise the basic signs and symptoms of the most common sporting injuries and conditions.

Applied anatomy and physiology

You are more likely to be able to improve sporting performance if you have a sound knowledge of how the body works. This section deals with the body systems most important in sporting action.

The world of sport covers a wide variety of activities. Enjoyment is the main reason why we take part in sport and physical recreation. We do not know in which sports you will specialise. Therefore, we have designed our book to give you the knowledge, principles and skills that underpin sporting performance. We recognise that we all learn in different ways, so we have included many different types of activities throughout the book. We hope that not only will you enjoy them but that they will stimulate you and lead you to success in your Edexcel Physical Education examination.

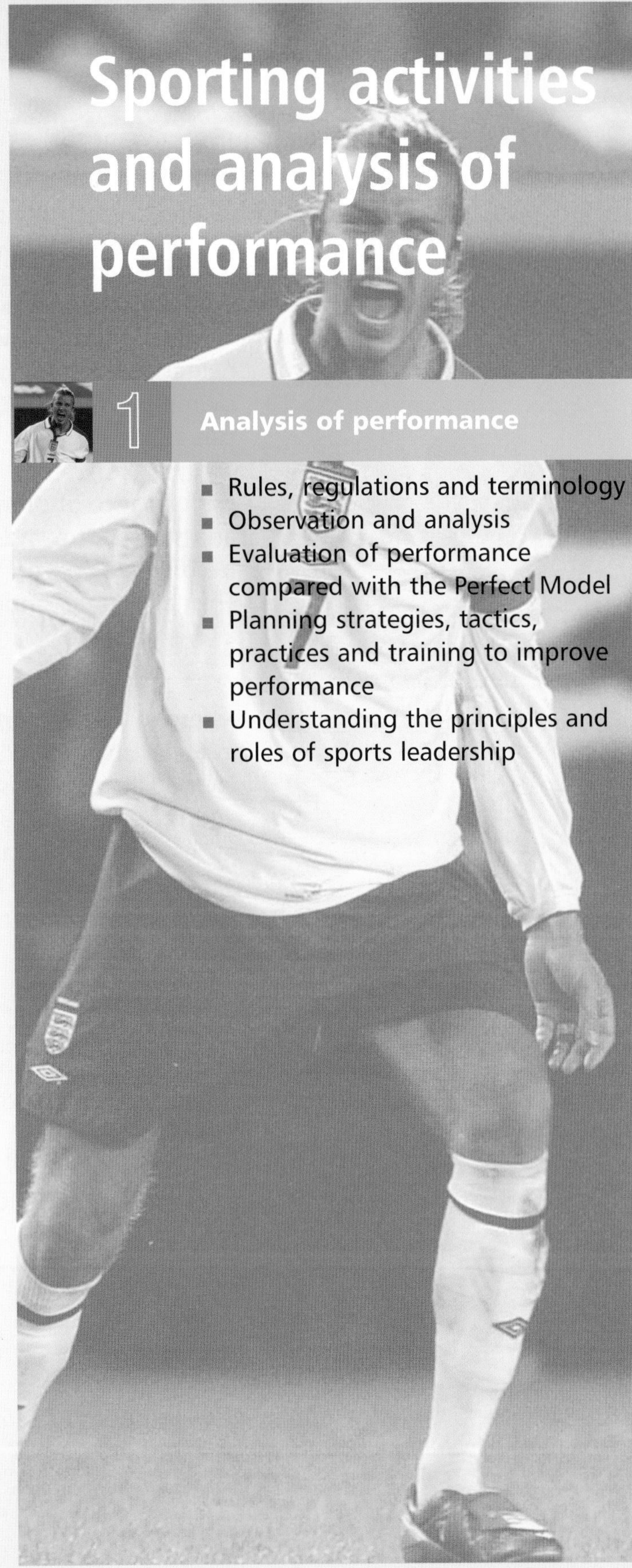

Sporting activities and analysis of performance

1 Analysis of performance

- Rules, regulations and terminology
- Observation and analysis
- Evaluation of performance compared with the Perfect Model
- Planning strategies, tactics, practices and training to improve performance
- Understanding the principles and roles of sports leadership

1 Analysis of performance

All of us involved in sport want to improve our **performance**. We train hard and practise our skills so that in competition we can produce our very best. To improve our performance we must first be able to **analyse** it. Learning the skills of analysing sporting action will help us to improve our own performance. We can also learn to analyse the performance of others and so work towards becoming a coach. This takes time, effort and experience.

Assessing analysis of performance

In this part of your GCSE course, you will be assessed on your ability to analyse your own and others' performance and to suggest ways to improve. Although you should have a good understanding of all sports and events you can select one sport for assessment purposes. You must be able to demonstrate your knowledge and understanding in five areas of coaching and leadership. These are:

- rules, regulations and terminology
- observation and analysis
- evaluation of performance compared with the Perfect Model
- planning strategies, tactics, practices and training to improve performance
- understanding the principles and roles of sports leadership.

activity

Analysing performance

Watch a group of your classmates playing a small sided game, for example, indoor hockey or netball. Try to decide who is the most effective player. Now explain why his or her performance is so effective. Is the player fitter? Faster-thinking? Harder-working? More skilful?

You can use the checklist on Worksheet 1 to help.

KEYWORDS

Analyse: to examine in detail and to explain

Arousal: level of alertness

Data: facts or information

Drill: training by repeating a technique or skill

Evaluate: to decide what is good and what needs to improve

Feedback: information about the outcome of a performance

Game plan: a set of tactics for use in a particular game

Motivation: determination to achieve

Observe: to watch carefully

Perfect Model: a mental image of the correct technique

Performance: how well a task is completed

Skill: the learned ability to choose and perform the right techniques at the right time

Strategy: long-term plan for success in sport

Tactics: methods used to put strategies into a game

Technique: basic movement in sport.

Key to Exam Success

For your GCSE you will need to know:

- the rules and regulations of your chosen sport and how to apply them as a player, coach, referee or judge. You should be able to use technical terms when describing your sport
- how to observe and analyse a performance and how to give feedback to the performer
- how to evaluate a performance, how to compare it with the Perfect Model and how to provide comprehensive and detailed feedback
- how to plan strategies, tactics, practices and training to improve performance with evidence from your own Personal Exercise Programme (PEP)
- the importance of leadership in sport and the different roles of sports leadership.

“ KEY THOUGHT ”

'Preparation is the key to success in sport.'

Rules, regulations and terminology

activity

What would happen if...?

Imagine if these sports changed their laws:

- cricket – no lbw law
- football – no offside law
- hockey – the ball is allowed to touch the feet during play
- athletics – no lanes for the 200m
- tennis – no second service.

Discuss how each sport might change as a result of these new laws.

Think about your favourite sport. Have any rule changes been made in recent years? You may need to research the official rules.

Why do you need to know the rules and regulations?

You will often be asked to referee, umpire or score during PE lessons. GCSE assessment includes your ability to apply the rules and regulations, also called laws, as an official in charge of a match. When refereeing you must think about the rules of the activity and how to make sure that the players obey them. Every time you are asked to referee you should take the opportunity to practise, as you will then improve. As an official you need to show the players that you understand the rules thoroughly. They also want to see you make confident decisions and to control the game fairly but firmly.

Your teacher will assess your knowledge and understanding of the rules of your chosen sport.

You will need to demonstrate this knowledge by refereeing or umpiring a game or a match. You will also be asked questions about the rules and basic tactics. You should take a pride in knowing the rules and also playing and refereeing fairly at all times. Ultimate Frisbee has included this idea in the official rules of the game. There is no referee. All players – even at the world championships – referee the game as they play!

Why do you need to keep up to date with the rules of your sport?

You should also keep up to date with rule changes. Every governing body reviews the rules of its sport on a regular basis. It may change the rules to make the game safer; for example, in rugby union, players must now stay on their feet at rucks. Rule changes may also be introduced to speed up the game; for example, in volleyball, teams now score a point every time they win a rally, not just when they win from their own serve. Often changes affect the way that the game is played and coached. In 1992 FIFA changed the rules so that goalkeepers could not pick up a ball that was passed to them by their own team. This stopped teams wasting time or using the goalkeeper as a 'safety' player. Defenders had to change their tactics as a result. Attackers began to run down back passes instead of leaving the goalkeeper to pick up the ball. The pace of the game increased and now we see many goalkeepers being forced into mistakes.

activity

Sports quiz

Choose a sport. It would be good if this is your Analysis of Performance assessment sport. Research the rules and produce a ten-question quiz to test participants' knowledge of the rules. Look for some obscure rules or situations to baffle your friends. If you like, create your quiz on a computer in order to make it more interactive. DataPower and Powerpoint programs could be used.

Why do coaches modify rules?

Sometimes coaches and teachers modify the rules of the game in training to develop skills or to create a new challenge. In some football games, players may only be allowed to control the ball with one or two touches in order to encourage movement and passing. Some rules will complicate the game too much for beginners; for example, in PE lessons the three-second and other time rules are rarely used in basketball, and in hockey lessons young players do not have to worry about offside. Some sports have different rules for junior games: for example, high fives netball, which is a five-a-side game with players rotating positions and roles.

What is terminology?

When you talk about your sport you will often use technical terms such as 'lbw' or 'offside'. These technical terms are called terminology. You probably know a lot of sports terminology already, but if you are going to coach effectively you need to know which terms to use to describe your sport.

Look at this example of terminology from badminton:

> 'You may play a forehand or a backhand shot. It may be a clear, a drive, a drop shot, a hairpin drop shot or a smash.'

You should be able to describe each shot and suggest to a player when he or she could use it as a tactic. Once everybody knows the terminology it is much easier to talk about the sport. Terminology includes examples of techniques, skills, strategies, tactics and rules.

Observation and analysis

The first stage in coaching is observing and analysing a performance. We have to watch a sportsperson in action and try to break down the movement into parts. If we watched a long jump we would need to look at the run-up, the take-off, the action in the air and the landing. Only when we have completed this part can we go on to evaluate the performance and explain to the performer how improvement can be made. At this second stage we can compare the jump in our mind with what we would like to see and then suggest to the athlete how he or she could do better.

Many coaches today use technology to help them to analyse performance. However, most of the time you will have to carry out live observation. That is to say, you must watch a player performing and then make decisions about the quality of the performance. This requires

activity

Terminology test

Are there any special terms in your chosen sport? Think about equipment, rules, techniques and strategies. Produce a list of terms on small cards, then pass the cards amongst your class. Each person has to explain the term to the rest of the class. If they do not know the answer you will have to make sure that you can explain it.

a lot of planning and practice. You can use a four-step approach to learn how to **observe** and **analyse**.

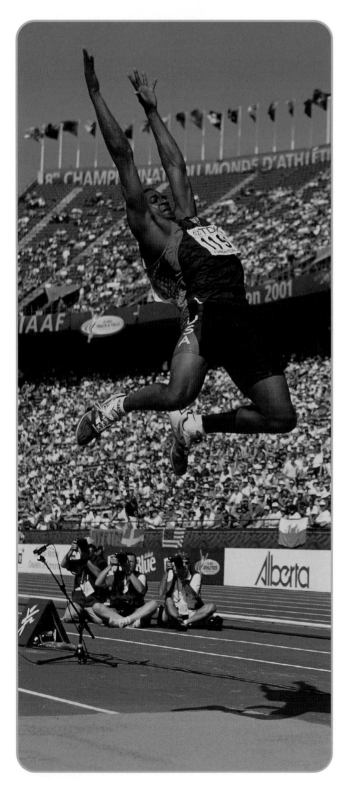

The four-step approach

The four-step approach begins with observing a simple activity involving one person. It builds up to a complex situation with many players in action.

Step 1
Observe and analyse a single technique – for example, a forward roll. In this situation you can control the environment, decide when the roll takes place and where you should stand to watch.

Step 2
Observe and analyse a single technique in action – for example, a forehand drive in tennis. This is a technique that requires a feed, that is someone to throw the ball for the player to hit. You are still in control of most of the situation, but the feed will vary and the player has to move to play the shot. There is much more to look at and to analyse.

Step 3
Observe an individual competitive performance – for example, a player in a badminton match. You can decide where to stand to observe the player, but you cannot decide which shots will be played. You will have to concentrate on just a few parts of the performance or you will get very confused. You will now be observing skill and tactics.

Step 4
Observe a competitive team performance – for example, a basketball team playing a match. In this situation you must focus on one or two aspects of performance and observe them carefully. Both team skill and team tactics can be observed.

Step 1: How do you analyse a specific technique?

You must know what the very best technique looks like. We call this the **Perfect Model**. You can then compare what you are seeing with the Perfect Model in your head. To build up this image you might use books, photographs, video footage or an expert performer. Your PE teacher, or one of your group, may be able to demonstrate during a lesson.

Before observing the technique you must break it down into a number of simple parts. You can then concentrate on each part in turn as the performer repeats the technique. Making a list of the different parts of the technique will help you to analyse in detail.

For example, if we were looking at a forward roll, we would look at the starting position, especially the hands and the head, the shape of the body during the roll and the finishing position, particularly of the arms. We would compare each part of the movement with the same part from our image of the Perfect Model.

You must decide where to stand to get the best view before observing any performance. You could view from either side, from the front or from behind, and also in some cases from above or below. The position you choose will depend on the specific technique that you are observing, the nature of the sport and on your knowledge of the sport. An experienced javelin coach will first note whether the athlete is right- or left-

handed and will then view the run-up and throw from a number of different positions. Safety would also be an important consideration for the coach in this event.

Step 2: Analysing a technique in action

When observing a technique in action you should use a help sheet to list the points you will be looking for before you begin.

Here is an example of a technique to analyse the overhead clear in badminton.

You might want to look separately at:

- movement into position
- foot placement and body position under the shuttlecock
- arm and racket preparation
- hitting action and follow-through.

Before observing this technique you must decide who is going to feed the shuttle to the player. A feeder in this context means another player or coach who throws, kicks or places the ball or shuttle in the best position so that the technique can be practised. If the feed is not accurate, the player will not be able to play the shot that you wish to see. Top coaches in sports such as volleyball have to pass tests to make sure that they can feed a ball accurately to the right place for each technique to be practised. When practising, the feeder has a very important role and should be told exactly how and where to feed. He or she must take the job very seriously.

Using ICT

Observation and analysis are much easier if you can slow down the action and study it in detail. Using ICT can help you to do this. There are many CD-ROMS and DVDs available which show footage of different sports. The web has examples too. If you have the facilities, you can make your own video using editing software. The simplest way of slowing down the action is to use a digital video camera and to watch the technique on the camera LCD screen.

activity

Where to stand

Choose a technique from a sport of your choice and consider where you should stand to observe it. Is it best to stay in one place? Do you need to observe from a number of different angles to get an overall picture – for example, from the side, the front and from behind? Are you better placed at ground level or should you observe from above?

activity

Observing a technique in action

Select a technique from a sport that requires a feeder. Write down a list of the parts of the technique that you wish to observe. Decide who is to feed and give precise instructions to the feeder. Then observe the technique in action and analyse the performance.

Step 3: How do you analyse a competitive individual performance?

A performer will use a range of techniques and skills very rapidly during competition. Your analysis must focus on these and also consider a number of other factors, such as fitness, tactics and strategies. Better performers will know both their own and their competitors' strengths and weaknesses. As a result they will be able to develop a plan or **strategy** in order to win. To achieve their strategy they will decide which particular **tactics** they can use during the competition. For example, suppose that a 1,500-metre runner knows that she has a much faster finish than the other competitors in a race. Her strategy is to have the race run at as slow a pace as possible in order that she has enough energy left for her sprint finish. Her tactic will probably be to take the lead and then try to keep the pace as slow as possible. Her opponents may have other ideas and she may have to rethink her tactics as the race progresses.

In planning your observation you should think about your performer's plan, performance and evaluation.

The plan

What overall strategy does the performer have and what tactics are they attempting to use? When you know these you can look at how effective they are within the game. If they are not effective you must look for reasons.

The performance

This includes the techniques and skills in action. By looking at these you can see if poor performance or technique is preventing your player from being skilful and carrying out his or her tactics.

The fitness level of your player is also a vital factor. Tired people perform less well. You must look carefully at fitness levels. If in doubt, ask the performer how he or she feels.

The evaluation

Good decision-making within the game is essential. If your performer is

activity

Analysing an individual competitive performance

Observe a group member playing a competitive game and assess his or her performance. Use the three factors, the plan, the performance and the evaluation, to focus your observation. Discuss your findings with the player and suggest ways to improve.

anticipating the opponent's moves and selecting successful moves then his or her performance will be good. You must analyse the decisions made by your player. This is especially important if your player is losing and needs your help as a coach to select better tactics.

Step 4: How do you analyse a competitive team performance?

In a team game you can observe either an individual player within the team or the performance of the team as a whole.

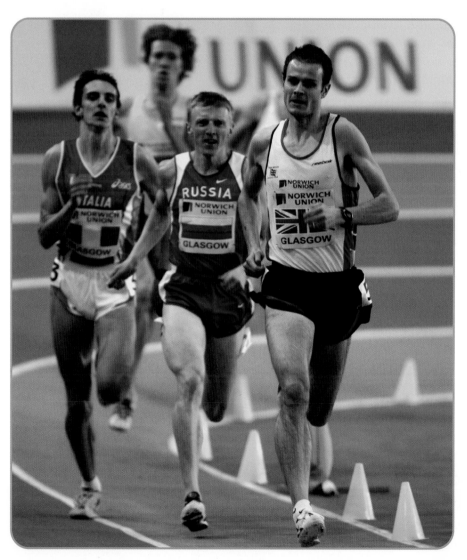

Individual performance

If you are focusing on an individual player you should not only look at his or her individual competitive performance, but at his or her contribution to the team effort. This will differ according to the sport, but might include running off the ball to support in attack, supporting in defence by covering others and getting back to mark opponents. The attitude of the player should also be assessed – for example, whether he or she encourages or criticises others – as this can play an important part in team games.

activity

Using data to analyse performance

Choose a sport and decide on the data to be gathered in order to analyse team performance. This may be the number of successful passes, tackles, attacks, etc. Have at least two observers for each team or player. Observe a team or player for a period of time and note everything that happens on a checklist. The checklist below can be used for football or hockey but you will need to adapt it to suit other sports. You may also wish to observe a particular player using a similar checklist.

Team performance

You can also observe and analyse the team performance as a whole. A team will have an overall strategy and a chosen set of tactics. You will need to decide which aspect of the performance will be your focus; top teams have a number of assistant coaches who only look at attack or defence. If you try to look at everything you will find that there are too many things happening for you to analyse easily.

The example below from football shows how **data** could be gathered on a number of aspects of a team performance:

Date:	Period of observation (minutes):	Tally total
Aspects observed	Record each incident with a tally mark	
Pass completed		
Possession lost		
Successful tackle		
Unsuccessful tackle		
Shot off target		
Shot on target		

How do you analyse a strategy?

A **strategy** is a plan for success in sport. A team of talented individuals will need to work together on their tactics and strategies to ensure success. Without a strategy team performance will suffer.

You can gather data to analyse the effectiveness of a strategy. Coaches and players have to select strategies in many sports. Sometimes the strategies are very different:

- A tennis player might stay at the baseline throughout a match or serve and volley – that is, run to the net to cut off shots from their opponent.
- Badminton pairs will often play 'front and back', with one player taking the short shots whist the other takes those to the rear of the court. Others choose to play side-to-side, with each player covering one side of the court from the net to the baseline.
- Basketball teams might use a 'man-to-man' defence or 'zone' defence.
- Some athletes in middle distance events will run as fast as they can from the start and hope to 'hang on' to their lead. Others will pace themselves then speed up and sprint to the finish.
- Throwers and jumpers often complete their first attempt at less than 100% effort to make sure that they do not produce a foul. Others try their hardest each time, but sometimes 'no-jump' or 'no-throw' throughout the competition.

Wise coaches will ensure that players are able to switch strategies and/or tactics to suit specific situations.

activity

Analysing a strategy

Consider this example from football and then decide how you could observe, gather data and advise the managers.

Mickey and Johanne are two experienced football managers in a local league.

Mickey believes that his team will be more successful in getting the ball into the opposition penalty area if his goalkeeper always plays the ball out to a full back to restart play. He thinks that his players will keep possession and create scoring opportunities for his strikers in the opposition penalty area.

Johanne has told his goalkeeper always to kick it as far up the pitch as possible. He thinks that this will lead to more scoring opportunities in the opposition penalty area.

Neither manager has any facts to back up their beliefs.

Can you find some facts to support one of the managers?

You could gather data by observing a number of live football matches on TV. You will need to decide what to look for, and create a rota of observers so that each match has at least two people watching the entire 90 minutes. Once you have collected enough information you will know which is the best strategy.

You might wish to send the results to your local club to help their manager!

Evaluation of performance compared with the Perfect Model

We have seen that the first stage in coaching is observing and analysing performance. The second stage is to evaluate the performance and to provide feedback to the performer.

- **Evaluating** a performance means deciding what is good and what needs improvement.
- Providing **feedback** means giving information about the performance to the performer.

Giving feedback is a very important stage as the performer needs to know how to improve. The coach must be careful to provide accurate feedback in a positive way. Providing incorrect advice or giving feedback in a thoughtless manner can damage the performer's confidence. A good coach will always allow the performer the opportunity to comment on his or her performance. You can use the coaching model on the right to guide your observation, analysis, evaluation and feedback.

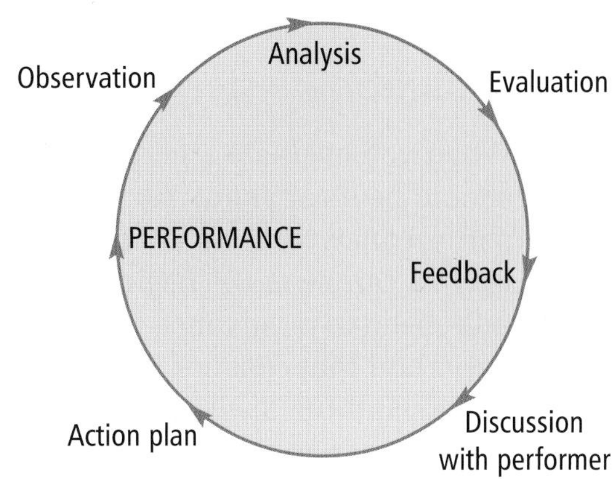

Back to basics

For this activity you need to put yourself in the position of a complete beginner. Attempt a simple technique in your chosen sport – for example, a set shot in basketball or netball, a serve in tennis or badminton, or a penalty kick in football – but use your non-preferred hand or foot. Do you have to think about the action? Are you able to perform it as quickly? How different was it? What expectations do you have of yourself when playing like this?

Coach the basics

Try coaching a group member to perform a simple technique with the non-preferred hand or foot. How easy is it to correct errors?

Evaluating a performance

When you evaluate a performance you should be clear about the standard of performance that you are expecting. Players can be at the beginner, intermediate or advanced level. It is important that coaches and players understand the level at which the players are performing. A lack of understanding can lead to unreasonable expectations of novice players. This in turn can create pressure and tension, which affects performance and slows the learning process.

The Perfect Model

We have seen earlier (page 8) that in order to analyse a particular technique we need to have a clear picture in our mind of what the technique looks like when performed very well. We call this mental image the Perfect Model. When we watch the performances of either ourselves (by means of video) or others, we compare these performances with our mental image of the Perfect Model. We gain our mental image of the Perfect Model by watching good performers in competitive action, either live or on video. Video footage is particularly useful if we are able to slow it down or freeze-frame it. This helps us to see exactly what is happening and helps us to understand why the movements we have in our mind are particularly effective.

Strengths and weaknesses

Whenever you observe a performance you should look for strengths and weaknesses. When giving feedback it is important to tell the performer about the good things you have seen before talking about the weaknesses.

Feedback

Feedback is essential for skill learning. We would find it very difficult to improve without knowledge of how well we are doing. However, when we are coaching we must take care to give the right kind of feedback at the right time if we are to get the best from our performers. The feedback given will mainly depend upon the ability and experience of the performers.

How much feedback?

Beginners only need a small amount of verbal or visual feedback, that is comments or demonstrations. They find

it difficult to use their own internal feelings about their performance and they cannot handle a great deal of detailed information. As performers become more experienced they get the 'feel' of successful movements and they can rely more on internal feedback, backed up by their coach's observations.

When is feedback given?
Comments should be made at key moments, but not after every attempt. Sportspeople will usually be trying to do the right thing and will know when they have made a mistake. Coaches should always allow a little time for performers to consider their performance. They should also check that performers have understood what was expected of them. It could be that they did not understand earlier instructions, or they might have been trying to achieve something different. Above all, feedback needs to motivate as well as correct the performer.

Using technology and data to improve performance

There are a number of different types of aid that coaches can use to help improve performance. These are:

- technical information
- video recordings of player performance
- statistical analysis
- fitness monitoring and analysis equipment
- interactive white boards.

You may have the opportunity to try some of these during your GCSE course. They can provide a lot of evidence to support your feedback to performers.

Which is the Perfect Model?
Working in pairs, look at the two long jumpers in the photographs. One is the Perfect Model. The other is also a very good performer. Discuss the strengths and weaknesses of each performer with your partner. What do they both have in common? Look at the take off, action in the air and landing.

Planning strategies, tactics, practices and training to improve performance

After observing, analysing and evaluating performance, you must plan to improve performance. You have looked at performances, compared them with the Perfect Model and decided what needs to be done to improve them. Now you have to consider how you can ensure that this improvement takes place. You must be able to plan practices and training sessions to improve fitness, techniques and skills. You will also need to show that you understand the strategies and tactics of your sport. Chapter 5, Principles of Training, shows you how to construct an exercise programme and how to organise a training session. Your Personal Exercise Programme (PEP) will include research into training methods. In this section you will learn about the practical side of coaching.

activity

Looking at arousal

Work in groups of about 12. Each player in turn attempts three free shots in netball or basketball under normal conditions. They then repeat it with a supportive audience, a totally silent audience and a hostile audience. The rest of the group provide the audience.

Discuss the results. Did the audience affect performance? How did the performer feel about each type of audience?

How do coaches plan to improve performance?

It is vital that coaches know their players so that they can plan programmes that match the player's level of ability and experience. Analysis of performance plays a large part in enabling a coach to prepare training sessions. It provides specific information which enables him or her to select activities and drills to suit the needs of the players. A good coach will also understand the personality of each player and will know how best to motivate each individual in the team.

Motivation and arousal

In sport the level of motivation is called **arousal**. If your arousal level is not high enough, you may feel bored and you will perform badly. If your arousal gets too high you may become anxious and worried. This creates tension, which causes your performance to become less effective. Coaches must look very carefully at the personality of different players and the nature of the sport before deciding on the level of motivation needed. For example, most snooker players need support to remain calm and focused before a major competition. Increasing their level of arousal is likely to lead to poor performance.

Inverted U theory

Performance: high, low
Arousal: low, moderate, high

How do coaches improve different types of skill?

We can put skills in sport into two different groups.

- **closed** skills are skills not affected by the sporting environment.
- **open** skills are skills that are affected by the whole sporting environment such as other players and the weather.

Closed skills

Closed skills are relatively easy to train. In gymnastics and archery, for example, competition is very similar to training. Closed skills are also found within 'open' games, for example, bowling the ball in cricket, taking penalties in football or taking a free throw in basketball. In all these activities the coach has to try to create the pressure that a player may feel within a competitive situation if the player is to be fully match-prepared. This can be done by:

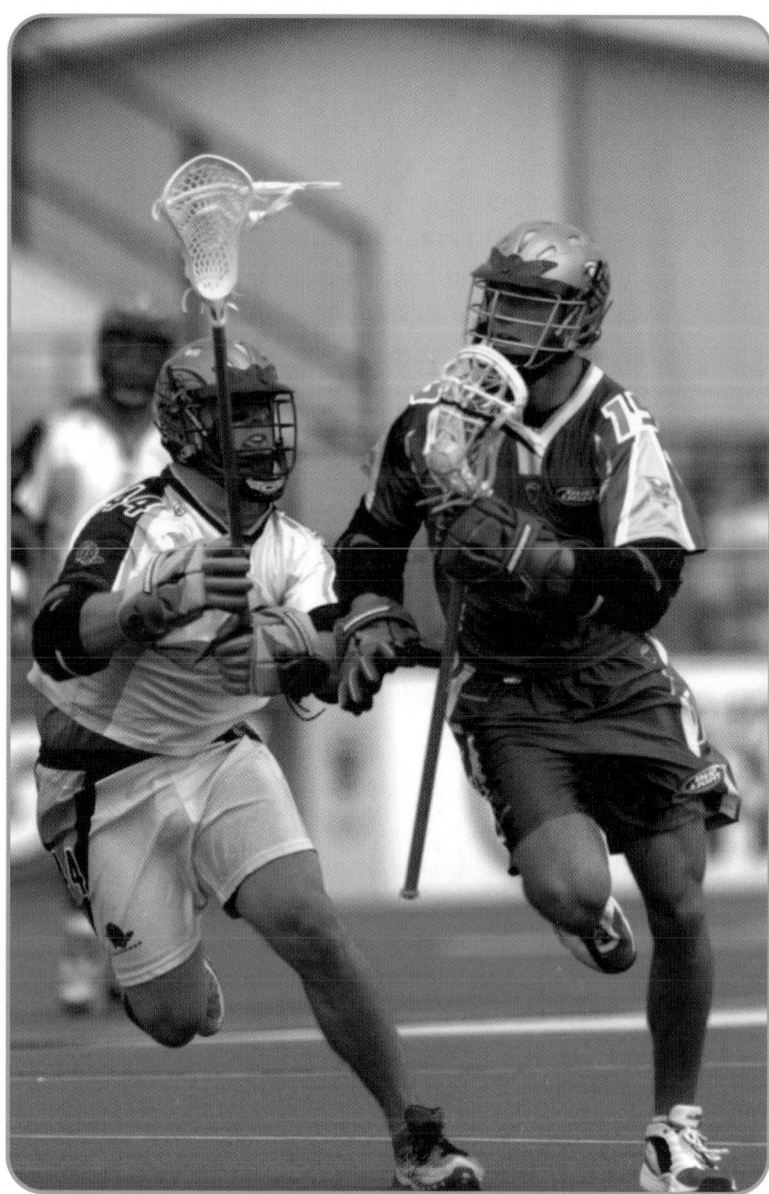

- setting 'closed' drills when the player is tired
- creating pressure by rewarding success or punishing failure (in the sporting sense, of doing an extra run)
- simulating the match with recorded crowd noise
- creating pressure by having team mates talking at, and trying to put off, the performer.

Open skills

Open skills are performed within open activities where it is difficult to predict what will happen next. Most sports are open in this sense, including invasion games and racket sports. Coaches need to provide their performers with as wide a variety of experiences as possible so that they can practise their skills in many different situations. To help them perform skilfully and develop tactical understanding, the coach needs to allow them to make their own decisions during game play. The best coaches know when to advise and when to let their players take control for themselves.

Putting skills into action

Tactical skill is the ability to choose the right plan of action when taking part in sport. Different types of sport require us to use different strategies and tactics. In order to develop our tactical skill we need to understand the needs of our sport.

What are strategies and tactics in sport?

- **Strategies** are plans that we think out in advance of the sporting competition. They are methods of putting us in the best position to defeat our opponents.
- **Tactics** are what we use to put our strategies into action. Tactics can also be worked out in advance, but they will often need to be adapted to the real situation during competition. Tactics involve planning and team work.

Strategies and tactics will be very different for different types of games. For example, an invasion game like rugby involves large numbers of players, a variety of set plays as well as an opportunity for individuals to respond to many different situations. It gives many choices to players, such as kicking, passing or running with the ball. By contrast, in a judo competition there is only one opponent to worry about and there are a limited number of attacking moves to make or defend.

Beginners are not able to cope with complex strategies. They will need simple tactics such as 'Pass the ball to a player who is free'. More skilful players are able to give time and attention to strategies and tactics.

What sort of strategies and tactics are used in sport?

Strategies and tactics become more important as the level of competition increases.

When developing a strategy the coach will focus on:

- teamwork
- the game plan
- team formation
- restarts and set plays.

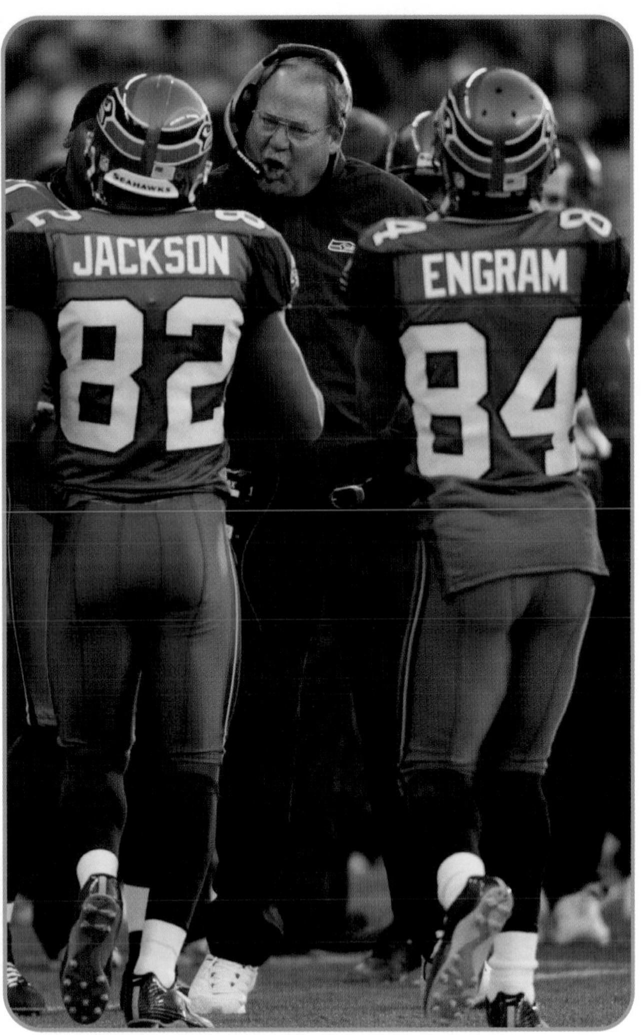

Teamwork

A successful team will have good teamwork. This means that all members of the team understand the agreed strategy. They also put the tactics for each game into practice by working as a unit. Managers, coaches and captains have important roles to play in teamwork. The motivation to work hard for each other has to be developed through training and team-building activities. A coach will also try to make sure that all the players are in their best positions during the game. For example, a tall, powerful footballer is likely to be in the centre of defence or attack, not expected to play in the middle of the midfield area where a quicker, more mobile player is required.

Game plan

In some matches and competitions, players and teams talk of a **game plan**. This is the set of tactics for use in a particular game. The game plan will be based on their own strengths and the weaknesses of the opposition.

Team formation

Teams can use different formations; that is, the players can take up different positions on the field of play. Some sports have rules limiting where the players can move during the game. In netball these restrictions present certain problems to be solved. In basketball there are few restrictions on the positions of players, so teams can be more flexible. Everyone discusses the formations in football. Some teams choose to have four defenders, four midfield players and two attackers (4:4:2). Others play with three central defenders, five midfielders and two attackers (3:5:2). Attack-minded teams or teams trying to score an equaliser in a cup-tie might play 4:3:3 or even 2:5:3.

Restarts and set plays

All games have restarts. In net games these are the serves. In invasion games they are free hits, throw-ins, corners, scrums, etc. These restarts give the team an opportunity to have free possession of the ball. At these times many teams use set plays which are practised during training.

How to develop strategies and tactics

To develop a strategy you will need to know:

- your own strengths and weaknesses
- the strengths and weaknesses of the opposition
- your level of fitness
- the importance of the competition
- any important environmental factors.

In a net game such as tennis, you might have considered all the factors above and decided your strategy. Let us say it is to move your opponent around the court in order to get her out of position and to tire her, allowing you to play a winning shot or to force an error. The tactic you use to achieve this might be to serve wide on both sides of the court and to come in to the net quickly.

In the game you might find that your tactics are not working because your opponent is returning your serve very well. In this case you will have to decide whether or not to continue with the same tactic or change it. If you change it you might stay at the baseline, but try to play disguised drop shots to draw the opponent forward and then lob or pass the ball beyond her. Alternatively, you might notice that her backhand is weak so you could decide to play most of your shots to her backhand side. Your tactics must be flexible to respond to the situations you meet during each game.

activity

Changing tactics

Working in groups, consider the following situations and make suggestions for strategies and tactics to help the individual player or improve team performance. You must explain to the whole group how you think your tactic or strategy will make a difference.

1 Your basketball team is losing heavily at half time. One player of average height but excellent all-round court movement has scored most of the opposition's points. Your zone defence has been unable to cope with him.

2 Your hockey team is winning 1–0 with 15 minutes remaining in the match. The opposition are playing almost entirely in your half. Your defenders are tired and keep hitting the ball away, but the opposition regain possession very quickly.

3 You are a middle distance runner. Both you and your rival have personal best times of 5 minutes for the mile (4 laps of the track). You plan to race at 75 seconds per lap and then out-sprint your rival to the finish. You begin the race and stay at the shoulder of the leader. However, after the first lap your rival speeds up to a pace of 65 seconds per lap.

Training to improve performance

The objective of every training session must be to improve performance. Your analysis of performance will provide a focus for your training sessions. Each session must be well planned. The coach must guide the players through techniques and into skills. They must also develop strategies and tactics in preparation for competition. The players' fitness will have to be maintained or improved. Training must include three essential parts:

- Warm up
- Main activity including skills training, fitness training, game and tactical development
- Warm down.

Warm up and warm down

These are an essential part of any training session. They must be linked closely to the sporting activity. Full details are given in Chapter 5, pages 90–91.

Skills training

Skills practices in sport are often called **drills**. They are used to teach techniques and skills. A drill is a movement or number of movements that are repeated until they can be performed easily. You might practise techniques individually even if you are training for a team game. Small groups, or units, might also practise their skills separately from the rest of the team. An example might be the defenders working on defending crosses in hockey.

A series of techniques are often linked into a skilled movement that mirrors the game situation. This is a very important aspect of training because skill practices should always reflect the reality of the game situation.

How to design a drill

If a drill is to work it must be prepared carefully. Before the coach begins to lead the drill, every aspect of it must be planned and all equipment must be in place. This checklist can be used to ensure that no detail is missed when you plan your drills. By answering all the following questions you will have prepared well.

activity

Design a drill

Training sessions often involve identifying areas for improvement and then practising skills or techniques. With your teacher, decide on a technique that could be developed and design a drill to teach this technique to your group. You must plan the drill in enough detail for someone else to be able to teach it.

- What is the drill trying to teach or improve?
- How many players are involved? What do they each do (feeder, performer, coach, ball collector)?
- What equipment is needed (bibs, balls, cones, goals, rackets, nets, posts, etc.)?
- What does the drill look like? Draw a diagram and write a key.
- What instructions will need to be given to explain the drill? Write them out.
- How many times do the players repeat the drill?
- What happens after the first player has completed the drill? Where does he or she go next?
- How do the players know if they have been successful?

Finally, you should evaluate your drill after it has been completed, as follows:

- Did it achieve what you set out to do?
- Were all the players able to follow your instructions?
- How would you change it if you did it again?

Types of skill training

Once a technique has been taught and learned, skill training can take one of four different forms, depending on the amount of opposition required.

Unopposed

We can learn techniques more easily if there is no opposition. In basketball, the shooter can practise the jump shot unopposed at first, and opposition can be introduced gradually as technique improves. In volleyball, team organisation often takes some time to learn. This is best practised with the coach feeding the ball rather than within the game itself, when the team will be under pressure from the opposition.

Passive opposition

Opposition is essential for some techniques to be learned. However, in the early stages of learning it is often best for opposition to be static or minimal. Learning how to tackle in rugby is far easier if the player with the ball stands still! This is known as passive opposition. It is much easier to learn how to keep control of a ball whilst dribbling in and out of a line of opponents when the opponents are not trying to steal it from you. Passive opposition drills are often used with beginners.

Active opposition

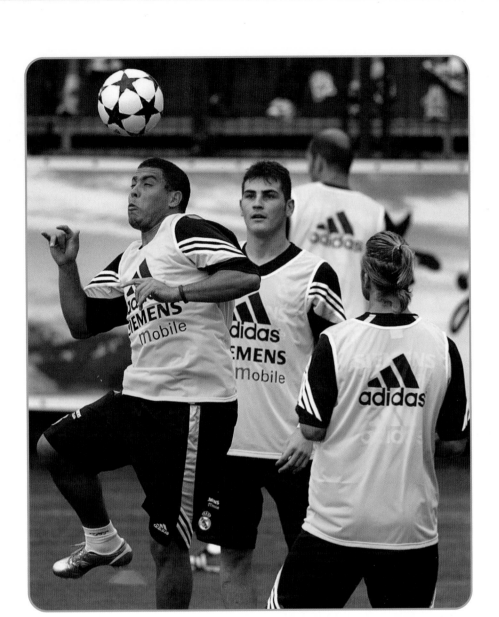

In order to make practices more realistic, the opposition must be real but limited in order for the techniques and skills to be learned. A common example of active opposition in football and hockey is the 3 *v* 1 possession drill in a grid square, where the player in the middle has to try to get the ball.

Pressure training

Pressure training is a method for putting a technique or skill under stress. It should only be used when a performer has developed the technique or skill to a high level. Pressure can be applied in a number of different ways:

- You might make the performer work very hard for a period of time. This combines skill and fitness work. As the performer tires, the skill level will drop. The practice will increase fitness levels and help the performer to play when tired. For example, in football, practice in heading the ball can be alternated with sprinting.

activity

Designing practices

Choose a technique or skill from the sport of your choice. Describe how you would set up a number of drills to improve performance using the techniques outlined above. Then try them out with your group. You may find that some of your group cope well with all types of practice. Others will find that their performance drops off as the pressure increases.

- Pressure can also be applied by forcing the performer to react very quickly. In basketball the jump shooter could receive the ball from a player who is between him and the basket. As he receives it, the player runs at the shooter and attempts to block the shot. The pressure to receive the ball, prepare and execute the shot in a short period of time is similar to the game situation. It will lead to improvement within the game.

How are games used to develop strategies and tactics?

Skills need to be transferred from the practice situation into the game situation. Practice games also let coaches try out strategies and practise tactics.

- **Modified** games give each player plenty of action and lots of time with the ball – for example, five-a-side hockey.
- **Conditioned** games have rule changes that focus on a particular skill or tactic. For example, two-touch football can develop good control and passing, but it also encourages support for the player with the ball. Conditioning the game can extend to providing areas of the pitch where the player with the ball cannot be tackled. If these are down both wings the teams are encouraged to play the ball wide because they can then keep possession until they wish to cross the ball. Once the habit of looking to create width in attack has been learned, the players will try to introduce it into normal games.

The use of games within training sessions also helps coaches to assess players' strengths, find out weaknesses and plan future sessions.

How do we plan and use fitness training?

Players must take responsibility for their own personal fitness. This includes eating and drinking sensibly, avoiding smoking and recreational drugs and getting plenty of rest. Nevertheless fitness training should be part of all training sessions. Further details can be found on pages 80–94. It can be part of the skills practices in the form of pressure drills, but should not exhaust players so much that they cannot concentrate on their skills. Regular fitness testing provides valuable feedback to coaches and players.

Understanding the principles and roles of sports leadership

When you analyse a team performance you look to see who influences the game. Players who influence those around them are leaders. Coaches, officials and others involved in sport can also be leaders. Your teacher will assess your own leadership ability, based upon your work during the GCSE course. It will include how well you demonstrate leadership through refereeing, organising and playing sport. You must always remember that good leadership has a direct impact on performance. If a game is refereed poorly, or a practice is disorganised, the players involved will not play to the best of their ability.

activity

Organising a club tournament

Imagine that you have to organise a tournament for your club involving players or teams from the surrounding area. Make a list of all the things that need to be done before the day of the tournament. Then list all the jobs that will have to be done on the day. Do not forget the clearing up afterwards! You will not be able to do everything, so divide all the jobs between a number of people. You can give them job titles, such as secretary, referee coordinator, referee, scorer, equipment organiser, equipment helper, etc.

What makes a good leader in sport?

A good leader in sport is likely to have one or more of the following qualities:

- outstanding ability in the sport
- great enthusiasm
- sound judgement
- good motivational powers
- ability to read the game or sporting situation.

Captains of cricket teams have a lot of responsibility for making tactical decisions during games. When fielding they must decide who is to bowl and where the fielders are to be placed.

activity

Follow the leader

Observe a competitive team performance. Look for leadership on the pitch. Give examples of when leadership is shown. Is it always the same players? Is it always the high-profile or popular ones, or can you find an unsung hero who leads well, but whose contribution is often overlooked?

Captains in other sports do not usually make as many crucial decisions, but they must set an example to the players in their team and motivate them. This is very important when a team is losing.

Motivators on the pitch are players who perform reliably under pressure. The other players look to them for inspiration. Some players drift in and out of games. They may be highly skilful but are not good leaders. Sometimes the most skilful players, or the most popular players, are given the captaincy of a team. However, the real leaders in the team may be doing an excellent job without being recognised.

What makes a good organiser in sport?

Sport needs organisers. Whether you are playing in a Sunday league netball team, or representing your country in the Commonwealth Games, you depend on many people to ensure that the event goes ahead smoothly. Sports organisers are needed at all levels in both professional and amateur sport and they carry out a wide range of roles. Some help to plan the event or take responsibility for the finance, while others will officiate. All these people are essential, although their work often goes unnoticed.

activity

Officials and sport

Do you know how many officials are required to control a game or event in your chosen sport? Research the answer and complete a checklist with details of each official and the roles they have.

Officials and sport

An official's central task, whether an umpire in tennis or a referee in rugby, is to enable sportspeople to take part in sport fairly and safely. Administrators organise events, but officials control the sporting action.

Officials must:

- have excellent knowledge of the sport and its rules
- apply rules firmly and fairly
- be patient, good with people and have a sense of humour!
- look after the safety of all those involved
- be in good physical condition.

Officials deserve respect and should not be taken for granted. Without them, organised sport would not exist.

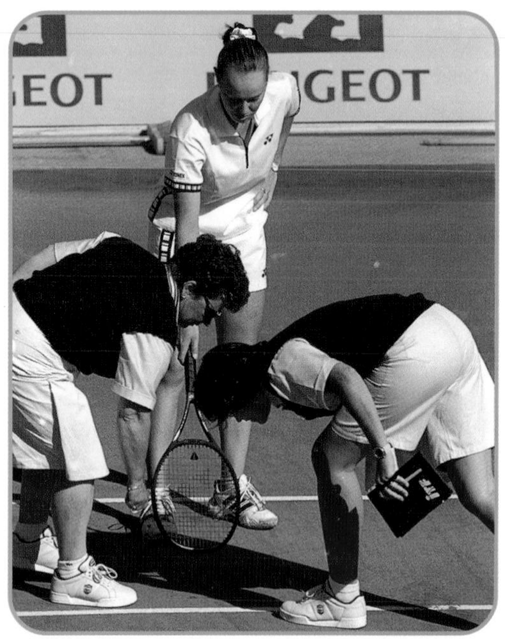

Exercise and training

2 Reasons for taking part in sport and physical activity

- Why do we take part in sport?

3 Health, fitness, exercise and performance

- What is health?
- What do we mean by exercise?
- Performance
- What is physical fitness?
- What is health-related fitness?

4 Skill-related fitness

- What is skill-related fitness?
- Factors of skill-related fitness

5 Principles of training

- Principles of training
- Meeting individual needs
- Planning a training programme

6 Methods of training

- How do our muscles work?
- Training methods
- Your Personal Exercise Plan (PEP)
- The effects of exercise and training on our body systems
- Anaerobic and aerobic activity in exercise

7 Diet, health and hygiene

- Why do we need a balanced diet?
- Diet and energy
- Food and sport
- Drugs and sport
- Hygiene and sport

2 Reasons for taking part in sport and physical activity

Sport is popular. Every weekend millions of us take part in sporting activities of one kind or another. Although we all realise that an active lifestyle will help to keep us fit and well, our reasons for taking part are many and varied. Why and how do we come to these decisions about sport? There are usually no simple answers. We are affected by many different factors in our lives.

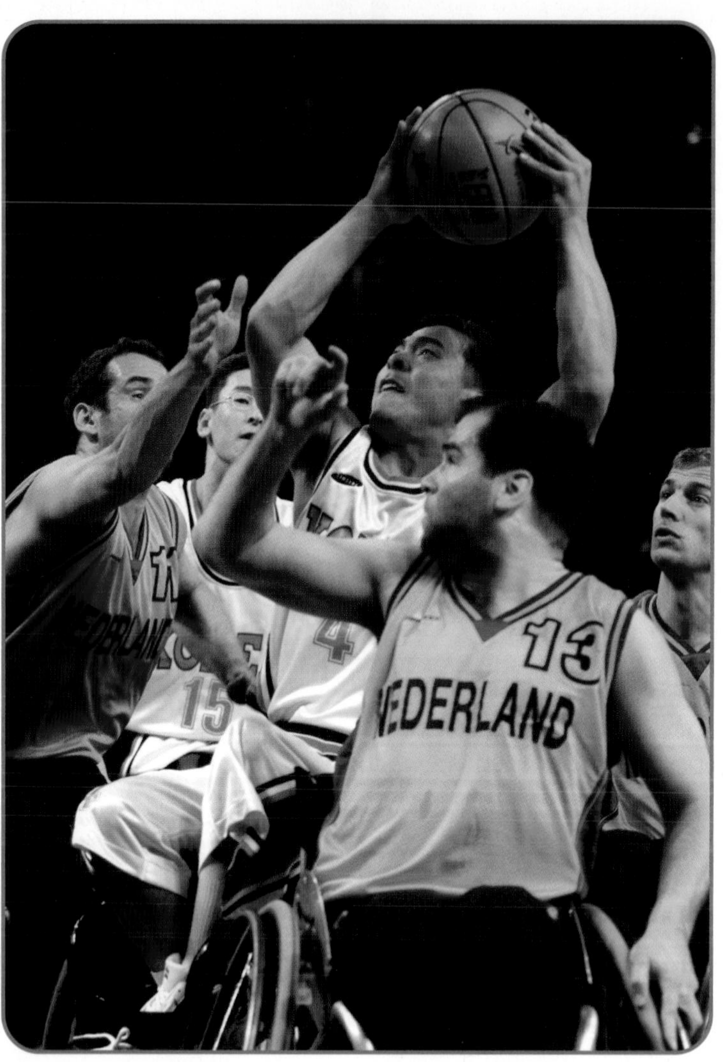

However, sport is not for everyone. Some people decide not to take part but enjoy watching sport. For others sport is of no interest and plays no part in their life. Society is made up of all sorts of people – men, women, different ethnic groups, able-bodied people, people with disabilities, people of different ages. If we belong to a particular group or groups of people, we may encounter a number of barriers to taking part in sport. Opportunities to take part in sport are not equal. Some groups have more opportunity than others. This is a complex issue. In order to be able to understand it properly, we need to understand why people take part in sports.

activity

Taking part in sport and physical activity

There are many reasons why we take part in sport. These reasons are linked to our particular lifestyle and the influence of our family, school and friends. Read the following pen pictures and then discuss why you think that each individual takes part in sport or physical activity.

John is a 26-year-old accountant and works in the City. His job is very demanding; he works long hours most days of the week, tends to eat out a lot and goes to the pub regularly. He visits the gym three lunchtimes a week and works out on both weights and aerobic machines. He also tries to have a run or a cycle ride each weekend.

Nisha is a freelance graphic designer who works from home. She is single and in her late twenties and has little contact with the outside world during her working week. She tends to eat a lot, has problems controlling her weight and worries about her appearance. As a student she enjoyed dance and has recently joined a modern dance group which meets twice a week.

Martin is 17 years old and has returned to college after failing most of his recent exams. He gets frustrated with his lack of progress and loses his temper quite easily. He has always enjoyed sport without making the school teams, but his PE teacher recommended that on leaving school he joined the local rugby club. He now trains twice a week with the club and plays a match every weekend. He has also started serious weight training at a local gym.

Ellie (18) is quiet and shy and took little part in PE and sport during her time at school. Through a friend at work she met a parascending group who eventually persuaded her to try the sport. To her surprise she not only enjoyed the thrill of the sport but realised that she was quite good. She is now group secretary, taking part every weekend and has also developed a growing interest in paragliding.

Can you think of any other reasons why people take part in sport? Think of your own experiences.

KEYWORDS

Aesthetic: the quality of the movement in a performance

Body shape: our physical appearance in terms of the distribution of muscle and fat

Competition: Testing our ability against others

Cooperation: working with others in order to achieve a task

Good health: a state of complete mental, physical and social well-being, and not merely the absence of disease and infirmity

Physical challenge: competing against our own best performances or against the environment

Stress: unhealthy pressure caused by factors such as family, work or finance.

Key to Exam Success

For your GCSE you will need:

- to know the reasons why people take part in sport or physical activity
- to understand the variety of factors which influence taking part in sport or physical activity
- to explain how taking part in sport or physical activity is good for us
- to understand the advantages of being a member of a sports club or group.

“ KEY THOUGHT ”

‘Sport – available to all, chosen by many.’

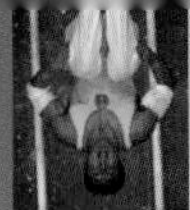

Why do we take part in sport?

We all decide whether or not to take part in sport or physical activity. Most of us who take part in sport do so in our own time, at our own expense and purely for our own pleasure. Only a relatively few people have the talent to play sport full time as professionals.

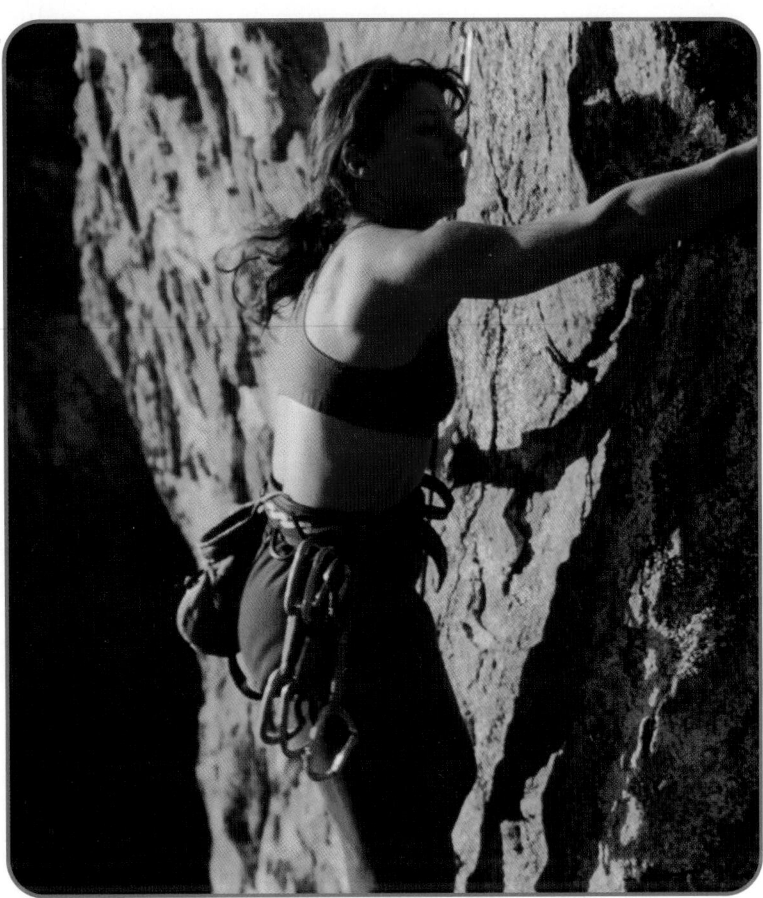

Our decision to take part in sport or physical activity is based on a variety of different reasons, depending on our personal situation and all the other influences on our life. These can be put under the two main headings of **health reasons** and **social reasons**.

Health reasons

We are very health-conscious today and most of us are aware of the benefits of regular physical activity and sport.

From a **physical** point of view, regular exercise and sport can help us to:

- feel and look good
- maintain good muscle tone and keep our body in good shape. This in turn improves our self-image and our confidence. We can follow a programme of activity which will increase flexibility and improve both the strength and tone of our muscles.
- enhance our **body shape**
- control our weight by burning up any excess fat. If we also control our calorie intake through a balanced diet, we will be able to improve our body shape and avoid the health risks of being unfit and overweight.
- maintain **good health** and enhance our enjoyment of life. In order to keep our bodies fit for the demands of daily life, we need to maintain minimum levels of muscular strength, muscular endurance, flexibility and cardiovascular fitness. We know that the more active we are, the better our health is likely to be.

Sport also enables us to test our physical qualities such as strength and endurance and our mental qualities such as determination and perseverance. We can compete against our own best performance in running, swimming or cycling. We can also compete against the environment when climbing, caving or sky diving. Meeting a challenge of this kind can be very satisfying.

From a **mental** point of view, regular physical activity and sport can:

- relieve **stress** and tension. Stress caused by the pressures of modern life is one of the greatest challenges to health today. Sport and physical activity will produce physical benefits including the reduction of blood pressure. Exercise in itself will not solve our problems but it may help us relax for a while, reduce our tension and, perhaps, allow us to take a fresh look at our worries. In this way sport and physical activity may help us to deal with stress-related illnesses such as depression, insomnia and anxiety.

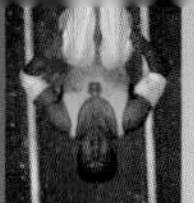

- offer us an **aesthetic** experience. Sporting movement can be, and often is, beautiful. We can all appreciate the speed and elegance of a sprint hurdler in full flow, the controlled power of a gymnast in a tumbling routine and the sweeping movement in rugby resulting in a try. All these activities appeal to our aesthetic senses. We can also reproduce this quality ourselves, if we have the talent. Dancers enjoy the experience of moving to the music and performing complex movements. Aesthetic appreciation is part of many sports and activities.

Social reasons

Sport also has social benefits. Many people enjoy relaxing in their leisure time and taking part in sport and physical activity with their friends. Membership of sporting clubs and participation in sporting activities can stimulate:

- **cooperation**: many activities take place in sports centres and clubs. We may attend regularly and develop an interest in a group or a club. Many people like being part of a team and choose to play together. Others may take on organisational responsibilities and help to run the affairs of a club. For sports involving teams, cooperation between team members is essential for success.
- **competition**: many of us are naturally competitive and sport provides a perfect opportunity to test our skill and fitness against others. We can compete directly with others in matches and tournaments in a variety of sports, from lacrosse to water polo, and from basketball to sailing. Competition can take place at many different levels, from Sunday football in the park to competing in the Olympics.
- **Friendship**: we all need daily contact with other people. Sport and physical activity gives us the opportunity to meet and talk to others. If we belong to a club or attend a class, sport acts as a common interest, stimulating conversation and encouraging friendship and social mixing.

Home and school influences on our sporting interests

Home influences

- **Family**: if our parents play sport regularly, we will be brought up in a sporting atmosphere. Sporting parents and older brothers and sisters provide us with role models to follow.
- **Friends and peers**: our peers are the people who are the same age as us. Our friends are often also our peers and their choice of leisure activity will usually affect our own choices. Friends often have similar interests. In school, peer pressure can be very strong.
- **Social class**: this can include a number of factors including type of employment, income level and family background. Our social class often affects the type of activity in which we take part.
- **Financial situation**: the amount of money coming into a family affects its standard of living and therefore the leisure activities of each family member. There is a cost in taking part

in any sport, as we will always need clothing and equipment. Some sports such as sailing are extremely expensive.

- **Environment**: where we live affects our sporting opportunities. Country areas may provide outdoor activities, but people living in the country often have to travel a long way to leisure centres and swimming pools. If we live near the sea there will be greater opportunities to take part in water sport.

School influences

- **The importance given to PE and sport**: although all schools are required to teach PE, the total amount of time given to PE and extracurricular sport varies a great deal. Sports colleges and the School Sports Coordinator Programmes are at the heart of the government's plan to increase the sporting opportunities for all and to help talented young sportspeople.
- **PE lessons**: skill development is at the centre of a sound PE programme. A wide variety of activities, well taught in a structured programme, will develop skill and motivate students to maintain their participation in sport beyond school.
- **PE staff**: many of us develop our love of sport through the inspiration of our PE teachers. Not only do they improve our skills, but their enthusiasm and encouragement can make a real difference.

QUESTIONS

2 Reasons for taking part in sport and physical activity

Answer questions 1–4 by choosing statements a, b, c or d. One mark for each question.

1 **An aesthetic performance refers to the:**

a overall effort made
b amount of strength seen
c type of flexibility shown
d quality of the movement.

2 **Physical activity helps to reduce stress by:**

a improving flexibility
b lowering blood pressure
c increasing muscular strength
d making us sweat.

3 **The main reason why people take part in climbing is the enjoyment of the**

a competition
b physical challenge
c aggression involved
d accuracy demanded.

4 **We take part in sport for social reasons because we all need**

a daily contact with other people
b fitness for everyday life
c sports skills
d to feel and to look good.

5 **Christof is an enthusiastic gymnast at school. He explains that he takes part in gymnastics for the competition, the physical challenge and the aesthetic enjoyment involved.**

a Explain each of these reasons and give an example of each from gymnastics. *(6 marks)*

b Give two reasons why Christof will gain health benefits from doing gymnastics. *(2 marks)*

c His PE teacher has suggested he join the local gymnastics club. Give two social reasons for joining the club. *(2 marks)*

6 **Anneli is a quiet and shy 16-year-old girl who excels at distance running. She is the school and county champion. She is coached at school but cannot be persuaded to join a club.**

a Suggest three social reasons why she might enjoy being a club member and relate each to a running club. *(6 marks)*

b Give four ways in which her running contributes to her physical health. *(4 marks)*

c What is meant by an **aesthetic** appreciation with respect to distance running? *(2 marks)*

d Explain what is meant by **stress** in modern life and suggest two ways in which running alleviates stress. *(4 marks)*

e Anneli says she enjoys the physical challenges of running. Explain what is meant by **physical challenge** and how it might be seen in distance running. *(4 marks)*

(Total 34 marks)

3 Health, fitness, exercise and performance

Being fit is central to our health and helps us to feel good about ourselves. **Health** and **fitness** mean more than just the absence of illness. If we are healthy and fit, then the physical, mental and social aspects of our lives are working together. Fitness is vital for success in sport.

activity

Lifestyle and health

Look at the pictures and descriptions below and decide what in the lifestyles of these people makes them healthy and unhealthy.

Phil is a 45-year-old married man with a wife and two young children. He has been unemployed for two years and is often depressed. His wife has a part-time job but does not earn very much. He watches a lot of television and likes fast food and beer. He supports his local football team but his regular exercise is limited to walking his children to and from school each day. He is overweight and would find running for a bus quite stressful, even though he is a non-smoker.

Sylvia is a 63-year-old widow who lives alone with her cat. She walks half a mile to the shops and back each day and most weekends she joins the local Ramblers on one of their walks. She likes the occasional glass of wine but watches her weight carefully. She smokes 20 cigarettes a day. She enjoys being with her many grandchildren and rarely needs to visit her doctor.

John is 16 and spends most of his spare time on his computer, often working until the early hours. He not only plays games but also uses the internet to keep up to date with his music and his friends. For PE at school he chooses archery and weightlifting but he does not participate in any lunchtime or after-school sport. His mother ensures he eats sensibly at home and she prepares sandwiches and fruit for his lunch every day.

Sarah, now 26, is confined to a wheelchair as a result of a road accident five years ago. Before her accident she was an outstanding hockey player and she now plays wheelchair basketball for her county. This involves regular training sessions including fitness work in the gym. She drives her own specially adapted car and has a boyfriend who plays rugby for a local team.

Try to decide, from the descriptions above, who has the most healthy lifestyle and why.

What advice would you give to the person above who you consider has the most unhealthy lifestyle?

KEYWORDS

Body composition: the percentage of body weight which is fat, muscle and bone

Cardiovascular fitness: the ability to exercise the entire body for long periods of time

Exercise: physical activity aimed at improving health and physical fitness

Fitness: the ability to meet the demands of the environment

Flexibility: the range of movement possible at a joint

Health: not merely the absence of disease or infirmity, but a state of complete mental, physical and social well-being

Health-related fitness: the level of fitness necessary for good health

Muscular endurance: the ability to use voluntary muscles repeatedly without getting tired

Muscular strength: the amount of force a muscle can exert against a resistance

Performance: how well a task is completed

Skill-related fitness: level of fitness necessary for success in a specific sport

VO_2 Max: the maximum amount of oxygen that can be carried to, and used by, the working muscles during exercise.

Key to Exam Success

For your GCSE you will need to know:

- how health, fitness, exercise and performance relate to each other
- the effects of exercise and fitness on performance
- the relationship between fitness and health
- the five factors of health-related fitness
- the importance of health-related fitness to your daily life and sports performance.

“ KEY THOUGHT ”

‘Thinking sportspeople will come out on top.’

What is health?

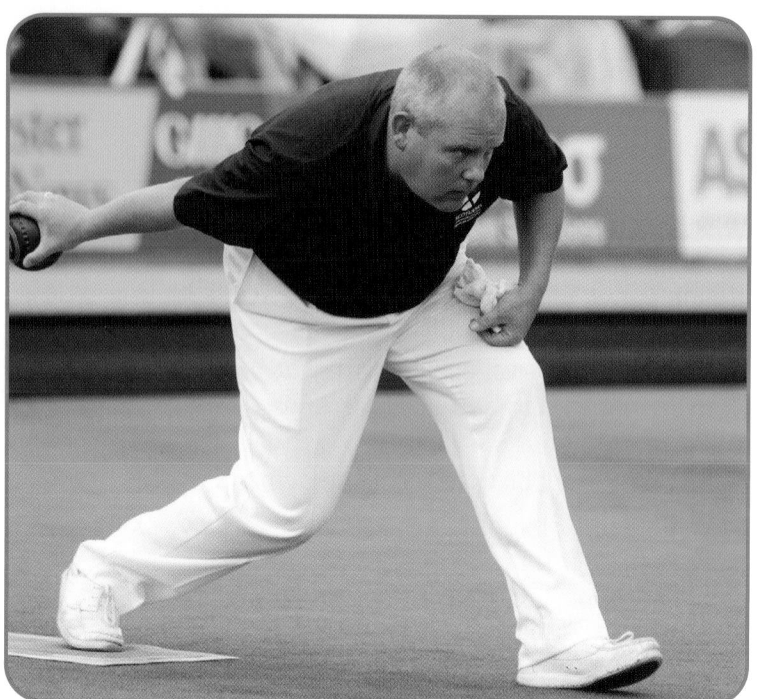

Health is defined as 'a state of complete mental, physical and social well-being, and not merely the absence of disease or infirmity'. (Edexcel).

Good health means that our mental state is sound, our body is working well and we are at ease socially. We are able to lead a full and active life, combining work, duties, recreation and social activities on a regular basis without becoming exhausted. We all need to lead a healthy lifestyle.

Good health comes from:

- eating sensibly
- taking regular physical **exercise**
- getting regular rest and sleep
- limiting our alcohol intake
- not smoking or taking social drugs
- improving our ability to cope with stress.

Good health requires physical, mental and social well-being.

Physical well-being

- Our cardiovascular system (heart and circulation) and our respiratory system (lungs) work well for normal activities and also emergencies.
- Our muscular system is strong enough to meet the needs of our daily life.
- Our body shape gives us confidence.
- We are able to resist and recover from illness.

Mental well-being

- We are able to cope with the stress and tensions of everyday life by relaxing and developing leisure interests.
- We are able to control our emotions, bringing stability to our behaviour.

Social well-being

- We need the company of other people in order to develop friendships and good personal relationships.
- We improve our own self-esteem and feel good about ourselves when we feel that other people value us.

Heredity

Heredity may affect our health. For example, problems such as high blood pressure and heart disease may run in families. If our grandparents and parents live a long and healthy life then we are likely to do the same, but we should not assume that this will be the case. We should all adopt healthy lifestyles to ensure good health.

What do we mean by exercise?

Exercise is defined as 'a form of physical activity done primarily to improve one's health and physical fitness'. (Edexcel)

We can exercise in many different ways, from judo to jogging and from swimming to sailing. We may exercise by playing sport, or by training to improve our performance in sport or for our own general health and enjoyment. Taking part in exercise that is related to our sport will not only make us fitter for our sport, but will also improve performance.

Exercise is only really valuable if it becomes a regular part of our lifestyle. It is recommended that we exercise at least three times a week. This exercise should last for at least 20 minutes, during which time our heart rate should be raised significantly.

All exercise has an effect on our physical, mental and social well-being and so helps to keep us healthy. The benefits of exercise depend on the type of activity.

Physical benefits

- stronger heart
- more efficient breathing
- stronger muscles with increased tone
- better **flexibility**
- improved body shape through the reduction of fat
- stronger bones
- prevention of heart disease and illnesses associated with high blood pressure.

Mental benefits

- relief of stress and tension
- satisfaction of meeting a challenge
- improved sleeping and relaxation
- emotional stimulus
- improved control of emotions
- improved self-esteem and self-confidence.

Social benefits

- opportunities to meet others and develop friendships
- improved communication skills
- opportunities to develop cooperation and teamwork.

Performance

Performance is defined as 'how well a task is completed'. (Edexcel)

Levels of performances differ widely. We can all applaud the performance of rowers who win Olympic gold medals. This is an extremely high-level performance. However, we can also feel happy about producing a good performance at our own standard, for example, in the dance studio, on the games field or in the gym.

Health, fitness, exercise and performance

It is clear that health and fitness are not the same thing. It is perfectly possible to be healthy provided that we are fit enough to carry out our normal everyday tasks. However, we may not be physically fit enough for sporting activity. This is because physical fitness is specific to a particular physical activity – sporting or otherwise. For instance, a person in their eighties could be very healthy for their age, be able to carry out all their everyday tasks and yet be unfit for most sporting activities.

It is also possible for a person to be very fit for a particular sport and yet to have an unhealthy lifestyle which may lead to long-term ill-health. For instance, a rugby player may train regularly and play for the first team, yet his diet, intake of alcohol and general lifestyle may be far from healthy.

Exercise is essential for good health, and specific exercise in the form of training will improve both health-related and sport-related fitness. Our performance in everyday life is dependent on our health-related fitness *and* the exercise we do. Our sporting performance is dependent on our sport-related fitness *and* the specific exercise we do.

What is physical fitness?

Fitness is defined as 'the ability to meet the demands of the environment'. (Edexcel.) The environment is everything around us, including home, school, family and friends.

Physical fitness is the ability of our body to carry out everyday activities with minimum fatigue and with enough energy left over for emergencies. Fitness means different things to different people. A man who is fit for work as a taxi driver may be dangerously unfit for a game of squash. A marathon runner may be quite unfit for lifting weights.

Physical fitness is made up of a number of physical qualities which work together. It can be divided into **health-related fitness** and **skill-related fitness**:

- Health-related fitness is the level of physical fitness which we all need to enjoy good health.
- Skill-related fitness is the level of physical fitness necessary for regular sporting activity.

We will look at skill-related fitness in detail in the next chapter.

activity

Physical fitness circuit

Working in groups of three, complete a circuit of tests designed to help you experience the different factors involved in fitness.

Circuit	Fitness circuit
Tennis ball pick-up	Place three tennis balls on the floor two metres away. Run, pick up the first ball and return both feet behind the starting line. Repeat with the second and third ball. Finish as quickly as you can. Record the time taken to complete the test.
Balancing ball	Extend your arm at right angles to the ground, fist clenched, back of the hand facing upwards. Place a volleyball on the back of your hand and time how long it can be balanced up to a maximum of 60 seconds. Your arm may be moved but not your feet.
The pinch	Have a partner pinch a fold of fat on the back of your upper arm, halfway between the elbow and the tip of the shoulder. Measure the fold in centimetres.
Two-ball juggle	Hold two tennis balls in your preferred hand. Juggle them up to 10 times without dropping either ball. Score one point for each catch up to maximum of 10.
Shoulder raise	Lie face down on the floor with your arms stretched out in front. Hold a metre rule with your hands shoulder-width apart. Raise your arms as high as possible, keeping your chin on the ground at all times and the rule parallel to the floor. Hold the highest position for three seconds. A partner measures the height reached from the floor.
Grip test	Squeeze a hand grip dynamometer as hard as possible with one hand. Record the reading.
Standing broad jump	Start with your feet comfortably apart and your toes immediately behind the start line. Then bend your knees and jump forward as far as possible. Measure the distance from your rear heel or any other part of the body which is nearest to the start line. You are allowed two attempts.
Press-ups	Complete as many press-ups as possible in 60 seconds. Girls can perform press-ups from the kneeling position.
Metre rule drop	Ask a partner to hold a metre rule so that the side edge is between your thumb and index finger at a point 30 cm from the end. When your partner releases the rule, catch it before it slips through your thumb and finger. Do not move your hand lower to catch the rule. Record how far the rule has fallen.
Double heel click	With feet apart, jump up and tap your heels together twice before you hit the ground. You must land with your feet at least 10 cm apart. Make three attempts. Record the number of successful attempts.
Shuttle run	Complete a 10-metre shuttle run as many times as possible over a one-minute period.

What is health-related fitness?

We all need a minimum amount of physical fitness to be healthy and to cope with everyday life. This fitness protects us from stress, accidents, injury, disease and other health problems. To have enough physical fitness for good health we need the five health-related fitness factors:

- cardiovascular fitness
- muscular strength
- muscular endurance
- flexibility
- body composition.

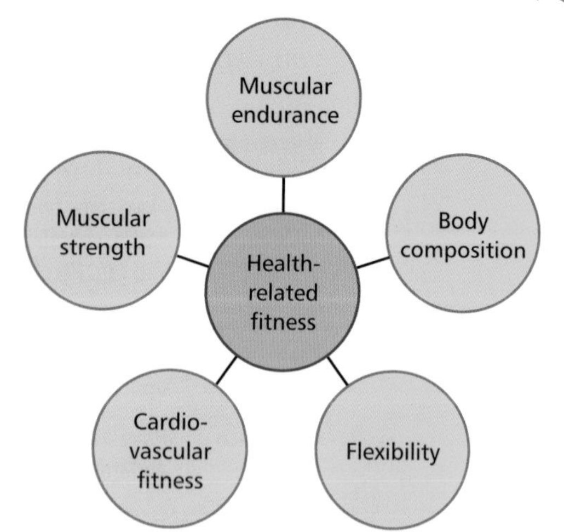

Muscular strength is the amount of force a muscle can exert against a resistance.

Muscular endurance is the ability to use voluntary muscles repeatedly without getting tired.

Body composition is the percentage of body weight which is fat, muscle and bone.

Flexibility is the range of movement possible at a joint.

Cardiovascular fitness is the ability to exercise the entire body for long periods of time.

Health-related fitness presentation

Working in pairs or small groups, your task is to prepare and deliver a brief presentation explaining one of the five factors of health-related fitness (see above). Include the following in your presentation:

- a definition of the fitness factor
- an explanation of the factor
- the importance of the factor in sport
- how the factor can be measured
- how the factor can be improved.

You may wish to use Microsoft Powerpoint for your presentation.

It is important to link your presentation to your Personal Exercise Plan (PEP). Use the appropriate sections of this chapter to gather your information. You will also be able to obtain more information from the internet. Be sure to include the analysis of the results obtained by your group in the fitness testing. You will be expected to explain your results.

Cardiovascular fitness

Cardiovascular fitness, also known as aerobic capacity, cardiorespiratory endurance or stamina, is the ability of our heart and lung systems to cope with activity over a relatively long period of time. It is essential for work and play in our everyday lives.

When our body works hard for a long period we must supply our working muscles with energy and get rid of waste products. To do this we need our heart, lungs and circulatory system to work well.

What is VO_2 Max?

Our maximum cardiovascular fitness or aerobic capacity is also called our **VO_2 Max**. This is the maximum amount of oxygen that can be carried to, and used by, the working muscles during exercise, and it is often used to measure fitness (see below). A person with a high VO_2 Max can use more oxygen, work harder for longer, and will have less fatigue, than someone with a lower VO_2 Max.

How do we improve our cardiovascular fitness?

We can improve our cardiovascular fitness by taking part regularly in any continuous whole-body exercise, for example, running, swimming or cycling. But we must keep our heart rate between 60% and 80% of our maximum heart rate in order for our cardiovascular fitness to improve. We should exercise at first for a minimum of 12 minutes, increasing this time to 40 minutes as we become fitter.

Continuous training, interval training and circuit training can all be used to improve our cardiovascular fitness.

Measuring cardiovascular fitness

We can measure our cardiovascular fitness by finding out our VO_2 Max. This is the amount of oxygen we can use in one minute of maximum exercise.

There are various tests to estimate our VO_2 Max: the Multistage (Bleep) Fitness Test, the Harvard Step Test and the Cooper 12-Minute Run.

Multistage (Bleep) Fitness Test

A pre-recorded tape plays 'bleeps' at regular set intervals while you make 20-metre shuttle runs in time to the bleeps. After each minute the time intervals between the bleeps get shorter so you have to run faster. You keep going until you can no longer keep up with the speed set by the bleeps. At this point you stop and record the level. You can then work out your VO_2 Max using the tables provided.

British National Team Scores in Multistage Fitness Tests

Sport	Male	Female
Basketball	11–5	9–6
Hockey	13–9	12–7
Rugby league	13–1	
Netball		9–7
Squash	13–3	

You can get an instant VO_2 Max score by using the VO_2 Max calculator at **http://www.brianmac.demon.co.uk.** Look for the links to 'Multistage Fitness test'.

Harvard Step Test

Before starting the test, you record your resting heart rate (pulse). You then step on and off a 45cm-high bench at the rate of 30 times a minute for five minutes. You must start with the same foot each time and fully extend your leg at the top of the step. At the end of the test your pulse is taken three times, each time for 30 seconds. The first time is at 1 minute, then at 2 minutes and finally at 3 minutes after the end of the exercise. Your fitness score is calculated using the following formula:

$$\text{Fitness score} = \frac{\text{Duration of exercise in seconds } (5 \times 60 = 300) \times 100}{\text{Pulse after 1 minute} + \text{Pulse after 2 minutes} + \text{Pulse after 3 minutes}}$$

For example, if Tom's three pulse rates were 160, 120 and 90 after 1, 2 and 3 minutes, his score would be as follows:

$$\frac{300 \times 100}{160 + 120 + 90} = \text{81 which would be above average}$$

Harvard Step Test: comparative scores

	Males 15–16 years	Females 15–16 years
High score	Above 90	Above 86
Above average	89–80	86–76
Average	79–65	75–61
Below average	64–55	60–50
Low score	Less than 55	Less than 50

Cooper 12-Minute Run

The aim is to run as far as you can in 12 minutes around a marked area. The total distance you run is recorded. You can work out your aerobic capacity using this table:

Cooper 12-Minute Run: comparative scores

	Males 15–16 years	Females 15–16 years
High score	Above 2,800 m	Above 2,300 m
Above average	2,799–2,500 m	2,299–2,000 m
Average	2,499–2,300 m	1,999–1,900 m
Below average	2,299–2,200 m	1,899–1,800 m
Low score	Below 2,200 m	Below 1,800 m

The importance of cardiovascular fitness

Cardiovascular fitness is essential for an active lifestyle. It also enables us to cope with unexpected physical demands like running away from a dangerous situation. It is essential in all sporting activities lasting more than a few seconds. The better our stamina, the longer we can continue our activity, whether it is swimming, running, cycling or rowing. This is because our skill level declines as we get tired. It is often said that 'When fatigue sets in, skill goes out of the window.' This can be seen in team games when more goals and points are scored towards the end of matches as a greater number of mistakes are made. A player with a high level of cardiovascular fitness will be able to maintain his or her skill level for longer.

Muscular strength

In everyday terms, we think of strength as being the ability of our muscles to carry out daily tasks easily. This is the strength which is one of the factors of health-related fitness. But our muscles also work to produce three different types of strength.

The two types of strength that are important for health-related fitness are:

- **muscular strength**: this is also called static strength or maximum strength
- **muscular endurance**: this is also called endurance strength.

The third type of strength is known as muscular power, explosive strength or simply power, and is important for skill-related fitness.

The type of strength we use in sport can be broadly described as the ability of a muscle or a muscle group to apply force and overcome resistance. Many sports demand a combination of muscular strength, muscular power and muscular endurance.

What is muscular strength?

Muscular strength is the amount of force a muscle can exert against a resistance. It can be improved by training with heavy weights (80 – 100% of our maximum), using a low number of repetitions. In order to build up muscular strength it is necessary to exercise through the full range of joint movements and to work slowly when lifting.

How do we measure our muscular strength?

To measure our muscular strength, we need to find out the maximum force that a muscle group can apply. Special dynamometers can be used to measure muscular strength at different speeds and angles, and according to whether the muscles are lengthening or shortening. They can also be set up to make our limbs move in the same way as in our chosen sport.

The Repetition Max Test

We can carry out a Repetition Max Test using free weights or multigym equipment. The aim is to find out the maximum weight we can lift just once, by gradually adding weights. This is called our one repetition max. We must allow at least 2–3 minutes between each lift for recovery.

Hand Grip Strength Test

To test the strength of your hand grip, you can use a hand grip dynamometer. You simply squeeze the handle as hard as possible with your hand and record the reading on the dynamometer.

Hand Grip Strength Test: comparative scores

	Males 15–16 years	Females 15–16 years
High score	Above 56 kg	Above 36 kg
Above average	56–51 kg	36–31 kg
Average	50–45 kg	30–25 kg
Below average	44–39 kg	24–19 kg
Low score	Less than 39 kg	Less than 19 kg

The importance of muscular strength

We use our muscles to move ourselves and everyday objects. Without strong muscles normal life would become very difficult. We need muscular strength to lift shopping and to move furniture. Attempting these sorts of activities without sufficient strength or correct technique could lead to injury.

Muscular strength is extremely important in most sports. For example, a judo player needs strength when attempting to throw an opponent; a rugby player needs strength when pushing in the scrum, and an archer when drawing back the bow.

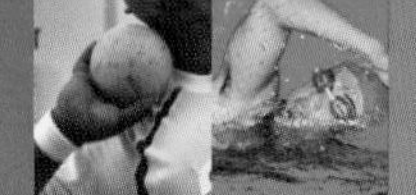

Muscular endurance

Muscular endurance or endurance strength is also called anaerobic endurance. It is the ability to use voluntary muscles many times without getting tired. It refers to the efficiency of the anaerobic system within the working muscles when performing high-intensity, repetitive or even static exercise.

A person who has a high percentage of slow twitch fibres will have an advantage in events involving muscular endurance. Muscular endurance is also closely linked with muscular strength.

You can improve your muscular endurance by training with light weights (40–60% of your maximum). The exercises need to be done at speed and with a high number of repetitions (20–30).

How do we measure our muscular endurance?

To measure muscular endurance you can perform repeated exercises such as press-ups or sit-ups for a given time or to exhaustion. Then you can compare your score either with those of others or with your own previous best.

The NCF Abdominal Curl Test

This test measures the muscular endurance of our abdominal muscles.

1. Lie on the mat with your knees bent, feet flat on the floor, hands resting on your thighs and the back of the head on your partner's hands. Your feet should not be held down to the floor.
2. Curl up slowly using the abdominal muscles and slide your hands up the thighs until your fingertips touch your kneecaps.
3. Return slowly to the starting position.

A complete curl should take 3 seconds, allowing 20 repetitions per minute. Repeat as many curls as you can at this rate and record the result.

NCF Abdominal Curl Test: comparative scores

	Males 15–16 years	Females 15–16 years
High score	60 and above	50 and above
Above average	45–59	40–49
Average	30–44	25–39
Below average	20–29	10–24
Low score	Below 20	Below 10

The importance of muscular endurance

Muscular endurance is important in a wide range of everyday activities, whenever the same muscle groups are used over and over again. Examples include ironing, cleaning the car and washing windows. It is particularly important in sports such as rowing, canoeing and other sporting activities where the same muscle groups work continuously with near-maximum effort.

Flexibility

Flexibility, also known as mobility and suppleness, is the range of movement possible at a joint, and it is necessary in order to stay healthy and avoid injury.

Flexibility does not depend on body shape. You can improve your flexibility by stretching your muscles and tendons and by extending your ligaments and supporting tissues beyond their normal range of movement – for example, by holding an extended position for 20 seconds and repeating the stretch after a short rest period.

When exercising in this way it is important not to overload your muscles unless you feel comfortable. You should also stretch the prime movers and then the antagonist muscles – for example, stretching the quadriceps followed by the hamstrings. This helps your muscles recover and adapt in a balanced way.

The effects of flexibility exercises are very specific. You can, for example, be very flexible in your shoulders and yet have little flexibility in your lower limbs.

Flexibility exercise, or stretching, should be part of all training programmes.

What are the different types of stretching?

There are four main types of stretching which can be used to improve flexibility. In each case you extend your limbs beyond their normal range and hold the position. How you get to the stretch position varies:

- **Static stretching**: you use our own strength
- **Passive stretching**: a partner or coach applies external force
- **Active stretching**: you move rhythmically and under control to extend the stretch
- **PNF stretching**: you contract the muscle before stretching it.

How do we measure flexibility?

The tests used depend upon the joints that are being measured.

Sit and Reach Test

This test measures the flexibility of the hamstrings. Sit on the floor, legs straight, feet flat against the table with shoes removed, fingertips on the edge of the top plate. Bend your trunk and reach forward slowly and as far as possible, keeping the knees straight. Hold this position for two seconds.

Measure the distance from the edge of the table to the position reached by the fingertips. Be sure you make a number of warm-up attempts before the actual measurement is taken. As the 'sit and reach' table has an overhang of 15 cm, a person who reaches 5 cm past their toes scores 20 cm.

Sit and Reach Test: comparative scores

	Males 15–16 years	Females 15–16 years
High score	Above 28 cm	Above 35 cm
Above average	24–28 cm	32–35 cm
Average	20–23 cm	30–31 cm
Below average	17–19 cm	25–29 cm
Low score	Less than 17 cm	Less than 25 cm

Shoulder Hyperextension Test

This test measures your ability to stretch the muscles of your chest and shoulders.

Lie face down on the floor with your arms stretched out in front. Hold a metre rule with your hands shoulder-width apart. Raise your arms as high as possible, keeping your chin on the ground at all times and the stick parallel to the floor. Hold the highest position for three seconds while your partner measures the height reached.

The importance of flexibility

We need a full range of movement in our joints for such everyday activities as

Shoulder Hyperextension Test: comparative scores

	Males 15–16 years	Females 15–16 years
High score	41 cm and above	46 cm and above
Above average	31–40 cm	36–45 cm
Average	21–30 cm	26–35 cm
Below average	11–20 cm	16–25 cm
Low score	0–10 cm	0–15 cm

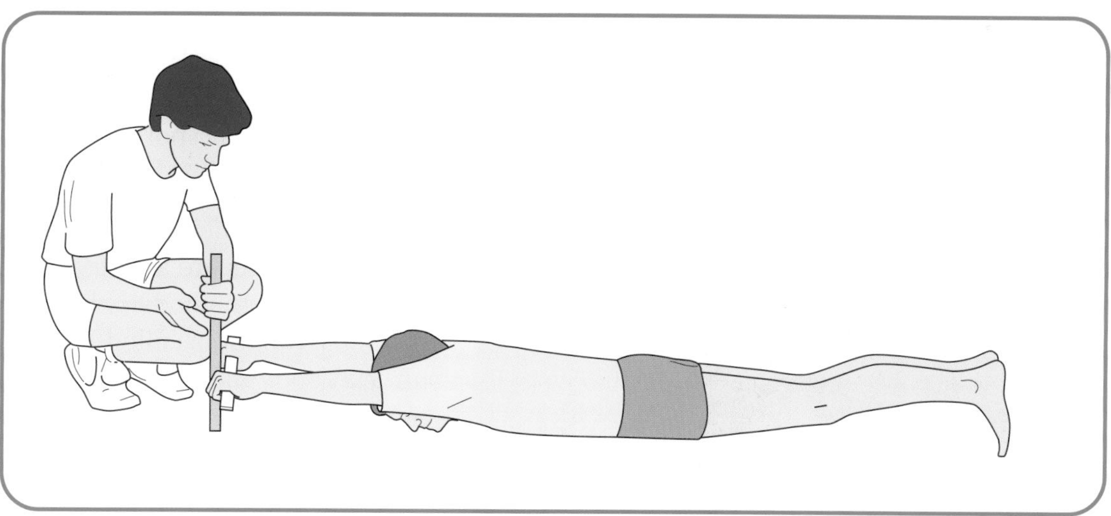

putting on our shoes, reaching up to cupboards and twisting round as we work in the kitchen or garden. Without flexibility our movements will be limited and we are more likely to injure our joints and muscles.

All sports need a flexible body. Sports such as gymnastics and hurdling need a great deal of overall body flexibility. Other sports – for example, javelin and volleyball – need flexibility in particular parts of the body. Flexibility exercises should form a part of all training programmes, as flexible joints are less likely to be injured when put under stress.

Sportspeople often need a combination of flexibility and strength. Flexibility allows us to use our strength through a full range of movement. Strength is needed to stabilise joints and avoid injury.

Body composition

Sporting success comes from a combination of ability, fitness and the right **body composition** for the sport. Usually we find that successful high-jumpers are tall and thin and gymnasts short and muscular. However, deciding what is the right body composition for each sport is complicated. We need to carry the right amount of fat and muscle for our particular sport.

Body composition is the percentage of body weight which is fat, muscle and bone. Scientists are able to work out how much of the body is fat. The rest of the body weight is called fat-free weight (or lean body mass) and includes bone, muscle, organs and connective tissue. Healthy adult males should have less than 18% body fat, while a healthy adult female should have less than 23%.

Body composition can be changed a great deal. We can reduce the amount of fat and improve the proportion of lean muscle in our bodies through careful diet and exercise.

How do we measure body composition?

Working out accurately how much of a person's weight is fat and how much of a person's weight is fat-free was once a very complicated procedure. However, today modern testing equipment accurately measures the amount of fat in the body by measuring the resistance to a very small electric current flowing from the right wrist to the right ankle. Alternatively, we can take skin fold measurements using a skin fold caliper and then refer to tables to estimate the body fat level.

Why is body composition important?

Too little or too much fat on our body can cause us problems in daily life. A certain amount of fat is necessary in order for our body to work properly. It provides the essential fatty acids that our body needs and is also a part of all cell membranes and nerves. Fat is a rich source of energy, particularly when we are resting or asleep, and it also cushions the internal organs. But too much fat means that we are carrying unnecessary weight, which will result in extra strain on our muscles, joints and cardiovascular system.

In most sports, the higher the percentage of a performer's body is fat, the poorer the performance. Moving extra kilos of fat around the football field, the badminton court or the swimming pool is not helpful. Therefore most sportspeople try to keep their body fat low and their fat-free weight – that is, their muscle weight – high. However, long-distance runners must keep both their fat and non-fat weights as low as possible because they have to carry all the extra weight during the race.

Standard height–weight tables give an ideal weight for a particular height. But these tables are not always helpful because they do not take into account body composition. If we are overweight due to extra muscle this is not a problem, but if we are over-fat our sporting performance will suffer and there are health implications.

Body composition is only one of three components of body build which are important for health and sport. The other two are:

- **body size**: height compared to weight
- **body type**: a way of describing a person's physique based on muscularity, linearity and fatness.

Body size

Height and weight are important factors in determining body size. We can compare our height with our weight. Body size will be affected by changing weight. A person's height will not change once he or she has reached

physical maturity. Both height and weight can be accurately measured.

Body size is generally not important in everyday life. However, extremes of height and weight can cause practical problems for us and pose a risk to health.

The ideal body size for sport depends on the type of sport or the position we play in the game. For example, a height of 1.9 metres would be short for a top basketball player but very tall for a gymnast. Long-distance runners keep their weight down in order to reduce the load they have to carry. If we watch a game of rugby we can see a variety of heights and weights. Some sports such as wrestling, boxing and weightlifting have fixed weight categories. It is essential that these athletes control their diets to prevent rapid weight loss through crash dieting and consequent weakness.

Body type

One method of body typing is known as somatotyping. This identifies and describes three extreme body types: endomorphs, mesomorphs and ectomorphs.

Endomorphs are wider front to back than side to side and have:

- a pear-shaped body
- wide hips and wide shoulders
- a rounded head
- a lot of fat on the body, upper arms and thighs.

Mesomorphs are narrow from front to back and have:

- a wedge-shaped body
- wide shoulders and narrow hips

- a massive cubical head
- broad shoulders and heavily muscled arms and legs
- a minimum amount of fat.

Ectomorphs have:

- narrow shoulders and hips
- a narrow chest and abdomen
- thin arms and legs
- a high forehead and receding chin
- little muscle and little fat.

sports. Tall ectomorphs may find that they are suited to basketball and high jump.

However, these extreme body types are rare: we are all part-endomorph, part-mesomorph and part-ectomorph. In general, body type is not important in everyday life, although extremes of endomorphy and ectomorphy can cause health problems. For more details of body type, see page 142.

How do we measure our body type?

We can be given a score (from 1 to 7) to indicate how far we fit the three body types described above. For example, '2,6,3' means low endomorphy (2/7), high mesomorphy (6/7), low ectomorphy (3/7). In this way we can compare our body type with that of other people. Height is not taken into account when measuring body type.

Most successful sportspeople are high in mesomorphy. They are suited to sport requiring explosive strength and power. Their muscular bulk also helps them in contact sports.

Those who are high in endomorphy should work to develop their strength and control their diet. Then they might be successful at sports needing power but with only a limited movement such as weightlifting and wrestling.

People who are high in ectomorphy could develop endurance and might be successful at long-distance events such as running or cycling events. By developing muscular strength they might also succeed in many non-contact

Body type depends very much on heredity and we cannot change our basic bone structure, but we can make some changes. Our body type will be affected by any long-term change in the amount of fat and muscle in our body.

Somatotyping is too lengthy and complicated a procedure to carry out in college or school. However, it is interesting to look at, for example, a college athletics team and sort the athletes into approximate body types. Typically, the throwers will tend towards endomorphy, the long-distance runners towards ectomorphy and the sprinters towards mesomorphy.

QUESTIONS

3 Health, fitness, exercise and performance

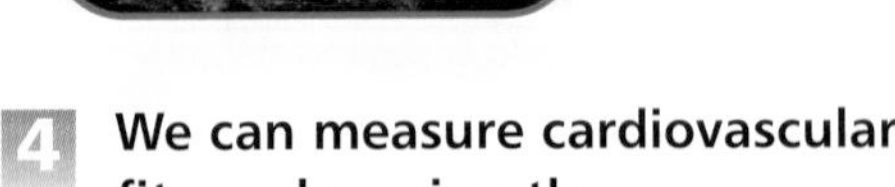

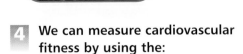

Answer questions 1–4 by choosing statements a, b, c or d. One mark for each question.

1 Fitness is:

a the capability of the heart, blood vessels, lungs and muscles to function at optimal efficiency

b a state of complete mental, physical and social well being, and not merely the absence of disease and infirmity

c the capacity to carry out everyday activities without excessive fatigue

d the ability to meet the demands of the environment.

2 One factor of health-related fitness is:

a flexibility
b speed
c coordination
d agility.

3 Muscular endurance is:

a the amount of force a muscle can exert against a resistance

b The ability to contract our muscles in one explosive act

c The ability to respond to a stimulus quickly

d the ability to use our voluntary muscles many times without getting tired.

4 We can measure cardiovascular fitness by using the:

a 'Bleep' Fitness Test
b Stork Stand
c Vertical Jump Test
d Hand Grip Test.

5 Rory is a good tennis player. He plays for the school team and is also a member of his local tennis club.

a Give a definition of health-related fitness.

(1 mark)

b Explain how playing tennis can improve Rory's health.

(1 mark)

c There are five factors of health-related fitness. Name four of them and, for each, explain how they can be improved by playing tennis.

(8 marks)

6 Francesca likes athletics, especially high jump, and trains regularly with the school team. She believes this exercise keeps her fit and healthy.

a Define the term 'health'.

(1 mark)

b Give three general rules for her lifestyle which will help Francesca maintain her good health.

(3 marks)

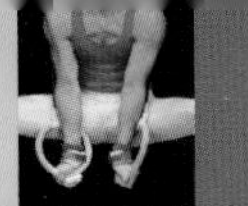

QUESTIONS

c Explain what is meant by exercise.

(1 mark)

d Exercise can bring physical benefits, mental benefits and social benefits. Suggest two benefits for each category that Francesca is likely to gain through training or competition.

(6 marks)

7 Suggest one way in which each of the following health-related fitness factors can be improved:

a cardiovascular fitness
b muscular endurance
c flexibility.

(3 marks)

d There are five components of health-related fitness. Name three which are important for high jumpers and explain why. Set out your findings in a table like the one below:

Component of health-related fitness	Why it is important in high jump

(6 marks)
(Total 34 marks)

4 Skill-related fitness

What is skill-related fitness?

Skill-related fitness is the level of physical fitness necessary for regular sporting activity. Although we may be fit from a health point of view, we may not be fit for sport. There are many different kinds of sporting activities and each makes its own particular demands on the body. For example, the fitness needed by a high jumper is totally different from the fitness necessary for a triathlete.

To be successful in any sport it is necessary to have health-related fitness. As well as this we need fitness related to our own sport. This skill-related fitness will include:

- agility
- balance
- co-ordination
- power
- reaction time
- speed.

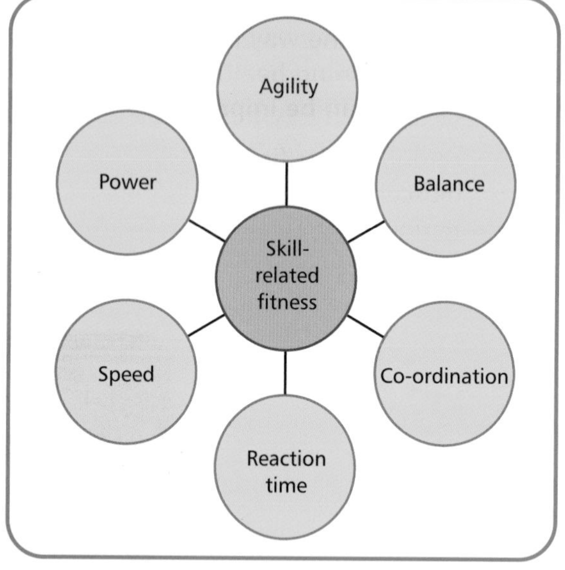

activity

Skill-related fitness presentation

Working in pairs or small groups, your task is to prepare and deliver a brief presentation explaining one of the types of skill-related fitness. Include the following in your presentation:

- a definition of the fitness factor
- an explanation of the factor
- the importance of the factor in sport
- how the factor can be measured
- how the factor can be improved.

You may wish to use to use Microsoft Powerpoint for your presentation.

It is important to link your presentation to your Personal Exercise Plan (PEP). Use the appropriate sections of this chapter to gather your information. You will also be able to obtain more information from the internet. Be sure to include the analysis of the results obtained by your group in the fitness testing. You will be expected to explain your results.

KEYWORDS

Agility: the ability to change the position of the body quickly and to control the movement of the whole body

Balance: the ability to retain the centre of mass (gravity) of the body above the base of support with reference to static (stationary) or dynamic (changing) conditions of movement, shape and orientation. More simply, the ability to retain equilibrium, whether stationary or moving

Co-ordination: the ability to use two or more body parts together

Health-related fitness: the level of fitness necessary for good health

Power: the ability to execute strength performances quickly. Power = Strength × Speed

Reaction time: the time between the presentation of a stimulus and the onset of a movement

Skill-related fitness: the level of fitness necessary for success in a specific sport

Speed: the differential rate at which an individual is able to perform a movement or cover a distance in a period of time.

Key to Exam Success

For your GCSE examination you will need to know:

- the effect of health-related fitness levels on skill-related fitness factors
- the six factors of skill-related fitness
- how performance in sport depends on the level of the skill-related factors.

“ KEY THOUGHT ”

‘Fitness is specific to our sport.’

Factors of skill-related fitness

Agility

Agility is 'the ability to change the position of the body quickly and to control the movement of the whole body'. (Edexcel.) It is a combination of speed, balance, power and co-ordination.

Agility can be developed by training and by rehearsing the movements you make in your sport. This has to be done at full speed and under conditions similar to those in a competitive situation. It is also important to improve your speed, balance, power and co-ordination, as all of these fitness aspects affect your agility.

How do we measure agility?

An expert watching us play our particular sport can make a very good assessment of our agility. We can also assess our general agility using a test such as the Illinois Agility Run.

Illinois Agility Run

Begin by setting up a course as shown in the diagram below. Lie face down on the floor at the starting line. When told to start, leap to your feet and complete the course in the shortest time possible.

The importance of agility

We need a basic amount of agility to carry out our normal everyday tasks – for example, moving through a crowd of shoppers, getting on a train or bus and getting into a car. We need to maintain our agility as we get older or it will deteriorate. Agility is closely linked to flexibility as it requires us to have a good range of movement at our joints.

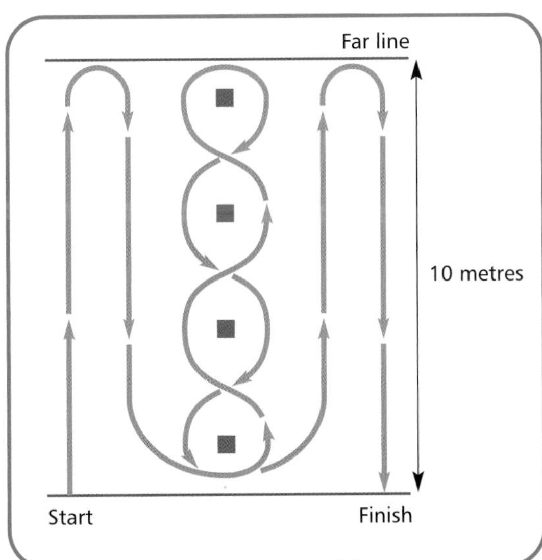

We need agility for all games and most sports. Gymnasts, basketball players and skiers all need specific agility if they are to be successful. Only in static activities such as archery and shooting will agility be of no importance.

Illinois Agility Run: comparative scores (seconds)

	Males 15–16 years	Females 15–16 years
High score	Faster than 15.9	Faster than 17.5
Above average	15.9–16.7	17.5–18.6
Average	16.8–18.6	18.7–22.3
Below average	18.7–18.8	22.4–23.4
Low score	Slower than 18.8	Slower than 23.4

Balance

Balance is 'the ability to retain the centre of mass (gravity) of the body above the base of support with reference to static (stationary) or dynamic (changing) conditions of movement, shape and orientation'. (Edexcel.) A simpler definition of balance is 'the ability to retain equilibrium whether stationary or moving'. We can also say that:

- **static balance** is the ability to maintain our equilibrium when stationary
- **dynamic balance** is the ability to maintain our equilibrium when moving.

Maintaining equilibrium means keeping the centre of gravity over the area of support. Our base of support is the area formed by those parts of the body which are in touch with the ground. For example, in a handstand we have a very small base of support, whereas in press-ups we have a very large base of support. If we do not keep our equilibrium we fall over. We maintain our balance through the co-ordinated actions of our eyes, our ears and the proprioceptive organs in our joints.

We can improve the balance needed in particular sports by developing the appropriate skills through practice and training. We can then put these skills to the test under the stress of competitive situations.

How do we measure our balance?

Dynamic balance is best measured by an expert watching us play our particular sport. Static balance can be measured in a number of ways. The Stork Stand described below is a test of static balance.

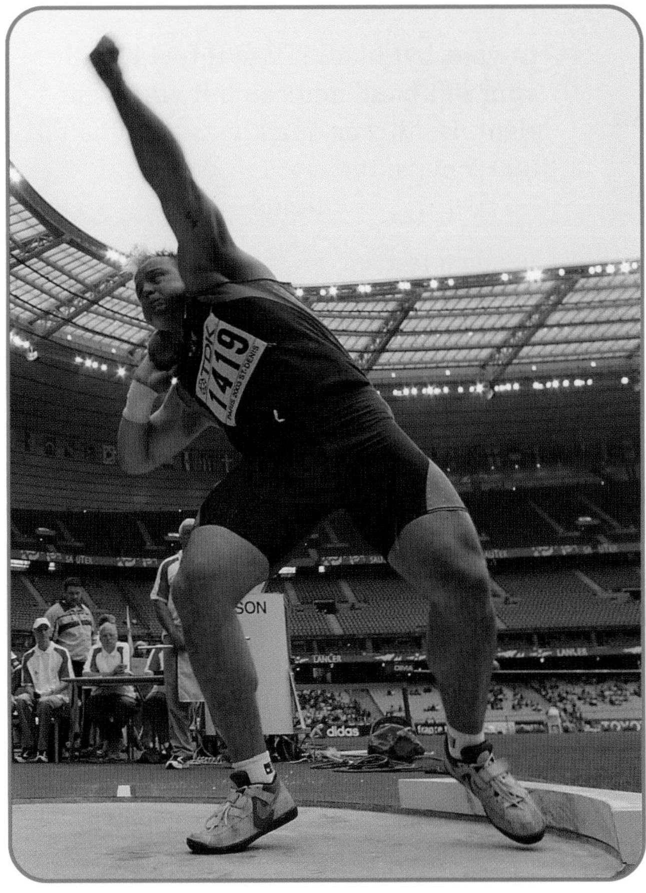

The importance of balance

Without the ability to keep our balance, life would be impossible. Fortunately loss of the ability to balance is rare and few of us ever have to worry about it. It is only when taking up a new activity such as skiing that we realise that we have to learn how to balance.

Static balance is only seen in a few sports such as gymnastics – for example, when holding a handstand. But dynamic balance is very important in most sports; for example, snowboarders and surfers who have to move very fast over uneven surfaces and who have to constantly adjust their positions need very good dynamic balance.

The Stork Stand

Stand comfortably on both feet and place your hands on your hips. Then lift one leg and place the toes against the knee of the other leg. On command, raise the heel and stand on your toes, balancing for as long as possible without letting either heel touch the floor or the other foot move away from the knee. Time your balance in seconds.

The Stork Stand: comparative scores (seconds)

	Males/females 15–16 years
High score	Above 49
Above average	40–49
Average	26–39
Below average	11–25
Low score	Below 10

Co-ordination

Co-ordination is 'the ability to use two or more body parts together'. (Edexcel.) Co-ordination involves carrying out a series of movements smoothly and efficiently. In order for this to happen the nervous and muscular systems need to work well together. We talk about hand–eye co-ordination being necessary to catch a ball and foot–eye co-ordination being necessary in football. Most of us are better coordinated on one side of our body than the other, and favour it in sport; for example, we tend to use a racket or throw a ball with one hand rather than the other.

Co-ordination improves with practice. Many of the toys we play with when young help to develop our hand–eye, foot–eye and whole-body co-ordination. Early PE lessons further develop our co-ordination through gymnastics and playing with balls, hoops and skipping ropes. Co-ordination improves with good coaching and regular practice.

How do we measure co-ordination?

An expert watching us play our particular sport can make a very good assessment of our co-ordination. Observers can also assess our hand–eye co-ordination using a test such as the Alternate Hand Wall Toss Test.

The Alternate Hand Wall Toss Test

Stand two metres away from a smooth wall. With your right hand throw a tennis ball against the wall and catch it in your left hand. Then throw it with your left hand and catch it with your right. Do this as quickly as possible for 30 seconds.

Juggling test

A fun way to test co-ordination is to try juggling with first two and then three balls. Some people are able to achieve the three balls juggling much more quickly than others.

The importance of co-ordination

We need to be well co-ordinated to cope with everyday life. Co-ordination is involved in every movement we make, from picking up a cup to cutting down a tree.

Alternate Hand Wall Toss Test: comparative scores

	Males/females 15–16 years
High score	Above 35
Above average	35–30
Average	29–25
Below average	24–20
Low score	Below 20

Good co-ordination is also essential for skilful performance in sport, from movements in gymnastics such as triple somersaults to saving penalties in football. We become only too aware of poor co-ordination when we try to learn a new sporting skill.

Power

Power is 'the ability to do strength performances quickly. Power = Strength × Speed'. (Edexcel.) More simply, power is the ability to contract the muscles with speed and force in one explosive act. Power, or explosive strength, is the combination of strength and speed of movement. The energy for our power comes from the anaerobic system.

We can improve our power by improving our strength and our speed of movement, or both. We can train with medium weights (60–80% of our maximum), but it is important to perform the repetitions at speed. Plyometrics training (see page 108) is also an excellent way of improving power. As power is a combination of strength and speed, it is important to develop both these areas of fitness.

How do we measure our power?

There are two simple ways to measure the power of your legs: the standing broad jump and the standing vertical jump.

Standing broad jump

Stand with your feet comfortably apart and your toes immediately behind the start line. Then bend your knees and

Standing broad jump: comparative scores (metres)

	Males 15–16 years	Females 15–16 years
High score	Above 2	Above 1.65
Above average	2.00–1.86	1.65–1.56
Average	1.85–1.76	1.55–1.46
Below average	1.75–1.65	1.45–1.35
Low score	Less than 1.65	Less than 1.35

jump forward as far as possible. Measure the distance from your rear heel back to the start line. You are allowed two attempts.

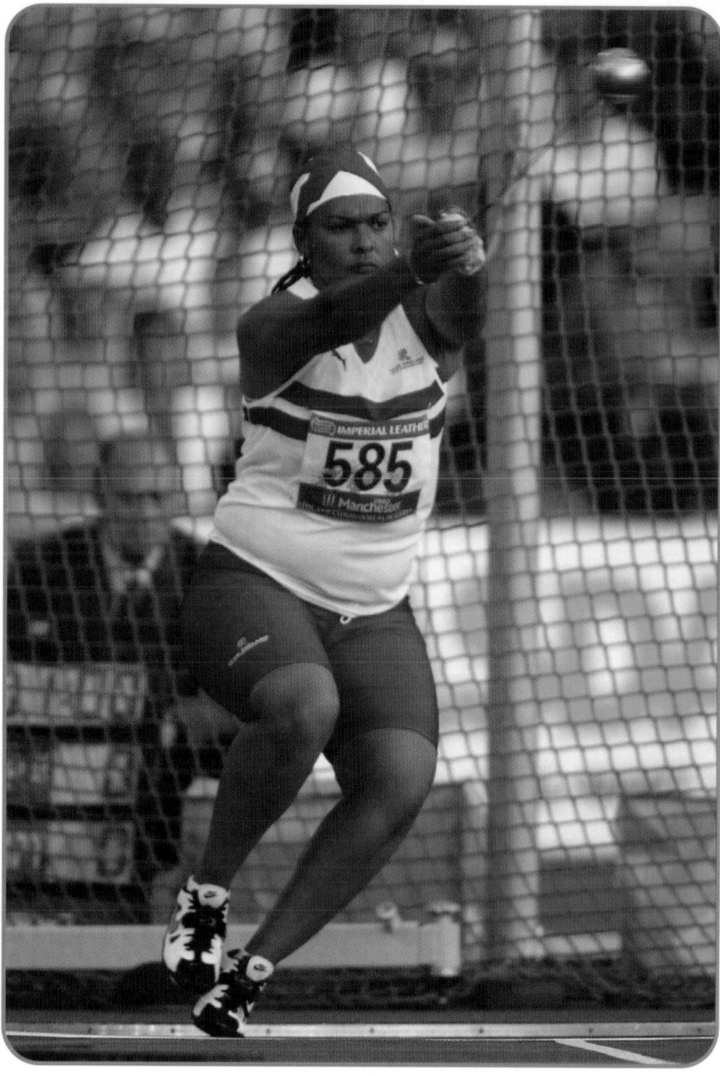

Standing vertical jump
Stand next to a wall and reach up with whichever arm is nearest to the wall. Mark the highest point you can reach with your fingers. Both feet must remain flat on the floor at this stage. Now chalk your fingers and perform a vertical jump, marking the wall at the highest point you can reach. The distance between the two marks gives a measure of how high you can leap from the ground from a stationary start. It takes into account your height and so is a fairer test than the standing broad jump.

The importance of power
Although power is not used a great deal in our everyday activities, we need it for certain physical tasks such as digging a hole or swinging a sledgehammer. Children often use power in their play, when they run, throw and jump.

Power is used a great deal in activities such as sprinting, throwing and jumping or when we try to move an object or ourselves as far and as fast as possible. Athletes need a lot of power, as do games players, racket players and gymnasts.

Standing vertical jump: comparative scores (centimetres)

	Males 15–16 years	Females 15–16 years
High score	Above 65	Above 60
Above average	65–56	60–51
Average	55–50	50–41
Below average	49–40	40–35
Low score	Less than 40	Less than 35

Reaction time

Reaction time is 'the time between the presentation of a stimulus and the onset of a movement.' (Edexcel.) A reaction can be simple, or it can involve choice:

- **Simple reaction time** is the time taken between the stimulus and our movement – for example, between the gun going off in a sprint race and a runner's first movement off the starting block.
- **Choice reaction time** is the time taken between the stimulus and an action which involves making a choice – for example, when we receive a ball from an opponent in a tennis match.

In both cases we have to react quickly; but in the first case, no choice has to be made. In the second case, we have to decide where and how to hit the ball. These decisions depend on where the ball is about to land, in which direction our opponent is moving and many other factors. We are therefore involved in making choices. The more skilled and experienced the player, the more likely he or she is to make the right choice and to hit the most appropriate type of return.

It is not possible to improve our simple reaction time through training. Speed of reaction to a single stimulus is due mainly to the efficiency of the nervous system. If we are lucky, our sensory and motor nerves will be capable of transmitting messages efficiently, and our muscles will get the message from our brain very quickly.

However, we can improve our choice reaction time a great deal through practice and experience. In a game like hockey, players will be receiving stimuli from their:

- **eyes**: about the position of the ball, other players and goal
- **ears**: from players, spectators and referee
- **kinaesthetic sense**: about their own body position and their options to pass, kick, etc.

Skilled players can reduce their choice reaction time by focusing on important information. They can anticipate the action of other players and the movement of the ball. This skill is developed mainly through training and experience.

Movement time

Movement time is the time that we take to move *once the decision to move has been made*. If we have a high percentage of fast twitch fibres, we will be able to respond faster than people with a high percentage of slow twitch fibres. We can improve movement time by improving our power.

How do we measure our reaction time?

A number of computer programmes are available to measure reaction time. They ask for a response as quickly as possible to a stimulus such as a sound or a visual cue. Some measure simple action times by only asking for one response to a single stimulus. Others measure choice reaction time by giving a variety of responses, only one of which is correct.

The importance of reaction time

All of us have to respond quickly to situations in everyday life. Examples include driving a car, riding a bike and crossing the road. Quick reactions can often prevent accidents – sometimes even save lives.

Simple reaction time is very important in sporting activities such as the 100-metre sprint on the track or in the pool. Choice reaction time is important in all games where we have to respond rapidly and effectively to the movements of other players, a ball, or both. However, movement time is critical in all sports and is most easily improved through training.

Speed

Speed is 'the differential rate at which an individual is able to perform a movement or cover a distance in a period of time'. (Edexcel.) More simply, speed is the ability to move all or part of the body as quickly as possible.

In order for our bodies to achieve speed, we have to supply energy to our muscles very quickly. The muscles then have to contract in the shortest possible time. We use our anaerobic energy supply system for speed work. If we have a high percentage of fast twitch fibres in our active muscles, we will have a natural advantage.

We cannot increase the percentage of fast twitch fibres in our bodies, but we can improve our speed in sport in other ways, such as:

- increasing our strength through a programme of weight training and plyometrics. Stronger muscles will give more power and therefore more speed.
- improving our reaction time
- improving our ability to change speed and direction when moving quickly (see page 66)
- improving our ability to cope with lactic acid (see pages 120–125)

- improving our skill in sport; for example, a more efficient swimming stroke will create less resistance and increase speed in the water.

How do we measure our speed?

Speed can be measured simply by recording the time it takes us to run a certain distance – for example, 50 metres – using a stopwatch. Reaction time, speed off the mark, time to reach top speed and deceleration times can all be measured as part of a training programme.

Why is speed important?

Children develop the ability to move quickly through play. Although adults do not need speed for everyday tasks, the ability to move quickly can be important in emergencies. Examples include moving out of the way of falling objects or moving to help another person at a time of need.

50-metre speed test: comparative scores (seconds)

	Males 15–16 years	Females 15–16 years
High score	Faster than 7.2	Faster than 7.8
Above average	7.2–7.8	7.8–8.4
Average	7.9–8.4	8.5–9.0
Below average	8.5–9.0	9.1–9.6
Low score	Slower than 9.1	Slower than 9.7

Speed is important in sports that require a great deal of effort over a very short period of time. Sprinters, speed skaters and sprint cyclists all need to develop speed. It is also important in many team games, when a sudden change of pace and direction is needed. Some sports require speed for the whole body, for example, long jumping; while for the javelin, shoulder and arm speed are of major importance.

activity

Fitness factors

Look at the photographs below:

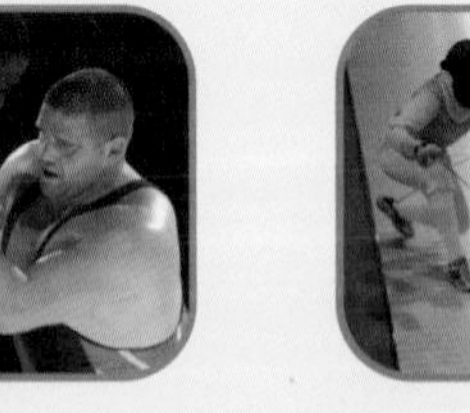

A Basketball **B** Wrestling **C** Fencing **D** Hammer

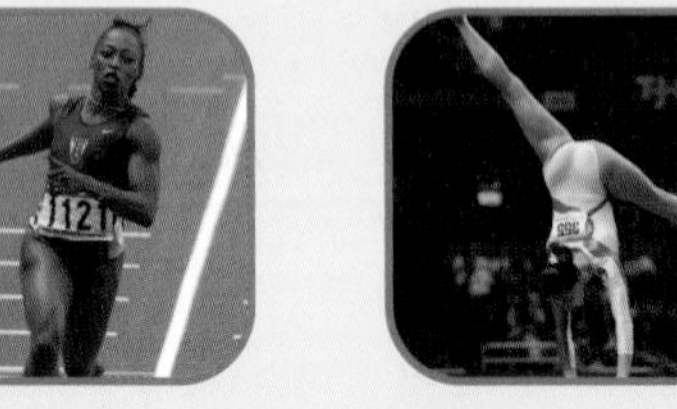

E High jump **F** Marathon **G** Sprinting **H** Gymnastics

activity

Write down the sport, or sports, in which you can see examples of the following fitness factors and present your results in the form of a table:

- good dynamic balance
- high level of cardiovascular fitness
- flexibility
- appropriate body composition
- muscular strength
- high level of power
- muscular endurance
- speed
- agility
- co-ordination
- quick reaction time.

Fitness classification grid

Referring back to the material in this chapter, gather statements about each of the six factors of fitness and arrange them in a table like the one shown below:

Fitness factor	Definition	Importance in sport	Measured by	Improved/developed by

Fitness Match

For this activity you will need to refer to the Fitness Match Grid which links fitness testing with the planning of your PEP. If you do not have this, ask your teacher for a copy.

Using the grid, decide the fitness requirements of your chosen sport, test your levels of fitness and analyse your results.

QUESTIONS

4 Skill-related fitness

Answer questions 1–4 by choosing statements a, b, c or d. One mark for each question.

1 The standing vertical jump can be used to measure:

a balance
b muscular endurance
c power
d flexibility.

2 Agility is:

a the amount of force a muscle can exert against a resistance

b the ability to change the position of the body quickly

c the ability to perform complex movements easily

d The range of limb movement possible at a joint.

3 Champion surfers need outstanding:

a muscular endurance
b speed
c stamina
d balance.

4 Co-ordination can be assessed by using:

a Stork Stand Test
b Illinois Agility Run
c juggling
d 60-metre sprint.

5 a Consider the following three sporting actions:

i a sprinter starting a race
ii a high jumper at take-off
iii a surfer riding a wave.

For each action state the major aspect of skill-related fitness and explain how it relates to the performance.

(3 marks)

b In order to be effective at basketball, the player uses different components of both health-related and skill-related fitness. Complete the following table by filling in the gaps:

(7 marks)

Component of fitness	Health-related (HR) or skill-related (SR)	Use of component by basketball player
		Ability to maintain equilibrium whether stationary or moving
Power		
Co-ordination		
	SR	Able to change direction at speed on court

QUESTIONS

6 Grace is a footballer who wants to improve her performance. She knows about the factors of skill-related fitness.

a Explain what each of the following factors means when applied to football:

i speed
ii reaction time
iii co-ordination
iv power.

(4 marks)

b Suggest one method for measuring Grace's:

i power
ii agility
iii balance
iv speed.

(4 marks)

c Suggest one way in which Grace could improve her:

i power
ii speed
iii agility
iv balance

(4 marks)

d Grace needs to have basic good health in order to train properly. Choose four of the factors of good health (muscular strength, muscular endurance, flexibility, cardiovascular endurance, body composition). Explain what is meant by each factor and say why it is important for Grace in her football performance.

(8 marks)
(Total 34 marks)

5 Principles of training

To be successful in sport, we need our energy systems and sporting skills to be at their highest possible level. We can reach these high levels by training. Training consists of a regular programme of exercise to improve performance. Our training programmes must be based on a number of basic principles. There are many different methods of training and ways of organising a training programme. We must be sure that our Personal Exercise Programme (PEP) is right for our sport and our levels of fitness and skill.

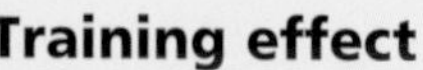

activity

Training effect

This activity is an experiment to see whether or not different types of training bring about an improvement in performance. To begin with, you will need to test your ability to juggle three tennis balls using both hands. You will count the number of successful catches and record your best of three attempts.

Next, you need to join one of three groups, and to practise the following for 20 minutes:

- Group A: juggling with two tennis balls using one hand
- Group B: bouncing a tennis ball continuously on the ground
- Group C: juggling with three tissues or scarves using both hands.

After your practice session, your juggling ability with the three tennis balls will be re-tested and the results entered in a table.

Use the information from your results to answer the following questions:

1. What sort of practice is most likely to improve your juggling skills?
2. Is this true for both boys and girls?
3. Is practising bouncing a tennis ball more likely to improve your juggling skills than practising with tissues or scarves?
4. Do you think your answers would apply to other sporting skills?
5. Does slowing down the skill, e.g. using the tissues or scarves, improve learning?

KEYWORDS

Aerobic threshold: the minimum rate at which our heart must work in order to improve our aerobic fitness

Aerobic training: training our cardiorespiratory system to provide the working muscles with enough oxygen to work for a long period of time

Anaerobic threshold: The minimum rate at which our heart must work in order to improve our anaerobic fitness

Anaerobic training: training our cardiorespiratory and muscular systems to work for a limited amount of time without enough oxygen

FITT principles: frequency, intensity, time, type – the basis for planning a fitness programme

Overload: training harder than you would normally in order to improve fitness

Periodisation: dividing a training programme into different parts – for example, pre-season, peak season and off-season

Progression: starting slowly and gradually increasing the amount of exercise you do

Reversibility: the principle that any adaptation that takes place as a consequence of training will be reversed when you stop training

Specificity: the principle that you must do specific kinds of activity or exercise to develop specific body parts

SPORT principles: specificity, progression, overload, reversibility, tedium – the basis for planning a training programme

Tedium: the result of lack of variety in training. Can also lead to increased risk of overuse injuries

Training: a well-planned programme which uses scientific principles to improve performance, skills, games ability and motor and physical fitness

Training threshold: minimum rate at which heart must work to bring about fitness improvements

Training zone: range of heart rate within which a specific training effect will take place.

Key to Exam Success

For your GCSE you will need to:

- know how training can be planned to improve health-related and skill-related fitness
- understand how training affects health and performance
- understand and apply the SPORT and FITT principles of training to any training programme, including your own personal fitness programme
- be able to monitor exercise training in order to bring about improvements.

“ KEY THOUGHT ”

‘Thoughtful training delivers the goods!’

Principles of training

Neither health-related fitness nor skill-related fitness can be achieved by chance. We need to work at all aspects of our fitness by following a training programme.

Our training must:

- be based on sound principles
- be systematic and planned
- take account of individual needs.

Training affects our health, our fitness and our performance. For steady progress, and to avoid injury, we should follow the SPORT principles:

- Specificity
- Progression
- Overload
- Reversibility
- Tedium.

Specificity

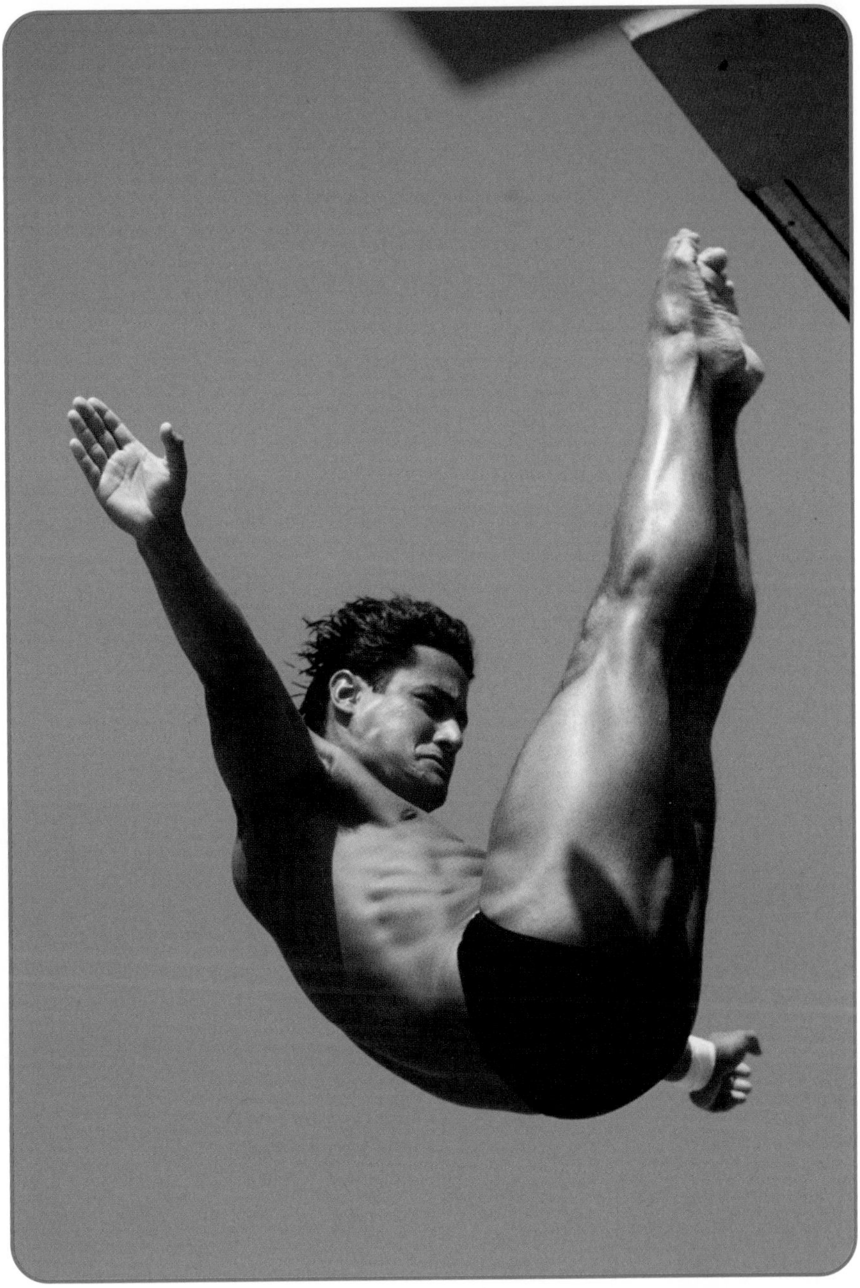

The principle of **specificity** states that 'you must do specific kinds of activity or exercise to build specific body parts'. (Edexcel.) Every type of exercise has a particular effect on the body. The type of training we choose must be right for the type of improvement we want to see. For example, if we want to improve the strength of our arms, then running will not help: we must use strength-training exercises that work our arms. We must always use a training programme that puts regular stress on the muscle groups or body system that we want to develop.

Our training programme must also be designed to suit the needs of our sport. For example:

- Sprinters need to include a lot of speed work in their training. This helps their fast twitch muscle fibres to develop.
- Endurance athletes need to develop their slow twitch muscle fibres. They train over longer distances or for a longer time.
- Games players need to include both speed and endurance training in their programmes to develop both types of muscle fibres.

Progression

Progression in training means that you should 'start slowly and gradually increase the amount of exercise you do'. (Edexcel.)

Our body takes time to adapt to more or harder exercise. We must build up the stress on our bodies in a gradual, or progressive, way – by lifting heavier weights or running further each time. If we build up the stress too quickly we will risk injury or find the challenge too great and give up. If we build up the stress too slowly we may become uninterested or bored and give up.

The body also needs time to recover and adapt to training. Our bones, ligaments and tendons may take longer to change than our muscles or other body systems. Our training thresholds will tell us if we are training at the right level.

If we are unfit, we can improve our fitness level quickly. The fitter we become, the harder it is to improve.

Overload

The principle of **overload** is that 'fitness can only be improved through training more than you normally do'. (Edexcel.) In other words, to improve the fitness of our body systems, we need to work them harder than normal. The body will then adapt to the extra stress and we will become fitter.

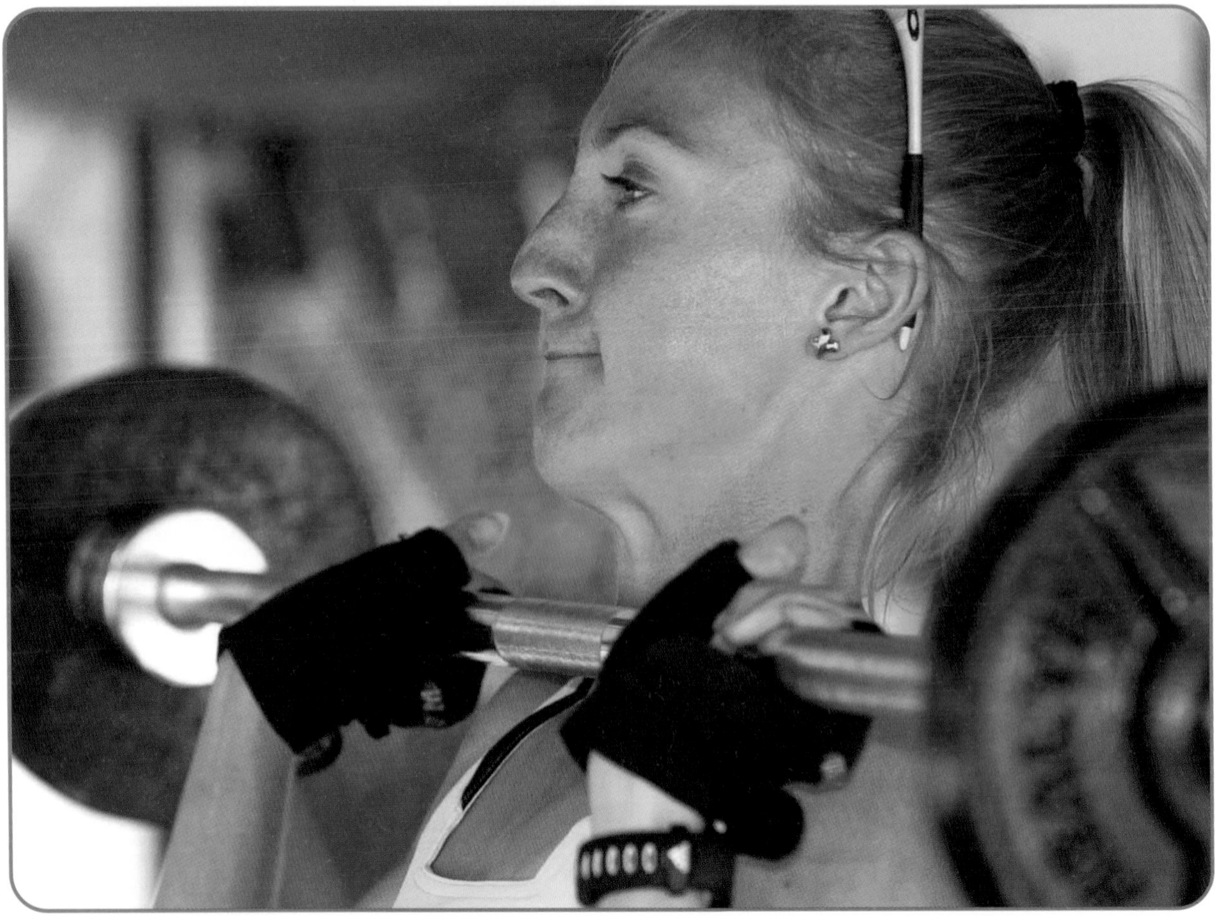

We can overload our bodies by training more often, by working harder or by spending more time on an exercise. For example, to improve aerobic fitness by running, we could run more often during the week, complete the run in a shorter time or increase the distance we run. Each one of these methods will overload the aerobic system. The aerobic system will gradually adapt to cope with the overload and we will become fitter.

Reversibility

Reversibility means that 'any adaptation that takes place as a consequence of training will be reversed when you stop training'. (Edexcel)

Our bodies adapt to the stress of exercise by becoming fitter. In the same way, we quickly adapt to less exercise by losing fitness. If our muscles are not used, they atrophy – that is, they waste away. We cannot store fitness for future use: it will decrease if we stop training. It takes only 3–4 weeks for our bodies to get out of condition if we are not exercising.

We lose our aerobic fitness more easily than our anaerobic fitness because our muscles quickly lose much of their ability to use oxygen. Our anaerobic fitness is less affected by lack of training. If we follow a strength-training programme for 4 weeks, we will lose our gains in strength after about 12 weeks of inactivity.

Although it is natural to want to achieve results quickly, it is important that exercise is done in moderation, otherwise ill-effects will result. We train to improve our performance. Overtraining – that is, too much training – can be bad for our health. Our bodies need to rest and sleep between training sessions. Overtraining can cause muscle soreness, joint pain, sleeping problems, loss of appetite and extreme tiredness. After injury or illness we must start training again only gradually.

Tedium

Our training programme must be varied to avoid **tedium**, or boredom. By using a variety of different training methods we will keep our enthusiasm and **motivation**. For example:

- We can follow a long workout with a short one, a hard session with a relaxed one or a high-speed session with a long, slow one.
- We can change where we train and when we train.
- We can avoid overuse injuries by varying the way we train. For example, shin splints can be avoided by running on grass rather than on hard roads.

Evaluating a training programme

Examine the following training programmes. Decide how far you think each programme has been based on the principles outlined above. Summarise your findings and be prepared to discuss them with the whole class.

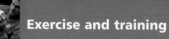

activity

Programme 1: Six-week programme for Sharon, a cross-country runner

	Monday	Tuesday	Wednesday	Thursday	Friday	Saturday	Sunday
Week 1 programme	10-mile run	Gym work, concentrating on upper body strength	Fartlek	Track work, 400-metre repetitions ×10	Rest day	Race	30-minute swim, continuous lengths
Following 5 weeks	No change	Increase weights gradually	Increase total distance run	Reduce rest time between repetitions	Rest day	Race	No change

Programme 2: Six-week programme for Errol, a badminton player

	Monday	Tuesday	Wednesday	Thursday	Friday	Saturday	Sunday
Week 1 programme	Skill practice for 1 hour	Endurance training on court – 1 hour	Light weights (high reps.) in gym	Gym work: 30-min. run, 20-min. bike, 20-min. rowing	Match practice	Stretching and plyometrics	League game
Following 5 weeks	No change	No change	Increase speed and reps.	Increase work rate	No change	No change	League game

Programme 3: Six-week programme for Mandy, a football player

	Monday	Tuesday	Wednesday	Thursday	Friday	Saturday	Sunday
Week 1 programme	5-aside matches	Power lifting in the gym	Match	Rest day	10-mile run	Match	Rest day
Following 5 weeks	No change	Heavier weights	No change	No change	No change	No change	No change

Programme 4: Six-week programme for Ahmed, a swimmer

	Monday	Tuesday	Wednesday	Thursday	Friday	Saturday	Sunday
Week 1 programme	100-metre repetitions – various strokes ×20	200-metre repetitions – various strokes ×10	1 hour technique improvement, including turns	2 miles continuous – fast	1 hour technique improvement, including turns	Competition	5 miles continuous lengths
Following 5 weeks	Reduce time for both reps. and recovery	Reduce time for both reps. and recovery	No change	No change	No change	No change	No change

Sharon

Errol

Mandy

Ahmed

Meeting individual needs

We have seen that training programmes must be designed to develop the specific fitness, strength and skills required for each sport. Training programmes must also be designed to meet the individual needs of the sportsperson. The following factors should be considered:

- **age and experience**: a training programme designed for a 30-year-old county player will not meet the needs of a 14-year-old student who wants to get into the school team
- **fitness level**: training programmes must start from our current fitness level and progress from there
- **sporting ability**: training programmes must develop the skills which we already have and introduce new skills in a progressive manner
- **motivation**: our training programme must ensure a good balance of challenge and success.

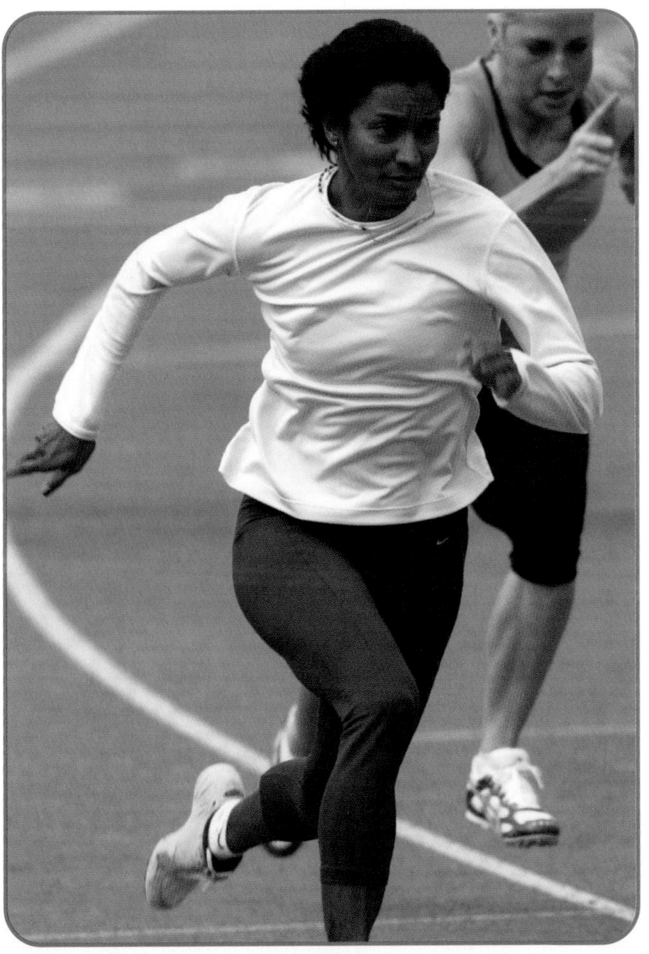

Thresholds of training

We need to know exactly how hard and how long we should train in order to improve our fitness and therefore our sporting performance. If we train at too low a level we will make little improvement in our fitness. If we try to train too hard we will quickly become exhausted or suffer injury and be unable to complete the programme. We need to calculate our own individual **thresholds** of training so that we can work to best effect.

To train effectively we must know:

- the amount of **anaerobic training** we need for our sport
- the amount of **aerobic training** we need for our sport
- our present level of fitness.

To calculate our individual threshold of training we can use our maximum heart rate (MHR). This can be estimated using the following formula:

- MHR (males) = 220 – age
- MHR (females) = 226 – age.

Our **aerobic threshold** can then be calculated by working out 60% of our MHR.

If we work above this level we will be improving our aerobic fitness.

Our **anaerobic threshold** can be calculated by working out 80% of our MHR.

If we work above this level we will be improving our anaerobic fitness.

	Males		Females	
	15 years	16 years	15 years	16 years
60% MHR Aerobic threshold	123	122	127	126
80% MHR Anaerobic threshold	164	163	169	168

Different sports require different amounts of aerobic and anaerobic fitness. For example, a marathon runner will rely almost entirely on aerobic fitness, whilst a 100-metre sprinter will not use aerobic fitness at all during the race. Sprinters need instant energy which is provided in the absence of oxygen. They will therefore need to develop their anaerobic fitness. Games players need both aerobic and anaerobic fitness and their training programmes will need to develop both types. The aerobic and anaerobic energy systems are dealt with in more detail on page 216.

activity

Calculating training zones

To achieve results, we must train in the appropriate ***training zone****. Consider the following training sessions for Floella, Jim, Janice and Mustafa. Calculate their individual* ***aerobic*** *and* ***anaerobic thresholds*** *and decide in which training zone they are working.*

- **Floella** is a 26-year-old racing cyclist. During a sprint training session she tries to maintain her heart rate at 155 beats per minute.

- 30-year-old **Jim** is doing a cross-country run and has maintained a heart rate of 158 for the last 15 minutes.

- **Janice** is 18-years-old and is doing interval training. Today's training session involves her completing ten 60-metre sprints with her heart rate raised to 170 beats per minute.

- **Mustafa**, who is 47 years old, swims regularly and keeps his heart rate above 105 throughout his swim.

Planning a training programme

We need to train to improve our fitness and therefore our performance. When planning a fitness programme we should follow the **FITT principles**:

- Frequency
- Intensity
- Time
- Type.

Frequency – how often we train

- We should train at least three times a week to improve our fitness.
- Our body needs time to recover from each training session.
- We should spread these sessions out over the week.

Intensity – how hard we train

- We will only get fitter if we work our body systems hard enough to make them adapt.
- We must start at the right intensity, depending on our current fitness.
- We must understand and use our training thresholds.

Time – how long we train

- To improve aerobic fitness, our training sessions should last longer and our working heart rate should rise.
- Each session must last at least 20 minutes to achieve real benefit.

Type – what kind of training we do

- We should analyse our particular sport to know the fitness and skills we need.
- Our training programme should include different types of activity to develop these skills and fitness.

Periodisation

If we take part in competitive sport we will naturally want to be at our best at the time of our most important competition. This is called peaking. Our training programmes will vary with the type of sport and the level of competition. We therefore need to plan well ahead. Dividing a training programme into different parts is called **periodisation**. For example, for many sports we could talk about three main periods: pre-season, peak season and off-season.

Pre-season

During the pre-season period you should:

- focus on fitness for your particular sport
- concentrate on muscular endurance, power and speed work
- develop the techniques, skills and strategies for your particular sport.

Peak season

During the peak season you should:

- emphasise speed
- practise your skills at high speed and in competitive situations
- add extra fitness sessions if you do not compete enough.

Off-season

Following the competitive season, you need a period of active rest at first. You then need to:

- maintain a high level of general fitness through moderate activity
- develop muscular strength, flexibility and aerobic fitness
- develop your sports skills.

activity

An annual training schedule

Draw up an annual training schedule applying the guidelines about periodisation outlined above to your own sport. This may help you in the planning of your PEP.

Planning individual training sessions

To avoid injury and to get the most out of training, we should divide each session into three phases: warm-up, main activity and warm-down.

Warm-up

Our warm-up should include:

- gentle exercise for the whole body, such as light jogging. This gradually increases heart rate, breathing and blood supply to the muscles. It warms up our muscles and prepares us mentally for the session.
- gentle stretching, to prepare muscles, ligaments and joints and to prevent injury
- practising techniques and skills to be used in the session.

Main activity

Our main activity could be fitness training, skill development or a combination of both, depending on our needs. If our sport is a game, then one activity should be a conditioned game.

Fitness training

Our fitness activities will depend on the demands of our sport, but we can design fitness activities to develop skills as well.

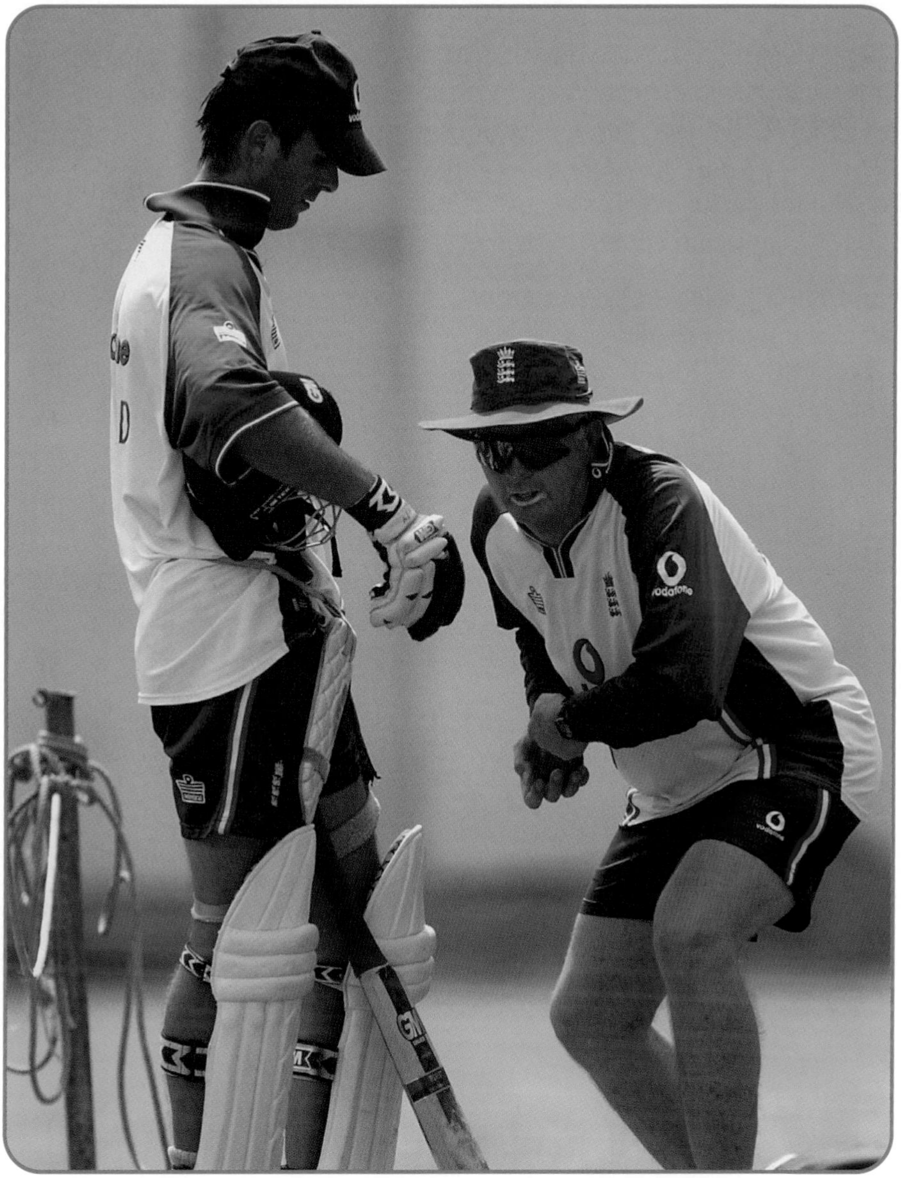

If training is too intense at the start of the session we may be too tired to practise our skills well later. However, games players need to practise their games skills when they are tired.

Skill development
The techniques and skills we need to develop will depend on our particular sport. We may need to work in pairs, in small groups, or in teams as well as on our own. We may play small-sided and modified games.

Conditioned game
Skill development practice must lead naturally into small-sided and modified games. In this way our skills will be transferred from training to the match situation.

Warm-down
Every training session should end with a period of lighter exercise. Always avoid going from hard exercise immediately to rest. Light exercise during the warm-down decreases recovery time by helping

to remove carbon dioxide, lactic acid and other waste products from the body. It also ensures that the blood continues to circulate well and prevents it pooling in the skeletal muscles, which may reduce blood pressure and cause dizziness.

While the muscles are thoroughly warm, flexibility exercises can be carried out with less chance of injury through over-stretching. Light exercise will also prevent muscle soreness and stiffness later.

Matching training to individual needs

The training programmes for an elderly, recreational tennis player and a young, competitive pole-vaulter would be very different. This is because training programmes need to be designed for the individual sport and for an individual sportsperson (or group of sportspeople at a similar level of ability).

Before planning the programme you must therefore find out about:

- the sport (skill requirements)
- the type of fitness needed (body composition, muscular strength, cardiovascular endurance, flexibility, power, muscular endurance, speed, agility, co-ordination, balance, reaction time)
- the principles of training (SPORT: specificity, progression, overload, reversibility, tedium and FITT: frequency, intensity, time, type)
- the types of training available (continuous, fartlek, interval, circuit, weight, flexibility, plyometric)
- the training year for the sport (pre-season, peak season, off season)
- the sportsperson's individual needs (age, health, fitness level, experience, sporting ability, motivation).

Your Personal Exercise Programme (PEP)

When developing a successful PEP, you must apply the principles of training (SPORT) and make it specific to your sport and to your current level of fitness. It must be progressive and involve overload, in order to increase your cardiovascular strength, muscular strength, muscular endurance and flexibility gradually and safely. You must maintain your programme over time in order to avoid reversibility and vary your training to avoid tedium. You must also remember that your body needs time to recover from training and that moderation in training is important.

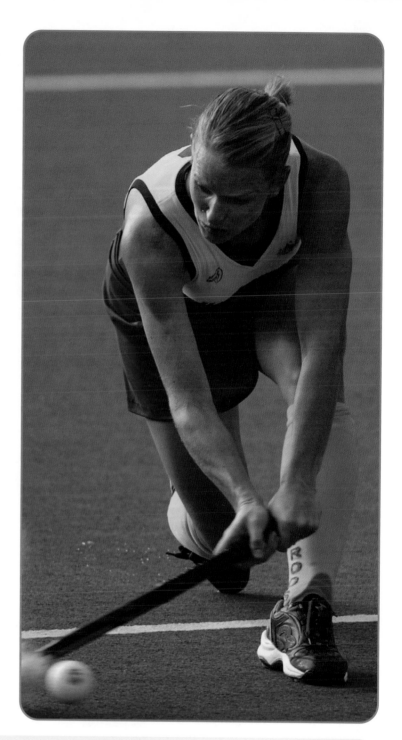

Detailed planning of your programme must also involve the FITT principles – that is, how often you train, how hard you train, how long you train and what type of training you do.

You must be aware of the aerobic and anaerobic demands of your sport and plan your training to ensure that you achieve the appropriate thresholds of training.

For each individual training session you must include a warm-up and warm down, whilst your main activity will be dependent on the particular skill development and fitness training required for your sport. Remember that your training programme must be designed to satisfy your individual needs in your chosen sport.

activity

Planning an individual training session

Prepare a training session specific to your chosen sport. Be sure to consider periodisation – in other words, match what you include in the training session with the training period, (pre-, peak or off-season) in which it is to take place. Include enough detail to allow someone else to lead the session if necessary.

QUESTIONS

5 Principles of training

Answer questions 1–4 by choosing statements a, b, c or d. One mark for each question.

1 In training, specificity means:

a gradually increasing the work done
b working harder than normal
c closely resembling the sporting activity
d varying training methods.

2 A training session should always finish with a:

a skill practice
b fitness session
c game
d warm-down.

3 The maximum heart rate for a 16-year-old girl is:

a 200 bpm
b 210 bpm
c 220 bpm
d 230 bpm.

4 In the FITT training principles, frequency means:

a how often we train
b how hard we train
c how long we train
d what kind of training we do.

5 Darren is a 16-year-old basketball player.

a Darren wants to apply the SPORT principles of specificity, progression, overload, reversibility and tedium to his training programme. Select three of these principles, explain what each means and give one example of the way that Darren can apply each in his training.

(6 marks)

b Darren has decided that he needs to develop both his aerobic and anaerobic capacity for basketball. Work out his aerobic and anaerobic thresholds.

(2 marks)

c Explain what is meant by periodisation when producing a year-long training programme.

(2 marks)

6 Ying is an enthusiastic 16-year-old footballer but finds it hard to get a regular place in the school team. She is advised to plan and follow a fitness programme based on the FITT principles of frequency, intensity, time and type.

a Give two ways in which each of the FITT principles could be applied to her training programme.

(8 marks)

b Ying has been asked to take a football training session for some younger players. She plans to include five sections in this training session. Name each of the five sections she should use and give an example of an activity which she could include in each section.

(10 marks)

c Suggest two differences between the training Ying might do during pre-season and in peak season.

(2 marks)

(Total 34 marks)

6 Methods of training

Success in sport only comes with dedicated training – and the key to success is to select the right methods of training. There are many different training methods available and it is important to understand their benefits and disadvantages. Together with the practical application of the principles of training, this will help you to achieve your potential in your chosen sport.

activity

Training for success

Look at these photographs of sportspeople in action. What methods of training do you think they used to reach this level of performance?

Discuss your ideas.

KEYWORDS

Aerobic activity: 'with oxygen'. If exercise is not too fast and is steady, the heart can supply all the oxygen the muscles need

Anaerobic activity: 'Without oxygen'. If exercise is done in short, fast bursts, the heart cannot supply blood and oxygen to the muscles as fast as the cells can use them

Fartlek: Literally 'speed play': a method of training in which pace and training conditions are varied

Interval training: any training using alternating periods of very hard exercise and rest

Isometric contraction: muscular contraction which results in increased tension but does not cause the length of the muscles to alter

Isotonic contraction: muscular contraction that results in limb movement

Oxygen debt: the amount of oxygen consumed during recovery above that which would ordinarily have been consumed in the same time at rest, resulting in a shortfall in the oxygen available

Lactic acid: waste product produced in the working muscles

Personal Exercise Programme (PEP): a programme of training drawn up for a specific sport and sportsperson

Plyometrics: training method using explosive movements to develop muscular power, for example, bounding and hopping

Recovery rate: length of time needed for the cardiorespiratory system to return to normal after activity

Target (training) zone: the range of heart rates which need to be achieved in order to bring about a specific training result.

Key to Exam Success

For your GCSE you will need to:

- understand the difference between isotonic and isometric muscular contraction
- know what is meant by circuit, weight, interval, continuous, cross, plyometric, flexibility and fartlek training
- be able to plan, perform, monitor and evaluate a six-week Personal Exercise Programme (PEP)
- understand the role of aerobic and anaerobic activity in relation to exercise
- describe the effects of exercise and training on the skeletal, muscular, cardiovascular and respiratory systems
- understand the meaning and use of recovery rates and target zones.

“ KEY THOUGHT ”

'Train well, play well.'

How do our muscles work?

Before looking at methods of training, we must understand the different ways our muscles work.

Our muscles can work in different ways according to the actions we are performing. Although they can only contract to cause movement, the way the muscles are positioned in our body means that this movement can vary enormously. For example, the very large muscles in our thighs not only drive us forward at a sprint start, they can also be used to help us hold a delicate balance in gymnastics.

There are two main types of muscular contraction: isometric and isotonic.

Isometric muscular contraction

Isometric muscular contraction results in increased tension but does not cause the muscle length to alter. During isometric muscular contraction, our muscle fibres do not shorten or lengthen and there is no movement around our joints. Throughout sport we can see isometric muscle contraction at work, for example, when we hold a handstand, hold the bow bent in archery and push in the scrum. Many of our muscles help to stabilise our body as our limbs move. They do this by working isometrically.

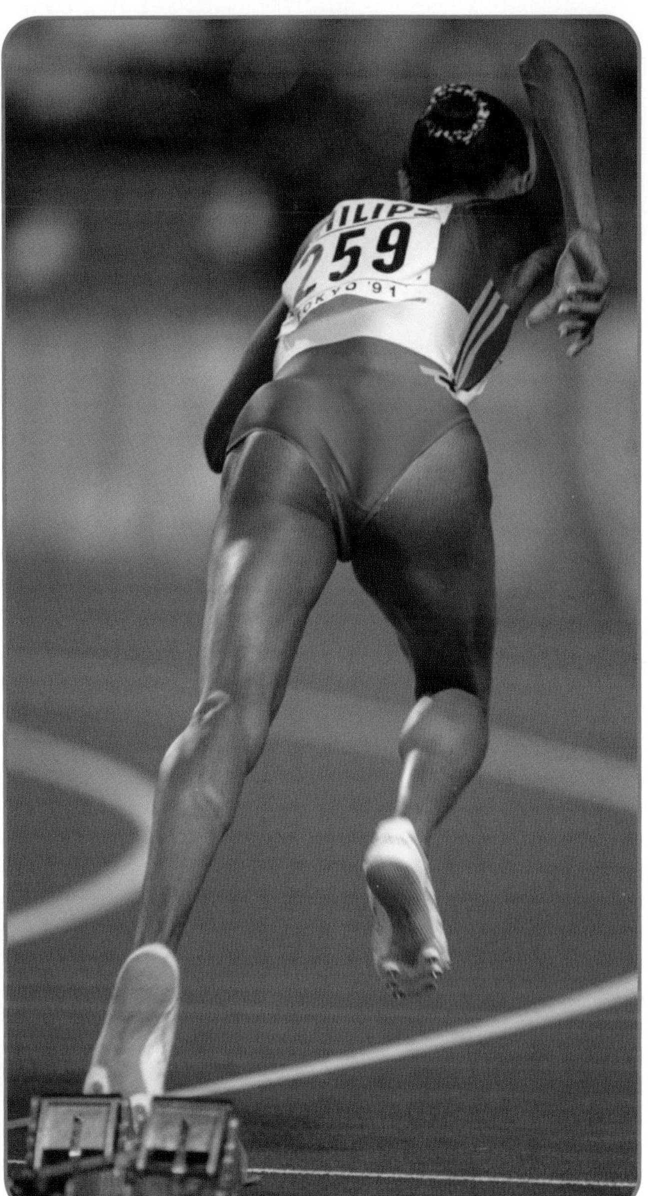

Isotonic muscular contraction

Isotonic contraction is 'muscular contraction that results in limb movement'. (Edexcel.) During isotonic muscular contraction our muscle fibres shorten or lengthen causing movement around our joints. Most sporting action involves isotonic muscular contraction of some sort.

Isotonic contraction can be either concentric or eccentric.

- **Concentric** muscular action takes place when the contracting muscle fibres shorten. This is the action we see most often in sporting movement. For example, when we do pull-ups on a bar, the muscle fibres in the biceps are shortening as they contract and bring the shoulder up to the wrist.
- **Eccentric** muscular action takes place when the contracting muscle fibres lengthen. For example, when lowering yourself from the pull-up position on the bar, the muscle fibres of the biceps are lengthening as they contract and lower the shoulder away from the wrist. Plyometric exercise uses eccentric contractions.

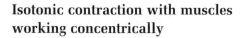

Isotonic contraction with muscles working concentrically

The muscles shorten as they contract

The ends of the muscle move closer together

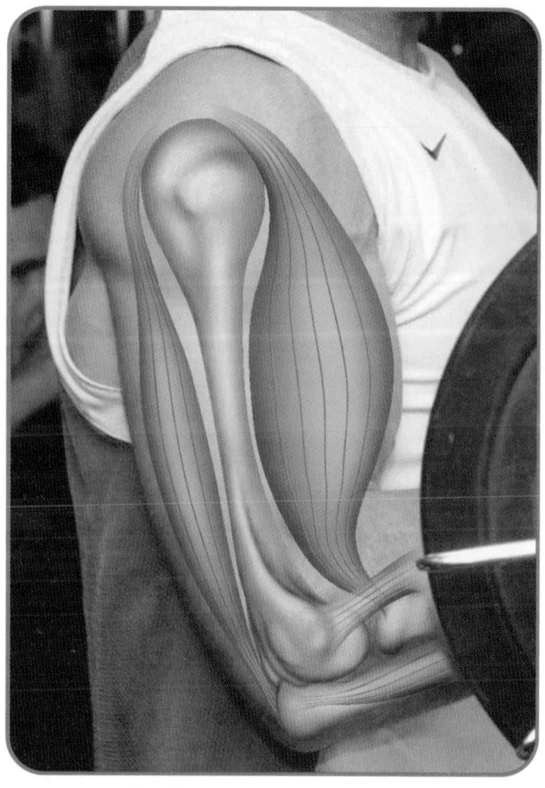

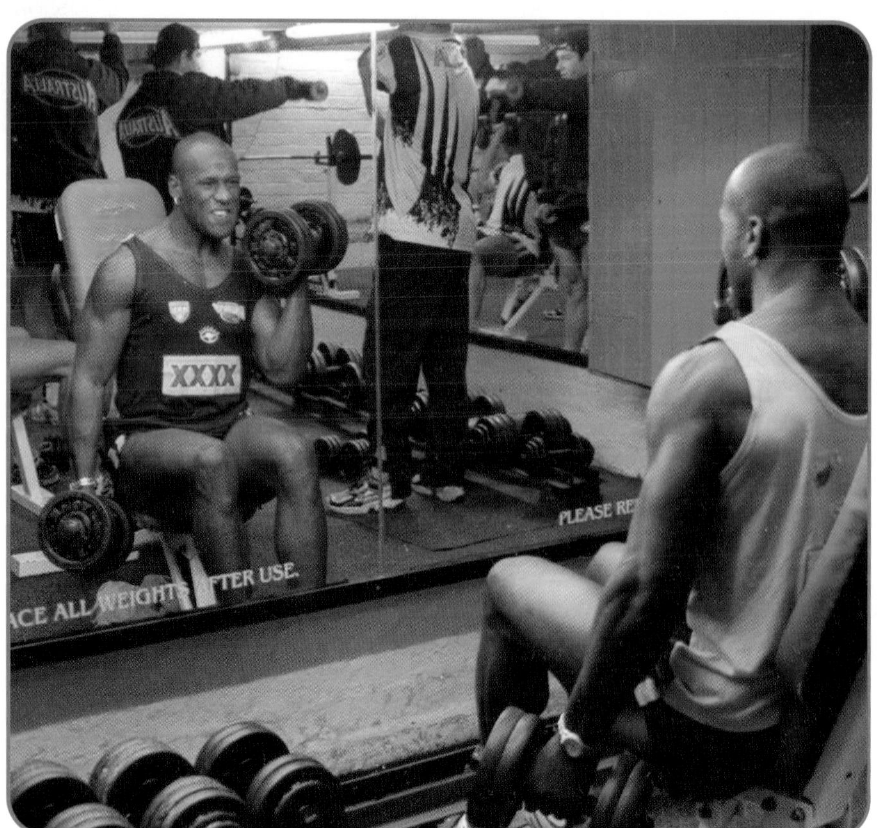

Isotonic contraction with muscles working eccentrically

The muscles lengthen as they contract under tension

The ends of the muscle move further apart

Isometric contraction

The muscles stay at the same length as they contract

There is no movement, so the ends of the muscles stay the same distance apart

activity

Feel the difference

This activity will help you to understand the three different ways in which muscles work.

1. Hold a textbook in your preferred hand with your arm extended by your side.
2. Bend your arm to raise the book to your shoulder. Place the fingers of your other hand on your biceps and feel the contraction. This is an isotonic, concentric contraction.
3. Slowly lower the book to the starting position and feel your biceps contracting as it lengthens. This is an isotonic, eccentric contraction.
4. Raise the book again but pause before your forearm is parallel to the floor. Hold the book steady and feel your biceps contracting. This is an isometric contraction as there is no movement taking place.

Training methods

There are many different training methods. They are all based on the different ways our body adapts to regular exercise, and include:

- continuous training
- cross training
- interval training
- fartlek training
- circuit training
- weight training
- plyometric training
- flexibility training.

Continuous training

Continuous training consists of working for sustained periods of time, using all major muscle groups of the body. Activity can include running, swimming, cycling, rowing, taking part in aerobics or any other whole-body activity.

Continuous training requires working at the same pace for between 30 minutes and two hours and being moderately active, that is, working in the aerobic training zone at 60–80% of MHR (Maximum Heart Rate).

Why use continuous training?

- to improve cardiovascular endurance
- to help improve health-related fitness
- to reduce amounts of body fat
- to maintain fitness in the off-season.

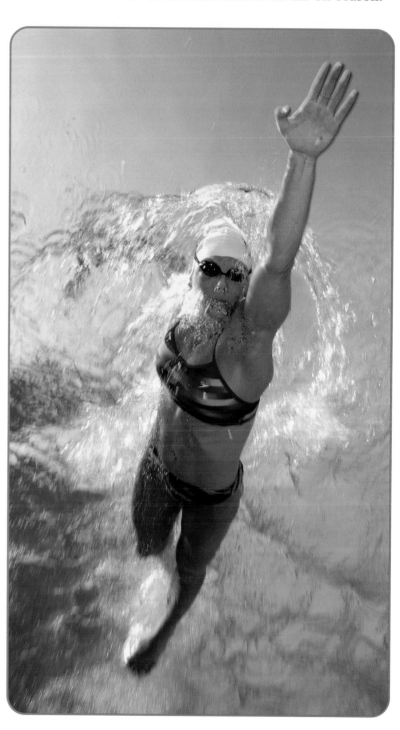

Who uses continuous training?

Everyone, because it forms the basis of all health-related fitness. In sport it is essential for all activities which continue over a period of time. Examples include all major team games, racket sports, swimming and running.

Cross training

Cross training involves using another sport or physical activity to improve your fitness for your own sport. For example, if you are a runner, you may cross-train on a bike. This will allow you to complete an intense workout, building up your quads and using up calories and at the same time minimising the risk of injury to your legs. Stair climbing will provide similar results. Not only will these activities provide variety, but they will give your legs a rest from the constant pounding they receive while running.

Why use cross training?

- to add variety to a training program and prevent tedium
- to prevent over-use injuries
- to rest well used muscles and yet at the same time complete an effective workout.

Who uses cross training?

Any sportsperson: for example, a swimmer may include weight training in his programme and rowers may train using cross-country skiing.

Interval training

Interval training consists of using alternating periods of very hard exercise and rest. Rest periods are essential for recovery and enable you to train for longer.

During interval training you can vary:

- the time or distance of each exercise
- the amount of effort (intensity) you put into each period of exercise
- the type of activity you take part in during each period of rest
- the number of exercise and recovery periods in the training session. For example, an interval training session on the track could involve six 200-metre runs in 30 seconds with 90 seconds rest between each.

Why use interval training?

The aim of interval training is to improve anaerobic and aerobic fitness. Your aerobic fitness will improve if you train for a long period at 60–80% of MHR. Your anaerobic fitness will improve if you train over a short period at 80–95% MHR.

Using this high-quality speed training you will need rests of 2–3 minutes, but it will develop your ability to work when tired.

Who uses interval training?

Interval training is a specialist training method for serious sportspeople and is not normally used for health-related fitness. It can be used to meet the needs of a variety of sports. Sprinters, for example, will allow sufficient time between sprints in order to recover fully. Games players will use programmes which alternate between working hard and light working – which is what happens in a game.

Fartlek training

The name **fartlek** comes from a Swedish word meaning 'speed play'. Fartlek involves deliberately varying the speed and intensity at which you walk, run, cycle or ski and the type of terrain over which you travel. A fartlek session normally lasts a minimum of 30 minutes.

Why use fartlek training?

- to improve aerobic and anaerobic fitness, depending on how you train
- to help games players who need both aerobic and anaerobic fitness
- to enable you to enjoy moving quickly but within your own ability
- to reduce tedium in training.

Who uses fartlek training?

Everyone can benefit from this type of training, as it can improve both aerobic and anaerobic fitness. In sport, it is regularly used in the training programmes of runners and skiers and can also be used simply to avoid tedium.

Circuit training

Circuit training involves performing a series of exercises or activities in a special order, called a circuit. A circuit usually consists of 6 to 10 exercises or activities, which take place at stations. At each station, a set number of repetitions is completed as quickly as possible, or as many repetitions as possible are completed in a fixed time, for example, one minute.

Circuits should be designed to avoid working the same muscle group at more than one station in succession. They should also include exercises that work opposing muscles around a joint.

As fitness improves, the circuit can be made more difficult by increasing:

- the number of stations
- the time spent at each station
- the number of repetitions at each station
- the number of complete circuits.

Why use circuit training?

Circuit training enables you to improve either aerobic or anaerobic fitness, or both at the same time. A great variety of exercises can be included, making it extremely adaptable for the needs of different sports.

Who uses circuit training?

Circuit training is a valuable training activity for almost all sports. For example, high jumpers can use programmes which concentrate on developing leg power, whilst basketball players can use programmes which develop leg power together with upper body strength and aerobic fitness. It is also possible to construct circuits for games players in which exercises are replaced by short skills practices – for example, passing a ball against a wall. At the same time, anyone who wants to achieve a basic level of health-related fitness can benefit from a suitably designed circuit.

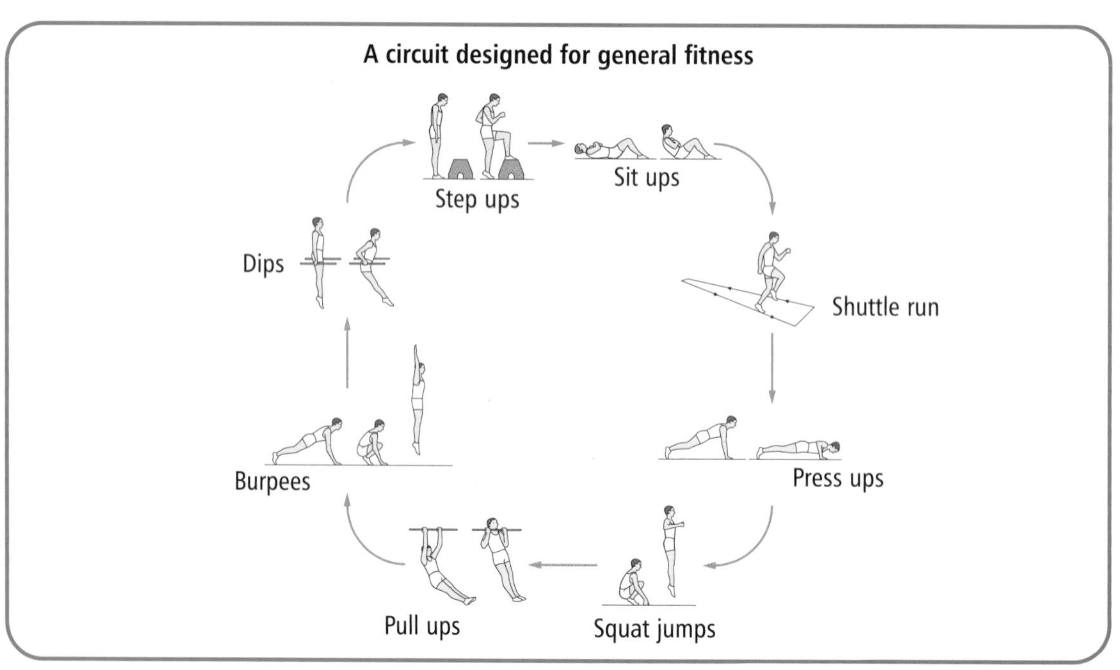

Weight training

In weight training, free weights or weights in machines are used to provide resistance to muscle power. Training consists of sequences or sets of exercises, and the weights used are gradually increased, allowing you to overload your muscles safely over a sensible period of time.

Any weight training programme can take account of your current state of fitness. Below are some guidelines for weight training:

- Decide which muscle groups are important for your sport and choose exercises to develop them.
- Aim for at least three training sessions a week.
- Make sure you are thoroughly warmed up before starting.
- Breathe out when you lift the weight and breathe in as you lower it.

- Never hold your breath, as this could make you faint.
- Work the different muscle groups in turn, to give time for recovery.
- Increase the weights as your muscles grow stronger.

Why use weight training?

The aim of weight training is to improve your strength, muscular endurance and power.

- Muscular strength is improved by using at least three sets of six repetitions at near-maximum weight.
- Muscular endurance is improved by using at least three sets of 20–30 repetitions. The weight should be 40–60% of the weight which you can lift just once (your one repetition maximum, or 1 RM).
- Power is improved by at least three sets of 10–15 repetitions. These should be done at speed, using 60–80% of your 1 RM.

Who uses weight training?

Anyone who wants a basic health-related fitness level can benefit from a suitable weight training programme.

Sportspeople looking to improve their sporting performance can design their own weight training programme by comparing the physical demands of their sport with their own current level of fitness.

Weight training programmes are included in the training programmes of most sportspeople. They are of particular importance to power athletes such as jumpers, sprinters and throwers.

Plyometric training

Plyometric training involves a series of explosive movements including bounds, hops, jumps (on to and off boxes) leaps, skips, press-ups with claps, throwing and catching a medicine ball, all of which are designed to improve muscular power (explosive strength). The muscles can be stretched before they contract. This stores up elastic energy. When they next contract, they will produce extra power.

For example, in a vertical jump, you:

- bend at the knees, which stretches the thigh muscles
- immediately contract these muscles as you jump upwards.

This movement converts the stretch into an elastic recoil, and the extra power enables you to jump higher.

Plyometric training puts great stress on the muscles and joints, so it is vital to warm up thoroughly first. Beginners should take special care and should start by training on grass (if outdoors) or on mats if indoors.

Why use plyometric training?

The aim of plyometric training is to improve power by training the muscles to contract more strongly, and to improve sports performance by using your own body weight in movements similar to those found in your sport.

Who uses plyometric training?

This is a specialist training method for serious sportspeople who need to develop power and is not normally used for health-related fitness. It can be used to meet the needs of a variety of sportspeople, particularly jumpers, basketball and volleyball players. It is of benefit to all games and racket players.

Flexibility training

Flexibility training involves using a series of exercises to improve and extend the range of movement at a joint by stretching and moving the tendons and ligaments just beyond the point of resistance. A variety of exercises can be used, involving static, active, passive and PNF stretching (see below).

Static stretching

In static stretching the limbs are extended beyond their normal range and the position is held for at least 10 seconds. After a few seconds the stretch is repeated. This is continued for at least five repetitions of 10 seconds, with the length of time the stretch is held being gradually increased.

Active stretching

In active stretching we extend a movement beyond our normal limit and repeat this rhythmically over a period of 20 seconds. It is very important that the muscles are warmed up before active stretching is started. Active stretches should be performed slowly at first, and bobs or bounces avoided.

Passive stretching

In passive stretching we increase the flexibility of our joints by using a partner to apply external force. He or she moves the limb being exercised to its end position and keeps it there for a few seconds. It is most important that this type of stretching is carried out carefully to avoid injury.

PNF stretching

PNF (proprioceptive neuromuscular facilitation) stretching is based on the principle that muscles are most relaxed (and therefore can most easily be stretched) immediately after contraction. The muscle is first contracted as hard as possible. It is then stretched fully and the stretch held for a few seconds. The muscle is then relaxed briefly before repeating.

Why use flexibility training?

The aim of all flexibility training is to improve flexibility and therefore performance. Good flexibility is important for most sports and can reduce the risk of joint injury as well as allowing us to use our strength more effectively through a full range of movement.

Who uses flexibility training?

Everyone who wants a basic health-related fitness level can benefit from a suitably designed flexibility programme. It is a valuable training activity for almost all sports and is particularly important for gymnasts, dancers, skaters and hurdlers.

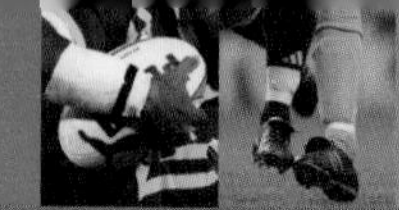

Your Personal Exercise Plan (PEP)

As part of your GCSE course you are required to produce a six-week **Personal Exercise Plan (PEP)**. This gives you an opportunity to show how much you know about fitness and training and also provides evidence of your knowledge for the Analysis of Performance assessment. It is very helpful if you select the same sport for the Fitness Match exercise (see page 77), your Analysis of Performance assessment and your PEP. In this way everything that you do combines into one project.

What is a PEP?

A PEP is a training programme that is specific to you and to your sporting activity. It is prepared using knowledge about your own needs, the needs of the sport for which you are training and a thorough understanding of fitness and training.

Your six-week plan must be designed to improve your levels of:

- flexibility
- cardiovascular endurance
- muscular strength
- muscular power
- muscular endurance.

What do you need to include in your PEP?

- **Introduction**: begin with an introduction, which explains what a PEP is and for which sport you are designing it.
- **Types of fitness**: in this section you define each of the fitness factors, so that the reader can see that you understand each one.

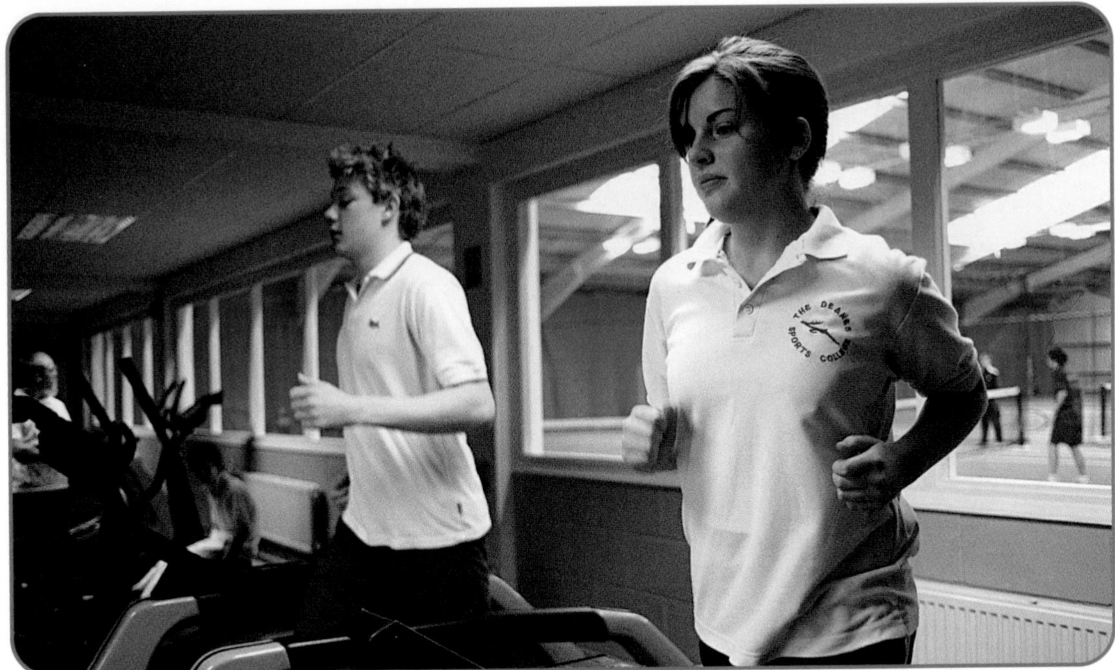

- **Effects of exercise on the body**: in this section you should show that you understand the effects of exercise on the body. Your explanation should include details about:
  - the difference between aerobic and anaerobic exercise
  - oxygen debt
  - the effect of lactic acid in the muscles
  - the difference in composition between inhaled air and exhaled air
  - the effects of exercise on breathing and heart rates.
- **Effects of training**: in this section you include a description of the effects that you expect to see from completing the PEP. You need to list the long-term effects of exercise on the circulatory system, the respiratory system and the muscular system (see pages 115–118). You should include details about:
  - how muscles change in size, strength and in endurance
  - changes to vital capacity and tidal volume in the lungs
  - changes to stroke volume, cardiac output, resting heart rate, recovery rate and blood composition in the cardiovascular system.
- **SPORT principles of training**: here you explain each of the SPORT principles of training (see pages 82–85) and show how they apply to your PEP. For example:

'I am planning to use cycling, running and swimming to increase my level of cardiovascular endurance. This will help to avoid tedium.'

When writing about specificity you should describe your individual needs using evidence from the Fitness Match exercise, and compare your levels of fitness with those required for your sport. This will produce a list of priorities. For example:

'I need to work very hard on improving my cardiovascular endurance, but my flexibility levels are high, so I just need to maintain them.'

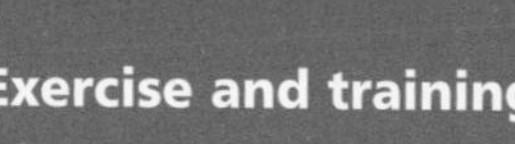

- **FITT principles of training**: here you need to explain the FITT principles and show how you will incorporate them into your PEP. You need to consider the types of fitness that you wish to improve and relate them to the types of training that will lead to improvement. Make clear statements. For example:

  'Plyometric training will improve my power.'

  You will also need to be scientific when explaining the intensity of your training. For example:

  'To improve my cardiovascular endurance I will train at 70% MHR for the first two weeks. By the sixth week I will be training at 75–80% MHR. This shows progression.'

- **Phases of a training session**: here you need to show your understanding of the three phases of a training session (see page 90), but you need to make it clear that the skill development section is not included in your PEP. However, you can use activities that are specific to your sport and you should provide examples of these. For example:

  'I will complete three sets of 15 blocking movements in volleyball to improve my muscular endurance.'

  In this section you should describe your warm-up and warm-down exercises in detail, but there is no need to write them out for every session during the six weeks! You can explain that the warm-up and warm-down are similar each time.

  If you are planning a flexibility programme you should describe it in some detail here.

Example of one-week PEP

Week 1	Venue: school field and gymnasium
Session 1	
Warm-up	See description
Cardiovascular endurance	20-minute run at 70% MHR
Flexibility	15 minutes active stretching of major muscle groups
Muscular strength	–
Power	Five sets of 10 reps plyometrics using two gymnastic box tops
Muscular endurance	Circuit of biceps, triceps, abdominals, shuttle exercises (2 x 30 seconds on each)
Warm-down	See description
Date/notes	

Week 1	Venue: local leisure centre
Session 2	
Warm-up	See description
Cardiovascular endurance	25-minute swim at 70% MHR
Flexibility	15 minutes active stretching of major muscle groups
Muscular strength	Weight training in fitness centre. Heavy weights, low reps
Power	–
Muscular endurance	–
Warm-down	See description
Date/notes	

Week 1	Venue: school field and gymnasium
Session 3	
Warm-up	See description
Cardiovascular endurance	25-minute run at 70% MHR
Flexibility	15 minutes active stretching of major muscle groups
Muscular strength	–
Power	Five sets of 10 reps plyometrics using two gymnastic box tops
Muscular endurance	Circuit of biceps, triceps, abdominals, shuttle exercises (2 x 40 seconds on each)
Warm-down	See description
Date/notes	

- **Training sessions**: here you need to outline training sessions for six weeks, taking into account all of the above. It is likely that you will train three times a week. This takes into account reversibility (which you will have covered in the FITT section when describing the frequency of training).

  You must be sure that the exercises are set at the right level of fitness for you. You can show progression by making the exercises a lot more demanding by the end of Week 6.

In the examples on page 113, the athlete is avoiding tedium by training in two different environments. Muscular strength training is only taking place in the fitness centre, where swimming is the chosen exercise to improve cardiovascular endurance. But your PEP must be designed for you. If you have access to a fitness centre you might choose to do all of the training there. If not, you may have to plan to use the school gymnasium, fields or local park.

As each session is completed you should add the date and notes about how it went, or any changes you made.

Monitoring and evaluation

Once you have prepared your PEP you have to actually do the work!

At the end of six weeks you will need to evaluate the PEP as a whole. A good way of doing this is to retake the fitness tests that you completed for your Fitness Match. It is important that you use the actual scores that you achieved before and after completing your PEP, because there may be a significant difference between the two. For example, your cardiovascular fitness level may have increased significantly from the low end to the high end of 'above average' in the norm tables. If you only look at the tables you will think that there has been no improvement.

Your evaluation should consider:

- if your fitness levels have improved – and by how much
- any changes to your heart rate at rest and when exercising
- changes to your recovery rate
- noticeable effects on your muscles
- good and bad points about your exercise programme and how you might improve it.

The effects of exercise and training on our body systems

If you follow a well planned, long-term training programme, changes will occur in your bones, muscles, cardiovascular and respiratory systems. Remember, however, that training is specific. This means that the actual changes that take place will depend on the type of training you have carried out. The long-term effects of aerobic, anaerobic and weight training will be different. On the pages that follow you will find all the major changes which can be brought about by exercise and training.

The effects of exercise on bones, joints and muscles

What are the immediate effects of exercise on bones, joints and muscles?

- little effect on bones and joints
- increased flow of blood to working muscles
- muscles take up more oxygen from the blood
- muscles contract more often and more quickly
- more of the muscle fibres contract
- rise in temperature in the muscles.

What are the effects of regular training and exercise on bones, joints and muscles?

- bone width and bone density increases
- strengthens muscles, tendons and ligaments surrounding joints
- joint cartilage thickens, improving shock absorption at joints
- increased range of movement at joints (flexibility)
- muscles adjust to greater workload
- muscles increase in size (hypertrophy)
- depending on the type of training, the number of fast or slow twitch fibres will increase
- muscles can work harder and for longer.

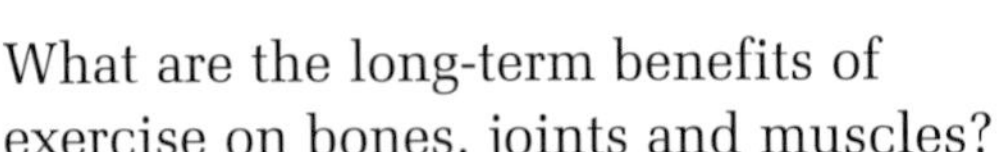

What are the long-term benefits of exercise on bones, joints and muscles?

- increases bone strength and thickness
- increases stability of joints
- develops a full range of movement at joints
- increases muscular strength, muscular endurance and muscular power
- improves the muscles' capacity to tolerate fatigue by coping with lactic acid and oxygen debt.

The effects of exercise on the cardiovascular system

What are the immediate effects of exercise on the cardiovascular system?

- the hormone adrenaline enters the blood system
- adrenaline causes the heart to beat more quickly – increased heart rate
- heart contracts more powerfully – increased stroke volume
- blood circulation speeds up with more oxygen carried to the working muscles
- blood diverted to areas of greatest need
- blood temperature increases, causing sweating response
- blood vessels to skin areas enlarge, allowing heat to be lost more easily.

What are the effects of regular training and exercise on the cardiovascular system?

- increased amount of blood pumped around the body
- cardiovascular system copes more easily with increased demands
- body able to carry and use more oxygen per minute
- body able to remove waste products (especially carbon dioxide) more efficiently
- increased recovery rate after exercise.

What are the long-term benefits of exercise on the cardiovascular system?

- healthier heart and blood vessels
- reduced risk of heart disease
- increased cardiovascular endurance
- reduced blood pressure

- lower resting heart rate and quicker recovery after exercise
- heart muscle increases in size, thickness and strength
- increased number of capillaries
- volume of blood increases.

The effects of exercise on the respiratory system

What are the immediate effects of exercise on the respiratory system?

- increased rate of breathing
- increased depth of breathing
- increased blood flow through lungs
- increased oxygen take-up and use by the body.

What are the effects of regular training and exercise on the respiratory system?

- increased strength of intercostal muscles and diaphragm allows deeper and faster breaths
- greater number of alveoli
- increased amount of oxygen delivered to the body
- increased amount of carbon dioxide removed from the body.

What are the long-term benefits of exercise on the respiratory system?

- healthier lungs
- increased vital and tidal volume
- increased capacity of lungs to extract oxygen from the air
- increased capacity of the lungs to remove carbon dioxide and other waste products from the bloodstream
- increased tolerance of oxygen debt as lungs can work harder for longer.

What are the immediate effects of exercise on our body systems?

We start to exercise
Our muscles work harder and use up more oxygen. The amount of carbon dioxide in our blood increases. Our brain detects this increase and releases adrenaline.

Action by our lungs
Our lungs breathe faster and deeper (increased tidal volume).
Increased exchange of gases:
- more oxygen taken into our blood
- more carbon dioxide removed from our blood.

Action by our heart
Our heart beats faster and stronger (increased heart rate and stroke volume).
More blood pumped to our lungs (increased cardiac output)
- to collect oxygen
- to remove carbon dioxide.

More blood pumped to our muscles (increased cardiac output)
- to deliver oxygen
- to remove carbon dioxide.

As a result:
- Blood pressure rises but blood vessels then expand to reduce the pressure.
- Body temperature rises, but surface blood vessels expand to reduce heat quickly through the skin, and sweating increases, producing water on the skin which evaporates and cools us.
- Blood flow is redirected away from parts of the body not involved in exercise such as the digestive system, towards our working muscles.

Anaerobic and aerobic activity in exercise

Our bodies need energy so that our muscles can contract and make our body work. Our muscles can use energy only when it is in the form of a chemical compound called adenosine triphosphate, or ATP. Our muscles have only very small stores of this high-energy compound. As soon as it is used up we have to remake it. We can do this by using either of our two energy systems: the anaerobic or the aerobic system.

- **Anaerobic system**: our body works without oxygen as we cannot get enough to the muscles for them to work at the high rate demanded.
- **Aerobic system**: there is a constant supply of oxygen to the muscles enabling them to work hard, but not flat out.

The anaerobic system

The anaerobic system gives us both immediate energy and energy for the short term. In our muscles there are small stores of ATP which give enough energy for 5–8 seconds of hard work. This means that energy is available instantly, but will not last for long.

We can remake ATP as quickly as we use up our muscle stores of ATP. To do this we use another chemical compound called creatine phosphate, which is stored in our muscles in small amounts. The extra energy we can gain from using up the creatine phosphate in our muscles will give us up to another 20 seconds of hard work.

When we work very hard the supplies of ATP and creatine phosphate in our muscles are quickly used up. As a result we breathe more quickly and deeply. This is in order to supply oxygen to the muscles to remake our ATP so that we can continue with the activity. Unfortunately, it takes some time for the oxygen to get into our bloodstream and to reach the working muscles. In the meantime, in order to keep our muscles working, our anaerobic system uses glycogen to remake the ATP.

We produce glycogen from the breakdown of carbohydrates in our food and we store it in our muscles and in our liver. Glycogen is carried in our blood and used to remake ATP in our muscles. However, if there is not enough oxygen available at the same time, then **lactic acid** will be formed as well as ATP. If lactic acid builds up in the muscle it makes muscular contractions painful and we become tired. Therefore we cannot use the anaerobic system for very long. The energy from the anaerobic system will be enough for a maximum of about one minute of hard work.

Oxygen debt and lactic acid

When we use the anaerobic system we produce an oxygen deficit – that is, our muscles need more oxygen than they can get at the time. As we saw above, we can continue the activity by using glycogen, but the disadvantage is that we also produce lactic acid.

A build-up of lactic acid causes muscle fatigue. This makes us feel tired and our working muscles stiffen and ache. This will force us to stop and rest eventually if no more oxygen is supplied.

If we are able to carry on, at the end of the exercise we have to rest and take in the extra oxygen we need to remove the lactic acid. This makes up our oxygen deficit.

The extra oxygen we have to take in at the end of the activity is called the **oxygen debt**.

Taking in oxygen allows us to remove the lactic acid, replace the oxygen stores in our bodies and to build up ATP and creatine phosphate supplies.

Feel the burn!

Feel the effects of lactic acid by straightening and curling your index finger as quickly as possible and for as long as possible. Discuss the effects as muscle fatigue begins to occur.

The anaerobic system and sport

This system is very important for many sportspeople. For example:

- for sprinters, throwers, gymnasts and judo players who need bursts of explosive speed
- for 100-metre swimmers, 200-metre runners or sprint cyclists who need to make a sustained effort over a short period of time
- for players of all games involving continuous short bursts of activity, including tennis, hockey, cricket and netball.

After the activity, we need to rest to allow our bodies to refill their creatine phosphate stores. Some sportspeople take food supplements containing creatine which they believe will help them improve their performance.

The aerobic system

The function of the aerobic system is to give us long-term energy. It can be used only when enough oxygen reaches the working muscles. The aerobic system is used for all light exercise, including most of our daily activities. It gives us energy much more slowly than the anaerobic system.

During exercise or activity, the working muscles use up the ATP stores in the muscle and glycogen and oxygen together remake the ATP. But as enough oxygen is now available, lactic acid is not formed and the waste products are carbon dioxide and water, which do not cause tiredness. Therefore we can continue to use the aerobic system for a long time.

The energy provided by the aerobic system comes from using glucose, formed by the breakdown of carbohydrates and fats, combined with a plentiful supply of oxygen. Although this gives us energy much too slowly for intensive activity, it can supply energy for a very long time.

The energy systems and sport

The aerobic system is important for nearly all sportspeople, particularly for those who need energy over a long period of time, such as runners, cyclists, swimmers and games players. But the energy we need for different sports varies a great deal.

- A shot-putter uses one huge burst of energy lasting just a few seconds. This comes from the anaerobic system; energy from the aerobic system would take too long to arrive.
- A 100-metre sprint swimmer needs a longer, but still quite short burst of energy. The swim will take more than eight seconds so the creatine phosphate supplies would soon be exhausted. The aerobic system will not be able to supply oxygen fast enough. The swimmer will therefore rely on the anaerobic system to supply the energy needed. At the end of the swim there will be an oxygen debt.
- A marathon runner needs a continuous supply of energy over a long period and has no need of the anaerobic energy system. He or she must rely on a well developed aerobic system to send a steady stream of oxygen to the muscles over a long period of time.

In many sports the two energy systems work together at different times to supply the particular type of energy needed. For example, a hockey player will need the anaerobic system when shooting for goal and when repeatedly sprinting short distances and the aerobic system when jogging into position when the ball is out of play.

Our anaerobic system works without oxygen and supplies our muscles with energy quickly. In contrast our aerobic system must have oxygen to work and only supplies energy slowly to our muscles.

To train your energy systems for your particular sport you need to know to what extent you use each energy system. You can then decide, with your coach, what type of training is likely to improve your performance. You will also need to think about training thresholds and **training target zones**.

Training thresholds and target zones

To train effectively you must know:

- your present level of fitness
- the amount of anaerobic training you need for your sport
- the amount of aerobic training you need for your sport
- your target, or training, zone. This refers to the range of heart rates within which you need to work in order to bring about a specific training result. For example, a runner may have an aerobic training zone of between 120 and 160 beats per minute. This means he or she must keep a pulse rate of between 120 and 160 beats per minute in order to have an effect on aerobic fitness.

Maximum heart rate

To work out our target zone, we need to know our maximum aerobic capacity (VO_2 Max), which involves scientific calculation. Fortunately there is a very close link between our VO_2 Max and our maximum heart rate (MHR), and we can use MHR instead.

As we saw earlier, maximum heart rate can be estimated in the following way:

- MHR males = 220 minus age
- MHR females = 226 minus age.

For example, a 16-year-old male has an MHR of 220 – 16 = 204 beats per minute. For a female of the same age, the MHR would be 210 beats per minute.

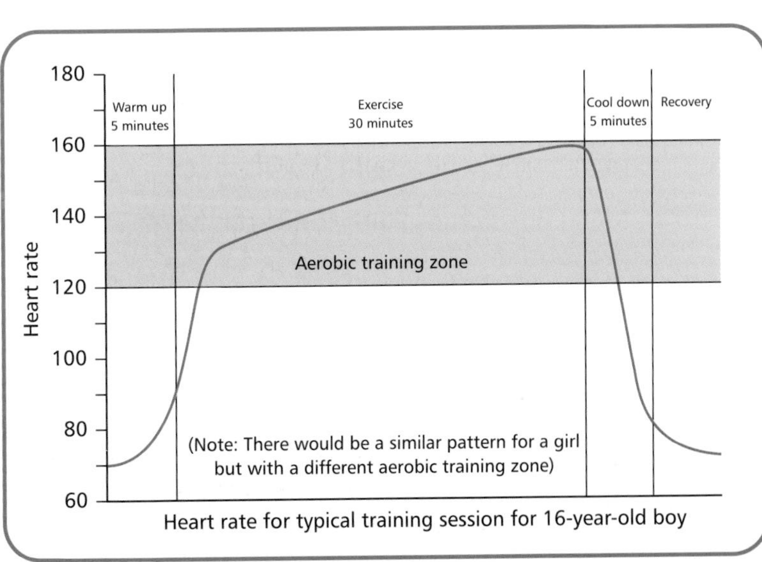

Heart rate for typical training session for 16-year-old boy

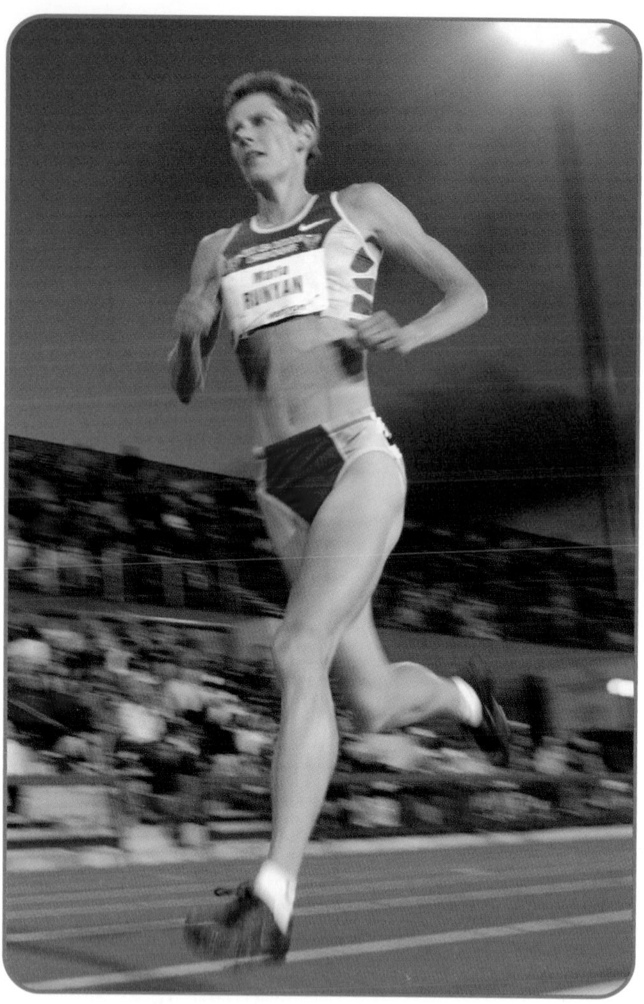

Aerobic target zone
When we train in this zone we improve aerobic fitness. To achieve this we need to exercise above our aerobic threshold, which means keeping our heart rate between 60–80% of our MHR.

For a typical 16-year-old athlete, the aerobic target zone would therefore be:

- Male: 60–80% of 204 = 120–160 beats per minute
- Female: 60–80% of 210 = 125–170 beats per minute.

Anaerobic target zone
When we train in this zone we improve our anaerobic fitness. To achieve this we need to exercise above our anaerobic threshold, which means keeping our heart rate above 80% of MHR. For a typical 16-year-old athlete, the anaerobic target zone would therefore be:

- Male: 80%+ of 204 = over 160 beats per minute
- Female: 80%+ of 210 = over 170 beats per minute.

Remember, however, that the percentages of MHR given here are only approximate. Personal levels of activity and fitness will cause differences. The less fit you are, the lower your training thresholds will be.

Recovery rates

Whenever we exercise, our heart rate increases to supply more oxygen to our working muscles. As a result our pulse rate increases from its resting level to a higher level depending on how hard we work. (Our pulse rate is simply our heart rate measured at the wrist or throat.)

A sportsperson's fitness can be estimated by checking his or her resting pulse rate. The fitter they are, the lower will be their resting pulse rate. A fit person will have a larger and stronger heart than an unfit person. This means that a fit heart can supply the same amount of blood to the muscles but uses fewer beats than an unfit heart. Therefore the resting pulse for the fit heart is lower.

Resting pulse rates: comparative scores

85 and above	Poor
70–84	Average
56–69	Good
55 and under	Excellent

However, a better way of measuring fitness is to work out how long a person's pulse rate takes to return to normal after exercise. This is called the **recovery rate**.

During the recovery period the body deals with the oxygen debt. This is achieved by breathing deeply, transporting more oxygen from the lungs and removing the lactic acid. The recovery process is helped by gentle aerobic exercise immediately after the vigorous activity. This aids the removal of lactic acid, reduces the possible effect of muscle soreness and improves recovery time.

activity

Measuring recovery rate

You can estimate your recovery rate by comparing your heart rate before and after exercise. Working in pairs, record your pulse rate at rest. Then run 400 metres as quickly as possible and after finishing, record your pulse every 30 seconds for the next five minutes. By recording and plotting your findings, you will be able to compare the results and discuss the reasons for any differences.

QUESTIONS

6 Methods of training

Answer questions 1–4 by choosing statements a, b, c or d. One mark for each question.

1 Plyometric training uses:

a a series of different exercises

b a variety of explosive movements

c alternating periods of hard work and rest

d weights as a form of resistance.

2 Anaerobic training means working:

a without oxygen
b with oxygen
c without glycogen
d with carbon dioxide.

3 The type of muscular contraction seen in a press-up is known as:

a isometric
b isokinetic
c isobaric
d isotonic.

4 One immediate effect of exercise on the cardiovascular system is:

a lower blood pressure

b decreased heart rate

c the hormone adrenaline enters the blood system

d increased blood flow to the stomach.

5 Sam wants to improve her performance in the school netball team. She is following a fitness programme including interval training and plyometric training.

a Explain what is meant by:

i interval training
ii plyometric training

– and give an example of each type of training.

(4 marks)

b i Explain why she needs to improve her power for netball.

(1 mark)

ii What particular way of weight training will improve power?

(1 mark)

c Two of the FITT principles are Time and Type.

i Name the other two.

(2 marks)

ii Explain what is meant by Type.

(2 marks)

QUESTIONS

6 **During training, the changes in Ricky's heart rate are recorded and plotted on a graph. The graph shows that in the first five minutes of activity, his heart rate climbs from 65 to 150 and remains there for the rest of the hour. Over the next half hour, it gradually declines back to 65.**

a Why does Ricky's heart rate increase in the first five minutes?

(2 marks)

b For a long period his heart rate is constant. Suggest the type of activity he was doing at this time.

(2 marks)

c In which target (training) zone is he working?

(1 mark)

d What is the relationship between his training activity and his oxygen supplies?

(1 mark)

e What happens to his heart rate after one hour?

(1 mark)

f What is this period called?

(1 mark)

7 **Carlos is a 16-year old sprinter.**

a Give two factors you would take into consideration when designing a training programme for him.

(2 marks)

b Name the target (training) zone in which he will be working.

(1 mark)

c Show how he could calculate his target (training) zone.

(3 marks)

d Name the type of training on the track which would be most suitable for a sprinter and give an example.

(2 marks)

e Complete the table by giving **one** possible effect of each training activity on the heart and muscular system.

Body part	Long runs	Weight training with heavy weights and few reps
Heart		
Muscular system		

(4 marks)

(Total 34 marks)

7 Diet, health and hygiene

Our sporting performance is influenced by many factors, including our inherited ability and our training programme. However, we must have a healthy lifestyle if we are to perform to our full potential. Our diet must match our sporting needs and we must be aware of the problems caused by alcohol and other social drugs. Following a healthy lifestyle when we are young will slow the ageing process and reduce the risk of an early death from disease.

activity

Body shape

All the sportspeople pictured here are performing well in their chosen sports. They have trained hard, but their body build and their lifestyle also help them. Working in small groups, look at the pictures and discuss the following questions:

- What is it about the body build (shape and size) of each person that helps them to excel at their sport?
- How will their training differ?
- Which person is likely to eat more food each day?
- Would you expect their diets to be different?

KEYWORDS

Carbohydrate loading: eating a large amount of carbohydrate before endurance events in order to increase the amount of glycogen available to working muscles

Cholesterol: fat-like substance found in blood which can build up on artery walls

Doping: use of illegal drugs to obtain unfair advantage in sport

Ectomorph: a body type with little fat or muscle and a narrow shape

Endomorph: a fat, pear-shaped body type

Energy equation: term used to describe the relationship between diet, weight and energy needs

Glycogen: chemical substance used to store glucose in the body

Hygiene: good personal habits which keep us clean and healthy

Mesomorph: muscular, wedge-shaped body type

Nutrients: basic elements of food that provide nourishment for the body

Obese: term used to describe people who are very overfat

Overfat: having excessive amounts of body fat

Overweight: having body weight in excess of normal. Not harmful unless accompanied by overfatness

Somatotyping: method of classifying body types.

Key to Exam Success

For your GCSE you will need to know:

- how different food types combine to form a balanced diet
- which food types help to produce energy
- the definitions of the terms overweight, overfat and obese
- the different body types and the effect they have on sporting performance
- why your diet should match your sports need
- how undereating and overeating can affect body weight and performance
- why your weight affects your performance
- the effects of smoking, alcohol and social drugs on health and physical performance
- the effects of performance-enhancing drugs in sport
- the importance of personal hygiene
- how to recognise, prevent and treat athlete's foot and verrucæ.

“ KEY THOUGHT ”

'We are what we eat.'

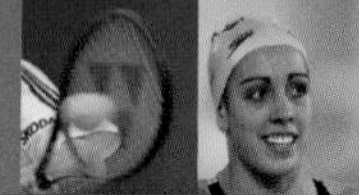

Why do we need a balanced diet?

To be healthy and successful in sport, we need to know about different food types, what makes a healthy diet and how food can provide us with the right energy for sport.

Why do we need food?

We need food for:

- energy
- repair
- growth
- good health.

We get energy from food for our muscles to work. Food contains the basic materials needed for growth and repair. We need many different **nutrients** for good health, and a balanced and varied diet will provide them. If we are following a regular training programme for our sport we must plan our diet accordingly. We will need extra amounts of energy-producing foods as well as sufficient foods to allow repair of tissues.

What is a balanced diet?

A balanced diet contains seven essential components:

- carbohydrates
- fats
- proteins
- vitamins
- minerals
- fibre
- water.

We should limit the amounts of the three main food types: carbohydrates, fats and proteins. The Department of Health recommends that a healthy diet should contain:

- 50–60% carbohydrates (mainly from starch and natural sugars)
- 25–30% fat (mainly from unsaturated fat)
- 10–15% protein (mainly from lean meat, fish, poultry and plants).

We should also:

- decrease the amount of salt that we eat
- increase the amounts of fibre, calcium and vitamin C that we eat.

Nutrients that provide energy

Carbohydrates

Carbohydrates are broken down in the body into different sugars. There are two types of carbohydrate:

- **Sugars** (simple carbohydrates): these are found in:
  - fruits
  - cakes
  - honey
  - biscuits
  - jam
  - beer
  - sweets
  - table sugar.

  Highly processed food such as sweets will give us a quick supply of energy but no other nutrients. Biscuits and cakes often contain a lot of fat.

- **Starches** (complex carbohydrates): these are found in:
  - vegetables
  - rice and cereals
  - bread
  - pasta.

  It is better to take most of our carbohydrates in the form of starches rather than sugars.

Why are carbohydrates important for exercise and energy production?
Carbohydrates give us the energy needed for our working muscles. We can also get energy from fats and proteins, but not as quickly or as efficiently as we can from carbohydrates. Large amounts of carbohydrates are stored as **glycogen** in the liver and muscles. Small amounts are stored as glucose in the blood. Intense exercise quickly uses up these stores, so active sportspeople need plenty of carbohydrates in their diet. Extra carbohydrates can be stored as fat around the body.

Fats

Fats are broken down in the body into saturated and unsaturated fatty acids. There are two types of fats:

- **Saturated fats**: these are found in animal products, and in foods made from them. These include:
  - milk
  - meat
  - cheese
  - cream
  - butter
  - cakes
  - biscuits
  - chocolate.

  Saturated fats can raise our cholesterol levels.

- **Unsaturated fats**. These are found in:
  - fish
  - nuts
  - corn
  - soya beans.

Why are fats important for exercise and energy production?

Fats provide energy, although much more slowly than carbohydrates. Fats need extra oxygen supplies to provide energy. Fats are the main source of energy when we are resting or asleep. Fats keep the skin in good condition, help to keep us warm and protect our vital organs. Extra fat is stored just under the skin. However, this extra weight will not help sportspeople. Too much fat can also lead to obesity and high cholesterol levels.

Cholesterol is a fat-like substance found in the blood. It is present in some foods, especially fatty animal products. Cholesterol which is not needed by the body builds up on our artery walls and may cause circulatory and heart problems.

Proteins

Proteins are broken down in the body into amino acids. There are two types of amino acids:

- **Non-essential amino acids**: for our bodies to function properly, we need 21 different amino acids. We can make 13 of these, which are called non-essential.
- **Essential amino acids**. These are the 8 amino acids that we have to take from our food because we cannot make them for ourselves. They are found in both animal and plant foods.

Proteins are found in:

- fish
- meat
- milk
- cereals
- poultry
- beans
- eggs
- cheese
- peas
- nuts.

Proteins from animal products contain all of the essential amino acids. However, plant proteins (with the exception of soya beans) lack some essential amino acids.

Why are proteins important for exercise and energy production?

Much of our body tissue is made up of protein, including our skin, bones and muscles. Proteins are needed for the repair, growth and efficient working of our tissues. Protein is only rarely used as

an energy source, when no carbohydrate or fat is available. Excess proteins cannot be stored in the body as protein. They are either used as an energy source, stored as fat or excreted.

Other nutrients that do not provide energy

Vitamins

Vitamins enable our bodies to work normally and efficiently. We cannot make vitamins. They must be supplied in our food. Some vitamins are water-soluble (vitamin C and the B vitamins). We need these vitamins in small regular amounts. Unfortunately, because they are water-soluble, they are 'washed' out of foods during cooking. Fat-soluble vitamins (such as vitamins A, D and E) can be stored by our body. We need to eat some foods containing fat in order to get these vitamins.

Sources of vitamins

Vitamin	Contained in:
A	Deep orange or yellow fruits and vegetables, dark-green vegetables, liver, codliver oil, dairy products
B1	Cereals, whole-grain bread, yeast, milk, potatoes, fish, sunflower seed
C	Most fruits and vegetables; high concentration in citrus fruits
D	Oily fish (mackerel, salmon, tuna), liver, codliver oil, butter, eggs
E	Beans, nuts, seeds, green, leafy vegetables, egg yolk, codliver oil

Why are vitamins important for exercise?
Vitamins do not provide energy. They regulate the activities of the body. They help in the working of muscles and in the release of energy from food. They also play a role in the growth and repair of body tissues.

The function of vitamins

Vitamin	Function
A	Good vision and healthy skin
B	Energy production, stress reduction
C	Fights viruses, keeps skin and gums healthy, heals wounds
D	Helps to build bones and teeth
E	Protects cells, helps immune system, aids growth

Minerals

Minerals are substances found in a variety of foods which enable the body to work normally and efficiently. They do not provide energy, and the body cannot make its own minerals.

We need small but regular amounts of minerals, and a balanced diet can provide them all. Too much of some minerals can be harmful: for example, sodium in the form of salt can cause increased blood pressure.

Sources of minerals

Mineral	Contained in:
Calcium	Milk, sardines and salmon with bones, vegetables, beans
Iron	Spinach, dark-green vegetables, liver, red meat, beans, peas, nuts
Magnesium	Dark-green vegetables, nuts, soya products
Potassium	Bananas, dried fruit, meat, vegetables, sunflower seeds
Sodium	Table salt, soy sauce, preserved meat, crisps, canned foods

Why are minerals important for exercise?

All minerals have their own function in helping the body to work well.

The function of minerals

Mineral	Function
Calcium	Strengthens bones and muscles
Iron	Aids production of red blood cells, helps get oxygen to the muscles, prevents fatigue
Magnesium	Helps muscles to contract and relax
Potassium	Aids muscle contraction, maintains normal blood pressure
Sodium	Maintains body fluid levels, aids muscle contraction

Fibre

Fibre is also called roughage or dietary fibre. Fibre is the part of a plant that cannot be digested. It does not contain any nutrients. Fibre is found on the outside of seeds, in vegetables, fruits and nuts.

Why is fibre important for exercise?

Fibre does not provide energy but adds bulk to our food. This helps the food to move through our digestive system and prevents constipation. Fibre is also involved in food absorption. It slows down the release of sugars from our food so that we get a more even release of energy. Dietary fibre adds bulk without adding extra kilojoules. A high level of fibre helps us to lose weight and to maintain good health.

Water

Although water does not provide energy it is essential for living. It comes from the fluids we drink and the food we eat. We lose water in our sweat, urine, faeces and in the air we breathe out. About two-thirds of our body weight is made up of water. It is the main component of blood and cells. As part of the blood, water carries nutrients, electrolytes, blood cells and waste products around the body.

Water in our blood also helps to control our body temperature by absorbing heat produced during exercise. This heat is then carried to the skin where it is lost to the air. Water helps to cool the body when it evaporates on the surface of the skin in the form of sweat. Heat is also lost in the water vapour in the air that we breathe out. Loss of water can lead to dehydration and heatstroke. Any adequate supply of water is vital during training, especially for strenuous exercise in the heat.

UBS
322
ZURICH
2003
2003

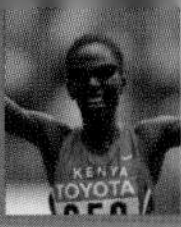

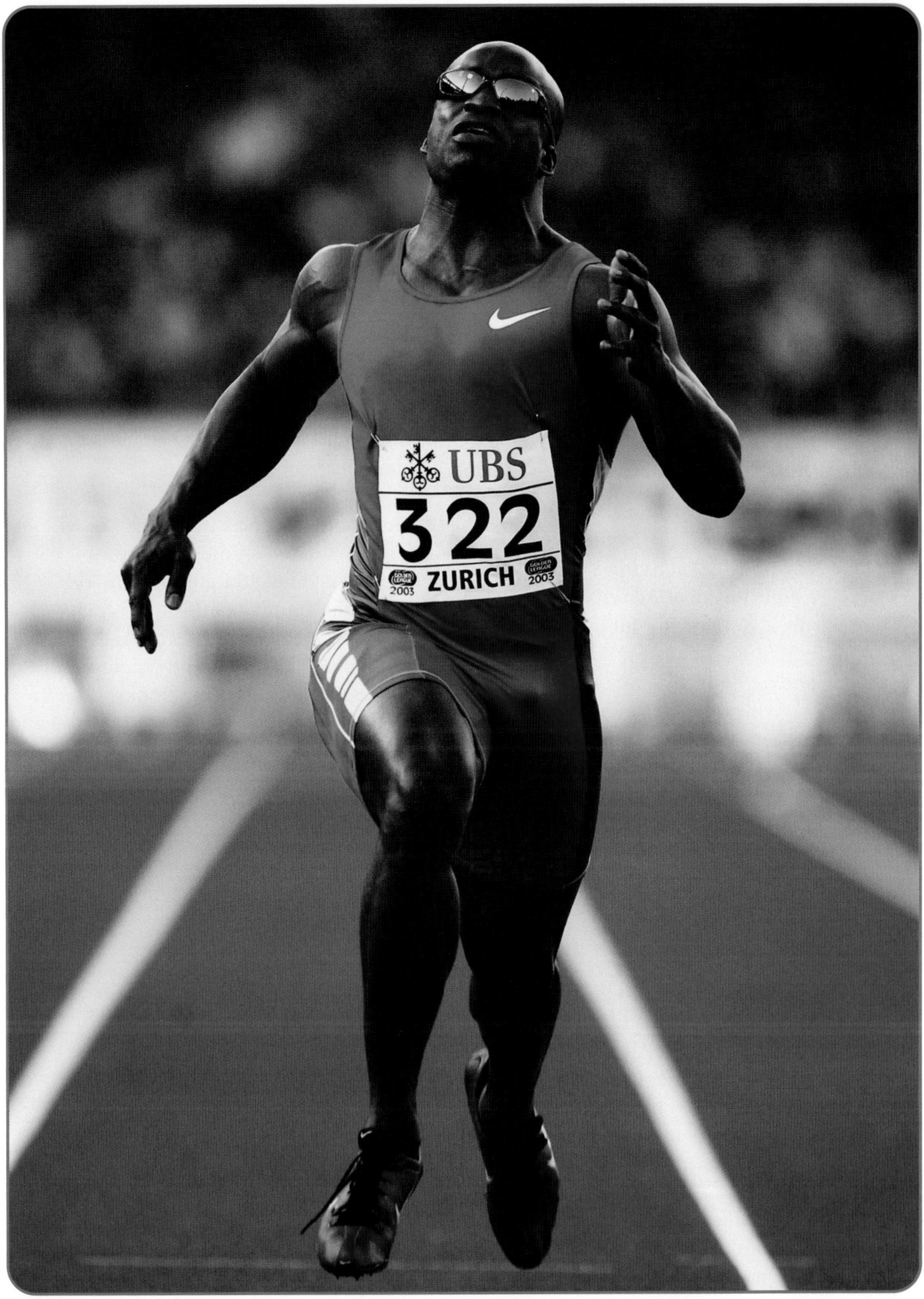

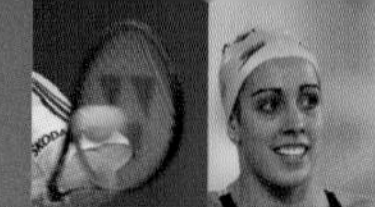

Diet and energy

Eating a balanced diet is vital for health. Eating the right food to provide energy and to maintain the correct body weight is a major factor in sports performance.

Why do we need energy?

The energy our bodies use has two main purposes:

1 **To keep our body systems going**. The amount of energy we need to keep alive and healthy is called our **Basic Metabolic Rate (BMR)**.We can think of it as the energy needed to keep us 'ticking over'. BMR is affected by our age, sex, body size and body composition.

2 **For physical activities**. This is known as our **Physical Activity Level (PAL)**. We use energy for all our everyday activities such as walking, housework and gardening. If we take part in sport we will use a lot more energy (depending on the type of sport, and how much activity is involved). Our age, sex, work, health and lifestyle will all affect our PAL.

Remember that:
our total energy needs = BMR + PAL.

How is energy measured?

Energy is measured in kilocalories (kCal) or kilojoules (kJ). One kilocalorie is the equivalent of 4.2kJ. All food contains an energy value, which is usually calculated as the number of kilojoules per gram of food. Exercise is measured as the number of kilojoules used per hour.

How much energy is contained in food?

The amount of energy in our food depends on how many carbohydrates, fats and proteins it contains. It is also greatly affected by the way the food is cooked. We can see from the table below that potatoes contain 3kJ per gram when boiled, but 15kJ per gram when served as chips. A baked potato may contain fewer calories than the butter that we spread on it!

How much energy do we need?

We need to match the amount of energy in the food that we eat with the amount of energy our body needs. We will lose weight if our body needs more energy than our diet is providing. We will put on weight if our body needs less energy than our diet is providing.

The energy equation

The link between diet, energy and weight is quite straightforward. The diagrams show the effects of an imbalance between the amount of kilojoules taken in and the amount of kilojoules burned up each day.

The energy content of food

Food	kJ per gram
Butter	31
Crisps	23
Milk chocolate	22
Sausage roll	21
White sugar	16.5
Chips	15
White bread	10
Boiled eggs	6.2
Boiled rice	5.8
Low-fat yoghurt (fruit)	3.8
Boiled potatoes	3
Milk (semi-skimmed)	1.9
Fizzy soft drink	1.5
Apple	1.4

Energy used per activity

Activity	kJ per hour	Activity	kJ per hour
Marathon running	4158	Cycling (moderate)	1260
Basketball	3360	Gardening	1260
Brisk jogging	2520	Cleaning	798
Disco dancing	2100	Studying	420
Badminton	1848	Watching TV	378
Golf	1428	Sleeping	252

Experts have calculated the energy needs, for growth and body maintenance, of teenagers as follows:

- An average 15-year-old male needs to eat about 11,500 kJ per day.
- An average 15-year-old female needs to eat about 8,800 kJ per day.

How much energy is used when taking part in activity?
The amount of energy people use depends upon the intensity of the activity.

There are many books and websites providing detailed information about the energy used in different activities.

Weight stays constant
Kilojoules taken in each day equals kilojoules burned up each day

Weight gained
Kilojoules taken in each day is greater than kilojoules burned up each day

Weight lost
Kilojoules taken in each day is less than kilojoules burned up each day

activity

Dietary advice

Interview a friend or family member about their diet and exercise levels. List the amount of food and drink that they consume in a typical day. Write down the amount of activity they have had during the day. Then write a summary about the effect that their diet and activity pattern will have on their weight. Finally, write down the advice you would offer them about this.

Weight and sporting performance

Our ability to perform well at sport is affected by our weight, and we can lose or gain weight through diet and exercise. However, our basic body type is the result of heredity and cannot be changed. Some body types are better suited to particular sports than others.

There are various terms to describe someone who is heavier than average. These should not be confused with terms used to describe body type. Each term means something different and it is important to describe each condition correctly:

- **Overweight**: 'having weight in excess of normal. Not harmful unless accompanied by overfatness.' (Edexcel.) Being overweight simply means being a little heavier than we should be for our height, according to the standard height–weight tables. Being 'overweight' is not a problem if it is composed of extra muscle.
- **Overfat**: 'a way of saying you have more body fat than you should have.' (Edexcel.) If we are overfat our body composition contains too much fat. A male body should not have more than 18% fat. A female body should not have more than 23% fat.
- **Obese**: term used to describe 'people who are very overfat.' (Edexcel.) If our weight is more than 20% greater than the standard weight for our height, we are **obese**. Obesity often leads to heart, circulation and other health problems. Being overweight can affect sports performance and it increases the risk of health problems.

It is important to recognise that undereating and loss of weight can also affect sporting performance.

Anorexia sufferers do not allow themselves to eat and often think they are overweight. Bulimia sufferers eat a lot of food, but get rid of it, usually by vomiting. Both conditions lead to extreme and dangerous weight loss. These are medical conditions and sufferers need urgent medical help.

How do overeating and undereating affect sporting performance?

Imagine that you have been asked to compete in a sports tournament, but that you have to carry your rucksack when playing! You would be very quick to complain that your chances of success were being harmed by the extra weight you had to carry. It is easy to see that being overfat or obese will slow you down when sprinting, make you less able to twist and turn in a games situation and will prevent you from

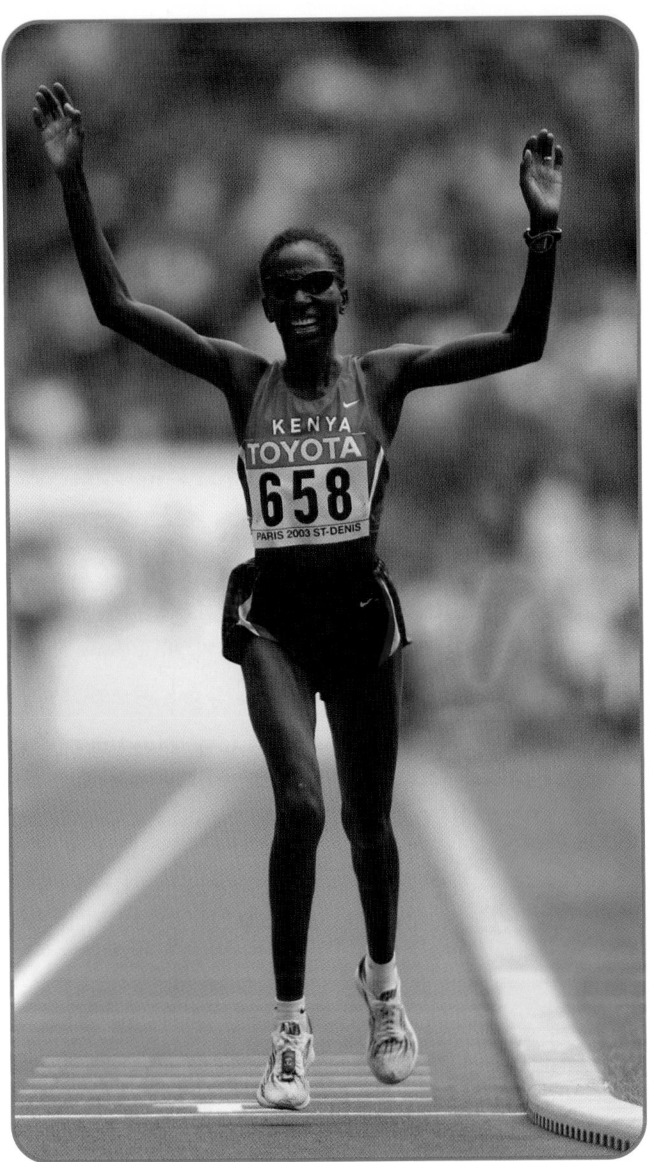

Other sports such as gymnastics, long-distance running and horse racing require athletes to be very light. Controlled diets are essential for these athletes to avoid problems caused by rapid weight loss through crash diets. Although they need to be light, they must make sure that they have enough energy reserves to compete and enough vitamins and minerals to stay healthy.

The ideal body size for sport depends on the needs of the individual sport or the position the person plays in the game. For more information see 'Body composition' in Chapter 3.

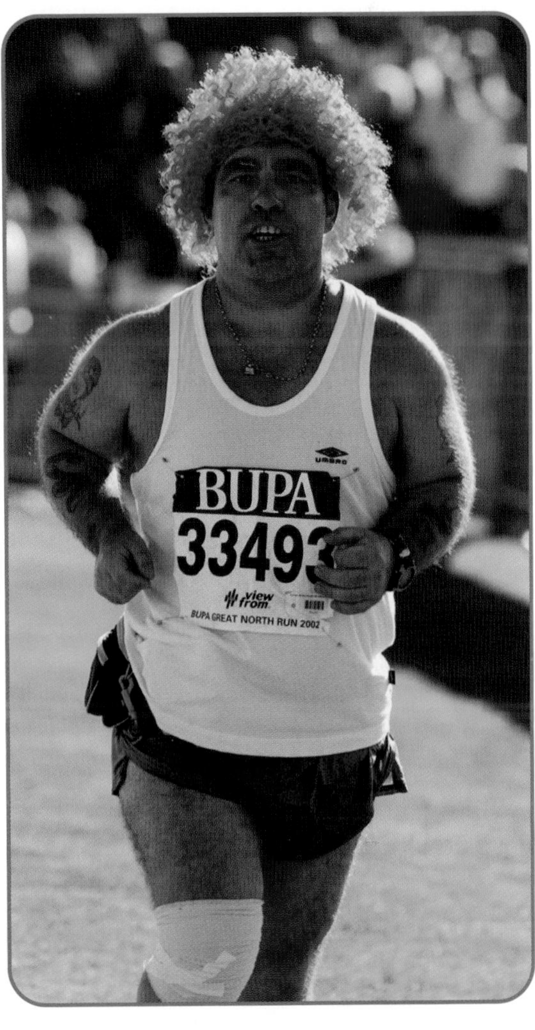

doing well in a long-distance race. Long-distance runners keep their weight down to reduce the load they have to carry. The lighter the load the further and faster they can run.

Some sports such as wrestling, boxing and weight lifting have fixed weight categories. Despite being able to compete when very heavy, top performers will have much more muscle than fat, because whilst eating a lot of food they will also be training very hard.

Food and sport

How do we get enough energy for sport?

When we work hard, the energy we use comes from stores of glycogen in the body. Glycogen is made from carbohydrates and also from fats. Our stores of glycogen are limited. To have enough energy for endurance activities we need to eat extra carbohydrates, which build supplies of glycogen. This is called **carbohydrate loading**. In order to carbohydrate load, we reduce our level of exercise for at least three days before competition. At the same time we increase the amount of carbohydrates (pasta, rice, etc.) in our diet.

Carbohydrates or fats?

Our bodies use carbohydrates, in the form of glycogen, and fats to produce energy. The mixture used depends on the length and intensity of the activity.

For example:

- When resting we use mainly fats.
- On a long walk we will also 'burn' mainly fat.
- If we start jogging we will begin to use glycogen.
- If we jog for a couple of hours, our glycogen stores will be used up and we will begin to utilise fats.
- Sprinting will lead to our muscles using glycogen.

Endurance training teaches our body to use more fat during exercise. This helps our limited supplies of carbohydrates to last longer.

Proteins are only rarely used as an energy supply. This happens when all other energy supplies have been used.

Eating for sport

We need to plan how we eat before, during and after exercise.

Before exercise we should:

- eat our main meal at least three to four hours and our snack meal at least one to two hours before exercise, to allow time for digestion
- include starches such as bread, cereal and fruit, to give a slow, steady release of energy
- avoid simple sugars (sweets) because they increase our insulin level, which in turn reduces our blood glucose and makes us feel tired
- avoid foods which are high in fat and protein as they take longer to digest
- include plenty of fluids to avoid dehydration.

During exercise we should:

- continue to drink water, not waiting until we feel thirsty, but taking small sips regularly
- drink a glucose-based sports drink if the activity lasts for more than one hour.

After exercise we should:

- eat foods rich in carbohydrate within an hour of exercising, even if we do not feel hungry, to restore glycogen stores quickly
- drink plenty of water to replace lost fluids.

Which sports foods will improve performance?

Food supplements for athletes are widely available and sports drinks are heavily advertised. Creatine monohydrate is becoming popular as it can help in the production of energy and in the recovery process. When we are trying to perform at our peak we are easily tempted to buy these products. However, we need to look at the scientific evidence and decide for ourselves if the product will help us.

Drinks

We only need to drink plain water before and during activities lasting 60 minutes or less.

Sports drinks containing carbohydrates and electrolytes (sodium, potassium, chloride and magnesium) can enable us to work hard for longer if our activity lasts more than 60 minutes.

Sports drinks can help after exercise as they help to restore lost fluids, energy and minerals. They also provide useful nutrition during whole-day tournaments.

But there is no need to buy sports drinks containing extra vitamins. We do not lose vitamins when we sweat and a balanced diet should supply all the vitamins we need.

Food and food supplements

A high-carbohydrate diet will allow us to work hard for longer, but we must also train well in order to do this. If we are training very hard, our diet should consist of 65–70% carbohydrates, but we should not increase fat consumption even if we are training very hard.

Remember also:

- Extra protein in the diet does not help to make extra muscle: it is broken down and stored as fat or used for energy. Using correct training techniques is the only way to increase muscle size.
- High-protein foods are difficult to digest and we should not eat them before training or competing.
- Creatine is found in large quantities in red meat. Our bodies can make it from amino acid.

What does it say on the label?

Collect a label from a sports energy drink and a snack bar. The labels will contain details about energy levels and other nutritional information. Compare a sports energy drink with an 'ordinary' fruit-based drink, or compare an energy bar with an ordinary snack bar.

Investigate and compare the claims made for each product. Some products have their own websites, but other information is also available on the internet. Decide whether or not you think the energy drink or snack bar will improve your sporting performance.

Body type and sport

As we saw in Chapter 3 (page 61), the method of body typing known as **somatotyping** identifies three extremes of body type called **endomorphs**, **mesomorphs** and **ectomorphs**. We need to be aware of our basic body type as it will affect our optimum weight and our suitability for our chosen sport.

Optimum weight means the ideal body weight for us in our particular sport. As we saw earlier in this chapter, diet is an important factor affecting our weight. We will now look at some other factors including height, weight, gender, bone structure and muscle girth.

Height

In general the taller a person is, the heavier they will be. However, short, heavy people and tall, light people are common. Body type is controlled by heredity. From a sporting point of view, some combinations of height and weight give an advantage. Tall, light people might become high jumpers and short, heavy people might do well in weight lifting. Optimum weight depends on the activity.

Gender

Men and women of the same height and body type will not necessarily have the same optimum body weight for the same sport. This is because women, in general, carry a greater percentage of their body weight as fat and their bones are not as heavy as those of men.

Bone structure and muscle girth

Bone structure and muscle girth are closely linked to body type, which is controlled by heredity. As we saw earlier (page 60), most successful sportspeople are muscular with a mesomorphic body type. Ectomorphs with less muscle and smaller bones will be less successful than mesomorphs. However, their body build will be helpful in such activities as long-distance running. Endomorphs, who are usually heavy and with high levels of fat, will find it difficult to succeed in sports involving speed and agility. However, if they can develop muscle, they many do well in activities such as weight lifting.

Drugs and sport

Drugs are chemical substances that affect our bodies. Medical drugs are made to fight illness and disease. The use of banned drugs in sport is known as **doping**. As sportspeople we need to know about social drugs and performance-enhancing drugs.

Guilty or not guilty?

Name: Alain Baxter
Sport: Slalom skiing
Event: 2002 Winter Olympics (bronze medal)
Tested positive for: Methamphetamine, a banned stimulant
Defence claim: Baxter regularly uses a nasal inhaler which does not contain any banned substance. He bought the same brand of inhaler in the USA without realising that it contained the banned stimulant methamphetamine.

Name: Kelli White
Sport: Athletics
Event: 100 and 200 metres World Championships, Paris 2003 (gold medallist for 100 metres and 200 metres)
Tested positive for: Modafinil, a stimulant
Defence claim: Drug is not on the IAAF banned list. It was prescribed to her to treat sleepiness caused by narcolepsy (sleeping sickness).

Name: Mark Bosnich
Sport: football
Event: Random testing
Tested positive for: Cocaine, an illegal banned stimulant
Defence claim: He took the drug unwittingly as his drink had been spiked on a night out.

Discuss the drug abuse cases above. Imagine you are one of the panel members meeting to decide whether or not the athlete should be banned from sport. In making your decision you should consider the effects on:

- the athlete who has tested positive
- other athletes in the same competition
- athletes in the sport worldwide
- young people who may see the athlete as a role model.

What are social drugs?

When we play sport we often become part of a social group that meets after training and after competition. Adult sportspeople often meet in bars after training. Many sports clubs earn money from running a successful clubhouse bar. The drugs that are available within social situations are known as social drugs. Some are legal and are widely used. Other social drugs are illegal, but are still used by a number of people. Social drugs are usually taken to help people to relax or to give users an enjoyable experience. We need to know about each social drug and how social drugs can affect sporting performance.

There are many different social drugs and each has a different effect. The most common are:

Name of drug	Type of drug	General effect
Alcohol	Depressant	Slows down how body works
Amphetamines	Stimulant	Speeds up nervous system. Fights fatigue
Caffeine	Stimulant	Increases heart rate. Increases alertness
Cannabis	Depressant	Reduces worry but slows down responses
Cocaine	Stimulant	Speeds up the nervous system. Creates feeling of well-being
Ecstasy	Stimulant	Increases confidence and sense of well-being
LSD	Hallucinogen	Changes the way we see and understand things
Nicotine (tobacco)	Stimulant	Increases heart rate. Increases concentration level

Of the drugs listed above, only alcohol, caffeine and nicotine are legal in the UK by law, but not in sport.

Alcohol

Alcohol has a number of effects on our sports performance.

- **reduced co-ordination, slower reaction time and poorer balance**: these changes affect our movements and skills, especially where catching and balance are involved, and reduce the steadiness needed in sports such as archery, gymnastics and shooting.

- **dehydration**: alcohol is a diuretic and increases urine production. This leads to water loss from the body. Dehydration seriously affects performance in endurance events and on hot days.
- **lower muscle glycogen levels and slower removal of lactic acid**: muscle glycogen is needed during endurance events. Lactic acid is produced during exercise and must be removed quickly. Therefore, drinking alcohol before any sport involving endurance will reduce performance. It will also take us longer to recover afterwards.
- **rapid loss of heat**: alcohol causes the blood vessels in the skin to open up. We lose heat quickly through our skin, which reduces our body temperature, although we feel warm. If we are in a cold environment, hypothermia can develop.
- **longer injury recovery time**: the RICE procedure (see page 173) is used to reduce the blood flow to an injured area. Alcohol has the opposite effect. Recovery time will be increased. If you receive an injury during a match you should not drink alcohol afterwards.
- **reduced size of arteries**: alcohol reduces the size of the arteries, so that less blood can flow along them. Heart rate and blood pressure both increase.

Alcohol also affects our:

- thinking, judgement, vision and hearing
- stomach (and can cause vomiting)
- liver, as it takes a long time to process
- weight, as it is very high in kilojoules.

Nicotine

Smoking has many effects on our sporting performance:

- **reduced lung efficiency**: the smoke damages the hairs lining the bronchial tubes. Dust is not removed from the air so our lungs become clogged and do not work efficiently. We need efficient lungs for all sport.
- **reduced oxygen-carrying ability**: carbon monoxide is taken into the lungs in the smoke and passes into the blood. It attaches to red blood cells, reducing the amount of oxygen we can carry in our blood. This affects endurance activities.
- **reduced fitness level**: even if we train hard, our fitness level will be reduced because of the damage to our lungs and circulatory system caused by smoking.
- **lowered resistance to illness**: colds are caught more often and we take longer to recover from chest infections. Smoker's cough is a special hazard, as is bronchitis. Sportspeople need to keep well to train and compete.
- **raised blood pressure**: nicotine causes our brain to release hormones which make the heart beat faster and the blood vessels in the skin to contract. This causes an increase in blood pressure and a feeling of being cold.

Smoking also affects our:

- **life expectancy**: smokers are at much higher risk of cancer and cardiovascular disease
- **social standing**: we breathe harmful and unpleasant fumes on people around us. We also smell of stale tobacco

- **senses**: by dulling our sense of taste and smell
- **appetite**: by reducing it.

Effects of other social drugs

- **amphetamines** increase heart rate and blood pressure. They hide symptoms of fatigue and reduce feelings of pain. They are addictive and can cause anxiety and aggression.
- **caffeine** is a mild stimulant found in tea, coffee and many soft drinks. It increases heart rate and blood pressure. This is not useful to endurance athletes.
- **cannabis**, or **marijuana**, can result in lack of motivation and poor judgement. Since it is smoked in tobacco, it causes the same problems as cigarette smoking. It has no role to play in sport.
- **cocaine** is a highly addictive stimulant. It encourages us to think that we are doing better than we are. This is no help in sport, where good judgement is essential.
- **Ecstasy** is a stimulant with mild hallucinogenic properties. It is not useful in sport because it affects our perceptions. Performance can also be affected the day after Ecstasy has been used, because of the negative effects of the 'come down'.
- **LSD** distorts reality and affects the ability to perceive situations and make decisions. The effects of LSD can often be felt in the form of 'flashbacks' long after the drug has been taken. This drug has no place in sport.

What are performance-enhancing drugs?

Some sportspeople try to gain an extra advantage in competitive events by using banned drugs. This is illegal, unfair and can be harmful to health. We need to know how performance-enhancing drugs work and how they can affect sporting performance.

Performance-enhancing drugs take many forms. In the table below, drugs that have similar effects are grouped together.

Some drugs are restricted in certain sports, but are not completely banned. These include all the illegal social drugs and alcohol.

Other proscribed methods of enhancing performance are:

- blood doping (see page 150)
- changing blood samples, or interfering with them in any way
- using masking agents to hide the use of a performance-enhancing drug.

Other restricted drugs

Drug	General effect
Beta blockers	Keep heart rate and blood pressure low, reduce tremble in hands; banned in archery and shooting
Corticosteroids (Cortisone)	Reduce inflammation and pain, masking effects of injury
Local anaesthetics	Reduce pain, masking effects of injury

Prohibited drugs

All the performance-enhancing drugs and methods described in this section are banned throughout sport. Even nicotine and caffeine levels have to be below a prescribed limit in most sports.

The list of prohibited drugs contains over 1,000 substances and is regularly updated. Sportspeople must check the list before taking any medicine, because some banned drugs are contained in everyday medicines. These include the steroid clenbuterol, which is used in asthma treatment. In January 2004

Doping class	Examples	General effect
Anabolic agents	Nandrolone, Testosterone, Stanozolol, Clenbuterol	Reduced recovery allows users to train harder and for longer. Increased muscle bulk and endurance when combined with regular exercise
Analgesics (narcotic)	Morphine, Methadone, Heroin	Pain-killing effect allows training and competing to continue even in times of injury
Diuretics	Frusemide, Probenecid	Rapid weight loss as result of reduction of fluid levels in body
Peptides, glycoprotein hormones and analogues	Human Growth Hormone (HGH), Erythropoietin (EPO)	Decreased fat mass. Thought to improve performance Increased number of red blood cells, more oxygen carried to body, endurance improved
Stimulants	Amphetamines, Cocaine, Ephedrine	Speeds up nervous system, quickening reactions. Masks fatigue and feelings of pain

caffeine and pseudo-ephedrine (contained in many over-the-counter cold remedies) were removed from the banned substance list.

Sportspeople must also be aware that drugs can sometimes be found in food supplements that are often given to athletes by their coaches. Following a

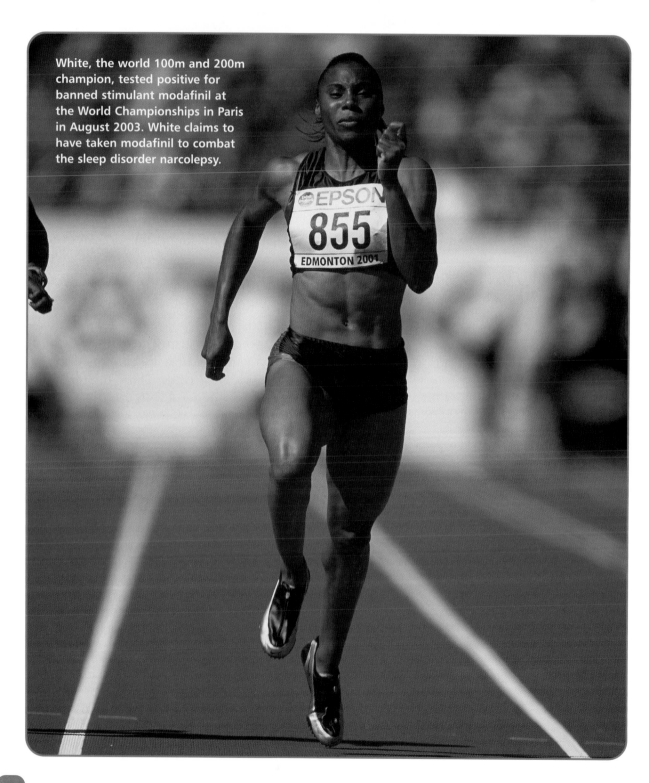

White, the world 100m and 200m champion, tested positive for banned stimulant modafinil at the World Championships in Paris in August 2003. White claims to have taken modafinil to combat the sleep disorder narcolepsy.

number of positive drugs tests in 2003, UK Sport issued the following statement:

> 'No guarantee can be given that any particular supplement is free from prohibited substances as these products are not licensed and are not subject to the same strict manufacturing and labelling requirements as licensed medicines.'

In May 2003 Czech tennis player Bohdan Ulihrach was suspended after testing positive for nandrolone, an anabolic steroid. He was the first of a number of professional tennis players to test positive during 2002/3. He has now had his punishment cancelled, as the food supplement was supplied to him by ATP (Association of Tennis Professionals) trainers.

UK Sport's Nandrolone Review Group have given this advice:

> 'Competitors are strongly advised that using dietary supplements carries the potential risk of unknowingly taking a banned substance.'

Michele Verroken, former director of Drug-Free Sport at UK Sport, commented: 'Athletes should look at suitable alternatives to taking supplements, the main one of course being to eat a balanced and healthy diet.'

Steroids

Anabolic agents, or steroids, can be taken orally or by injection. They have positive effects upon performance because, when combined with extra exercise, they increase strength, muscle growth, body weight and endurance. They enable sportspeople to train more often and harder. However, they have serious side-effects which, for men, include:

- increased aggression
- impotence
- kidney damage
- baldness
- development of breasts.

Disadvantages for women include:

- increased aggression
- development of male features
- growth of facial hair
- growth of body hair
- irregular periods.

Narcotic analgesics

Codeine, morphine, methadone and heroin are members of the opiate family. They have a positive effect on sporting performance by reducing the feeling of pain. By doing this they mask injury or illness and allow sportspeople to compete when they should not.

The dangers of taking narcotic analgesics are that:

- injuries can be made much worse and even permanent
- they are highly addictive.

Diuretics

Diuretics are mainly used by sportspeople in events where they have to 'make the weight' – that is, to fit into a weight category. These events include horse racing, boxing, weight lifting and martial arts. The diuretic works by removing fluid from the body as urine, so the result is rapid weight loss. They are also used to remove other drugs from the body in order to beat the drug-testers.

The disadvantages of taking diuretics are that they often result in:

- dehydration
- cramps
- dizziness
- headaches
- nausea.

These conditions seriously affect ability to play sport.

Peptide and glycoprotein hormones and analogues

These hormones are produced naturally in the body. Analogues are the same hormones produced artificially.

Erithropoietin (EPO) improves endurance by increasing the number of oxygen-carrying red blood cells. The disadvantages of using this type of drug are that it may:

- thicken the blood, so increasing the risk of a stroke and heart problems
- cause oily skin, acne and muscle tremors.

Blood testing for EPO has been introduced, in addition to taking urine samples, at many endurance events as the authorities have sought to keep sport drug-free.

Human Growth Hormone (HGH) encourages muscle growth, increases the use of fat and improves the body's ability to cope with fatigue. The disadvantages of using this type of drug are that it may cause:

- abnormal growth, including enlargement of internal organs
- atherosclerosis and high blood pressure
- diabetes, arthritis and impotence.

Stimulants

Drugs such as amphetamines, ephedrine and cocaine can lead to an improvement in performance because they give a 'lift', keeping us awake and competitive, speeding up reflexes and reducing feelings of fatigue.

The disadvantages are that they:

- increase heart rate and blood pressure
- hide symptoms of fatigue, putting high levels of strain on the body that can lead to death
- reduce feelings of pain with the risk of making injuries worse
- can lead to acute anxiety and aggressiveness
- are addictive.

Blood doping

Blood doping does not involve the use of drugs, but requires blood to be injected into the body to increase the number of red blood cells. Athletes usually inject their own blood, which has been removed earlier and stored, but it can come from another person. Blood doping makes the blood able to carry more oxygen to the working muscles. This increases aerobic endurance, which is an effect that can also be gained by training at altitude. Blood doping has a similar effect to the use of EPO.

Blood doping has disadvantages that are very dangerous. These include:

- overloading the circulatory system, increasing blood pressure and causing difficulties for the heart
- kidney failure
- risk of transmission of AIDS and other diseases.

The campaign against doping in sport

The desire to win is very high amongst competitive sportspeople. If they believe that a drug will help them achieve their goal, they may be tempted to use it – and the temptation is even higher when success will lead to great financial rewards. The pressure to succeed, from the media and public as well as from coaches and managers, can be very great.

Many sports performers rationalise their decision to use drugs by arguing that other competitors are using drugs, and that without them they will have no chance of winning. Some use anabolic agents while being treated for injury in order to speed up the recovery process. To them, the practice is risky but acceptable. Although out-of-competition testing may catch them and lead to a ban, they believe that they will not get caught and are prepared to cheat in order to win.

The case against doping

The International Olympic Committee (IOC) does not allow doping for three main reasons:

- to ensure that competition in sport is as fair as possible
- to protect the health of sportspeople
- to protect the wholesome image of sport.

Drug rules: who decides?

Each sport has its own international sports federation (ISF) which controls its activities worldwide. The ISFs make their own rules about doping. In the case of Olympic sport, the sport must also follow the drug code of the International Olympic Committee (IOC). Each governing body in a country has the responsibility for testing sportspeople in and out of competition. In Britain, drug testing is co-ordinated at the London office of UK Sport, with the support of national administrators in England, Northern Ireland, Scotland and Wales.

What penalties do drug-takers face?

Competitors who are found guilty of taking banned drugs are often banned from competing in their sport. Bans are usually for a minimum of two years. The competitor will also face a loss of earnings from competition and sponsorship and will have to live with the personal disgrace of being revealed as a cheat.

activity

Looking for doping offences

Imagine that you are a member of the UK Sport drug-testing team.

1. List all the banned and restricted types of drugs.
2. Make a list of sports in which you would be likely to encounter each type of drug. Conduct an internet search to confirm that each of the drugs on your list has been found in the sports that you have indicated.

Recent drug issues

THG (Tetrahydrogestrinone)

As we have seen, anabolic steroids can improve the body's ability to train and compete at the highest level. They reduce the tiredness linked with training and the time required to recover after physical exertion.

Steroids also promote the development of muscle tissue in the body that leads to an increase in strength and power. Doping tests for steroids have been in place for a number of years but recently, a designer drug based on the steroid THG (Tetrahydrogestrinone), has been uncovered. This drug has been altered by chemists so that it was undetectable by the usual tests.

The United States Anti-Doping Agency (USADA) was given a syringe containing THG (from an anonymous athletics coach), from which it was able to develop an effective test for the substance. Urine samples taken during an out-of-competition test conducted by the IAAF in August were re-tested using the new test. This resulted in a number of positive tests, including that of the British sprinter, and European 100-metre champion, Dwain Chambers.

International Anti-Doping Code

A World Conference on Doping in Sport in 2003 agreed an Anti-Doping Code that came into force at the start of the 2004 Olympics in Athens.

The Code works on the principle of strict liability, whereby sportsmen and women are responsible for any prohibited substances found in their system, regardless of whether or not they have performance-enhancing capabilities. The main reason for this new code is to protect those athletes who do not cheat.

Dwain Chambers tested positive for the designer steroid THG and in February 2004 was banned from competition for two years.

Rio Ferdinand (Manchester United and England), was found guilty of failing to turn up for a drugs test. He received an eight-month ban from the game.

Hygiene and sport

We should keep our bodies healthy as part of our preparation for sport. We should also develop hygienic habits after taking part in sport and ensure we get enough sleep and rest.

Hygiene means the different ways we look after our body to keep it healthy and clean.

Skin care

Our skin protects and maintains our body. If the skin is healthy, it can resist most infection. Soap and warm water removes the dirt and sweat which encourage bacteria and lead to body odour. We should wash our hands after going to the toilet, before meals and whenever they are dirty.

We can also keep our whole body clean by showering daily. It is essential to wash or shower thoroughly after taking part in any physical activity. Most of us use deodorants and anti-perspirants, but they are only really effective if the body is already clean.

Acne is a skin complaint which affects many teenagers. The glands in the skin, which produce grease, become particularly active at puberty and the openings of these glands can become blocked. Greasy material builds up under the skin if the blockage is not cleared and the skin becomes infected with bacteria. To prevent acne, it helps to keep the skin very clean, to avoid make-up, to eat fresh fruit and to get plenty of sunlight.

Nails and hair

Nails should be kept clean and cut regularly to reduce the risk of scratching yourself and others during sporting activity. You should also wash your hair regularly to keep it clean. Long hair can be a hazard in some sports and should be tied back.

Teeth

Teeth must be kept clean and free from decay. Avoid sugary foods and keep your gums healthy by eating foods that need chewing. Regular dental check-ups are essential.

Feet

Make sure your footwear fits well. Wash your feet regularly and dry them carefully, always checking for:

- **athlete's foot**: this is a fungal infection between the toes which makes the skin split, causing itching. It can be treated by drying our feet carefully and using anti-fungal powders.
- **verrucae**: these are warts found on our feet which are caused by a virus. They can be painful, but can be treated with appropriate medication.

Clothing

Clothes should be changed and washed regularly. You should have a complete change of clothes for sport, which should be thoroughly washed after each exercise session.

How do sleep and rest affect sporting performance?
You will not be able to train or compete effectively if you do not get enough sleep. Most people need between seven and nine hours' sleep each night. If your pattern of sleep is disrupted, your sporting performance will suffer. Sleep patterns can be disturbed by drinking alcohol or caffeine, smoking or eating high-protein meals shortly before sleeping.

Rest (which is not the same as sleep) is also essential in order to recover physically and mentally from the activities of the day. Rest is especially important for sportspeople who train and compete at a high level.

activity

How much sleep and rest do you get?

List the number of hours of sleep and rest you have had each day for the last week in a table like the one shown below. Add a comment if you wish to explain anything. Then analyse your sleep and rest pattern and explain the likely effect on your sporting performance.

Day	Hours of rest	Hours of sleep	Comment
Mon			
Tues			
Wed			
Thurs			
Fri			
Sat			
Sun			

QUESTIONS

7 Diet, health, hygiene and performance

Answer questions 1–4 by choosing statement a, b, c or d. One mark for each question.

1 Carbohydrates are:

- a essential for growth and repair
- b an aid to digestion
- c the main source of energy for exercise
- d used in the formation of bone.

2 The ideal body type for a 100-metre sprinter is:

- a endomorph
- b somatotype
- c ectomorph
- d mesomorph.

3 Which statement best describes a verruca?

- a a fungal infection between the toes
- b a wart found on the foot, caused by a virus
- c a sebaceous cyst on the foot
- d a harmless mole-like growth on the foot.

4 Anabolic steroids are used by athletes to:

- a give them more red blood cells
- b build muscle and allow them to train harder
- c boost their nervous system and make them more alert
- d help them to lose weight by reducing fluid levels.

5 a Which food type will provide most of the energy for each of the following activities?

i walking for 30 minutes *(1 mark)*

ii sprinting for 400 metres. *(1 mark)*

b Amy wishes to eat a balanced diet. Copy and complete the following table to remind her of what to eat and why. *(1 mark each)*

Food type	Source of food type	Why it is important
Carbohydrates		
	Dairy products	
		Helps growth and repair
	Fresh fruit and vegetables	

(Total 8 marks)

QUESTIONS

6 **Ross is a keen rugby player. His coach has told him to increase his body strength and body weight. Ross has changed his diet and has started a weight-training programme.**

a Name two food types that Ross should eat regularly to provide the energy for his new training programme.

(2 marks)

b Why should Ross's diet include protein?

(2 marks)

c Explain what fibre is and why it is important in any diet.

(3 marks)

A man at the gym has suggested that Ross takes a drug to gain weight and strength more quickly.

d Name the type of drug that is likely to have been recommended.

(1 mark)

e List two side-effects that might result from regular use of the drug.

(2 marks)

f Name the type of drug that might be offered to Ross to mask the use of the first drug.

(1 mark)

7 **The use of banned drugs is a problem in many sports.**

a Describe three reasons why sportspeople may be tempted to use banned drugs.

(3 marks)

b Name and describe a banned performance-enhancing procedure that does not involve the use of drugs.

(3 marks)

c EPO is now used by some endurance athletes and cyclists to gain an advantage. Describe the effects of EPO on the body and explain how this enhances performance in endurance events.

(3 marks)

(Total 34 marks)

Safety aspects and risk assessment in sport and physical activity

8 Prevention and treatment of sports injuries

- Preventing injury
- Risk assessment
- Sports injuries and their causes
- Recognition and treatment of sports injuries

8 Prevention and treatment of sports injuries

Many of us take part in sport because it is exciting and often unpredictable. This unpredictability can put great strain on our bodies and brings with it the risk of injury. Good preparation is important in trying to reduce the risk of injury.

If we are to perform to the best of our ability we must avoid injury when training and competing. To do this we must assess the risks, plan to be safe and take every precaution to stay safe. If we do get injured, we must know how to recognise and treat the injury so that we recover quickly. Knowing when to return to training is also important, because returning too soon can cause problems.

activity

Safety issues

Look at the following cartoons of sporting activities and copy and complete the grid listing all the potential safety hazards.

Sport	Facility	Clothing and equipment	Safety in general
Trampolining			
Climbing			
Gymnastics			
Rugby			
Cricket			
Basketball			

KEYWORDS

CPR: Cardiopulmonary Resuscitation – a procedure to follow if someone has no pulse

DRABC/Doctor ABC: Danger, Response, Airway, Breathing, Circulation – a checklist to follow when dealing with an emergency

Etiquette: special ways we are expected to behave in our sport

HARM: Heat, Alcohol, Running, Massage – things to be avoided in the first 48 hours of injury

Hypothermia: dangerous lowering of the internal body temperature through exposure to extremely cold conditions

Heat exhaustion: state of fatigue in hot conditions caused by dehydration

Heatstroke: when the body becomes dangerously overheated through exercise in extremely hot conditions

MMV: Mouth-to-Mouth Ventilation – a procedure to follow if someone has stopped breathing

Overtraining: continuing to train when the body needs rest and time to recover

Overuse injuries: caused by using a part of the body incorrectly over a long period of time

Sprain: when we overstretch or tear a ligament at a joint

Strain: when we stretch or tear a muscle or tendon

RICE: Rest, Ice, Compression, Elevation – a checklist to follow in the case of soft-tissue injuries.

Key to Exam Success

For your GCSE you will need to:

- understand how to prevent injuries by keeping to the rules of the game, wearing correct clothing and footwear and taking part in balanced competition only when fit enough and properly warmed up
- be able to assess the risks involved in sporting activities both to yourself and others
- recognise the signs and symptoms of a range of sporting injuries
- know the procedures for dealing with a sportsperson in an emergency situation
- identify how preventative measures can minimise the risk of injury to yourself and others.

“ KEY THOUGHT ”

‘Most sporting injury is both painful and avoidable.’

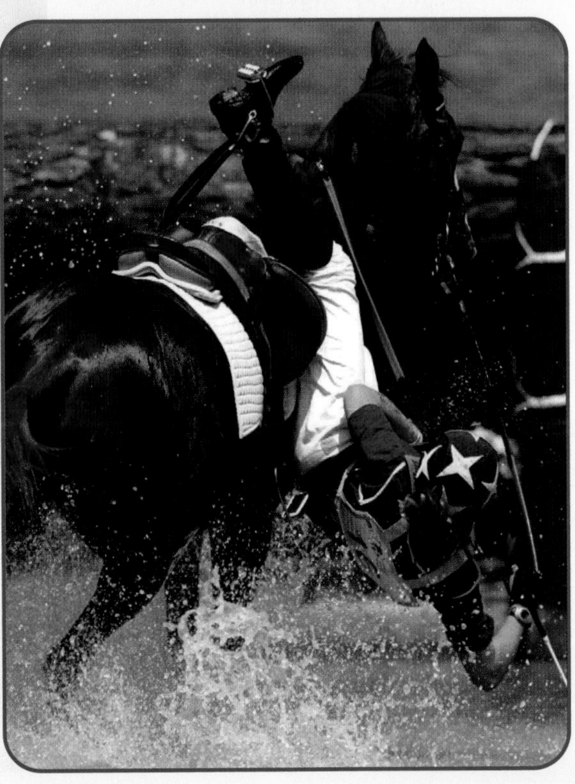

Preventing injury

We can look at prevention of injury in sport under a number of headings:

- rules of the game
- footwear, clothing and equipment
- balanced competition
- warm-up and warm-down.

Rules of the game

We need to know and understand the rules of our activity. Rules encourage good sporting behaviour, help games to flow and also protect players from injury. Rules must be followed and players punished if they break them. Injury causes pain and stops us from playing. In high-risk collision sports such as rugby, injuries will be part of the game. However, players who break rules and harm opponents must be dealt with severely. In recent years some players have been taken to court when their deliberate foul play has led to serious injury.

Some sporting activities such as mountaineering, pot holing and sky diving have no formal rules as such. However, failure to follow the appropriate safety guidelines in sports like these could lead to disaster.

Etiquette means the special ways we are expected to behave in our sport. Etiquette is not a set of written rules, but is something that has become part of each sport over a long period. Golf has many examples of etiquette; for example, when players complete a hole, they should immediately leave the green and record their scores elsewhere. Tennis players will always shake hands at the net after a match, and rugby players will clap their opponents off the pitch. Etiquette allows us to demonstrate fair play, sportsmanship, sporting spirit and respect for our opponents. In this way it helps to reduce violence in sport.

activity

Safety rules

All sports have rules designed to minimise the possibility of injury to those taking part. For example, in football girls are not allowed to play against boys after the age of 11, players who raise their feet too high close to an opponent are penalised and all players must wear shin guards.

Choose three sports and for each of them write down three rules designed to prevent accident or injury.

Footwear

Sports shoes should support and protect our feet as well as be comfortable. Shoes must also grip the playing surface and absorb impact when we are running or landing. This will reduce injury. Cross-trainers are useful for moderate performers who play a number of sports, but top players will always choose shoes that are specially designed for their sport. They will also make sure that their shoes can provide maximum support and response to movement by tying the laces tightly when training and playing.

Clothing and equipment

Always wear the correct clothing for the activity. Check your clothing and equipment regularly to see that everything is in good order. For example, a damaged fencer's outfit could be dangerous if used in competition or practice.

In extreme weather conditions appropriate clothing is especially important. Sports manufacturers now produce a wide variety of clothing suitable for very hot, very cold and very wet weather.

Some sports have rules to make sure that protective equipment is worn. For example, hockey goalkeepers and school-age batters in cricket must wear

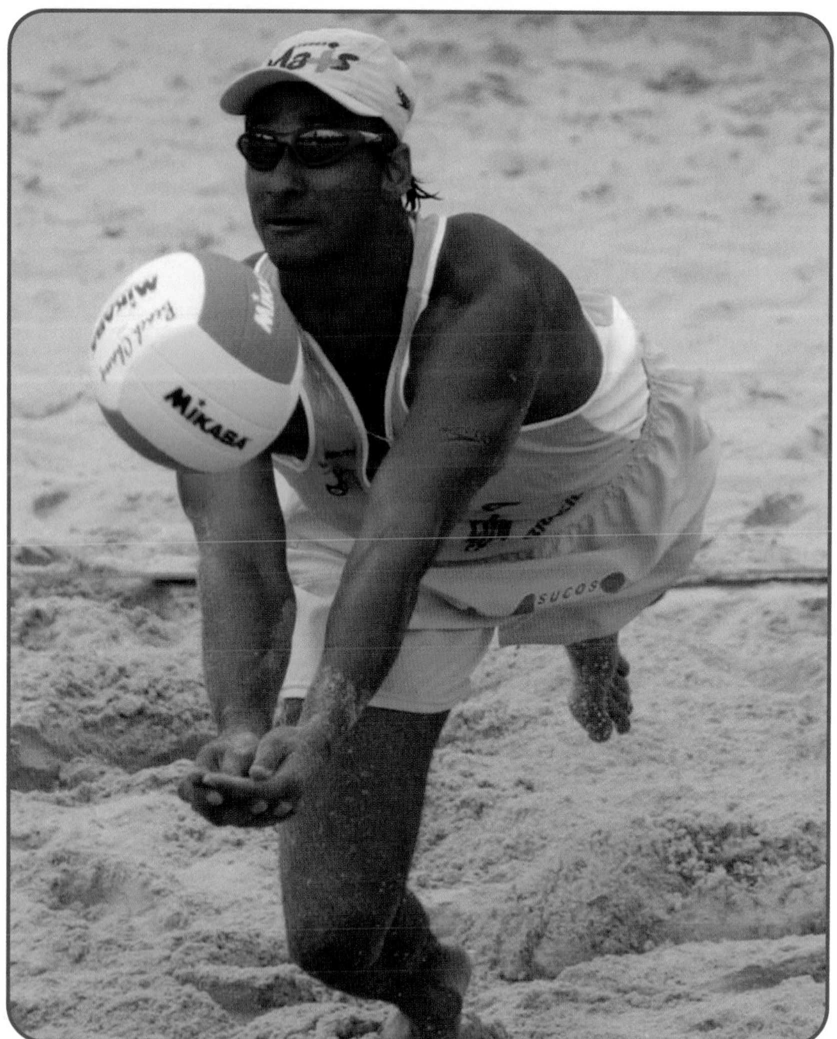

harmful ultraviolet rays, such as sunglasses, hats, long-sleeved shirts and skin creams.

Jewellery

Players should remove as much jewellery as possible before playing sport. The risk of accidents due to jewellery will vary with the sport. For example, rings on fingers will be a much greater problem in judo than in running. People taking part in contact or combat sports should wear no jewellery at all.

Balanced competition

Many sports try to make their competition balanced for fairness and the greater enjoyment of the competitors. For combat and contact sports, balanced competition is important for safety reasons. Factors taken into account include:

- **age**: most competition in school sport is based on age. However, competition between competitors of the same age but with different physical development can be both unfair and unsafe.
- **size and weight**: rugby and football can be very dangerous if there are large differences between the body size and skill levels of the players involved. For weight lifting and

helmets and other padding. Footballers must wear shin guards. For many sports, there are few rules about clothing, but players will still need to take sensible precautions.

Protective equipment must:

- properly protect the sportsperson
- allow freedom of movement
- permit air to flow around the body
- be comfortable
- be safe and reliable.

In very sunny conditions, players should wear protection against rowing there are weight categories to make competition fairer, whilst weight categories in boxing and wrestling make contests both fairer and safer.

- **gender**: mixed-sex teams are acceptable in tennis, volleyball, hockey and badminton, but not in netball. Rugby union has non-contact forms of the game which are suitable for mixed teams, whilst mixed teams are allowed in soccer up to the age of 11.
- **skill**: in karate and judo belts are awarded for different skill levels. In competition age, weight and skill level are taken into account for reasons of safety and fairness. Golf has a handicap system to make a game competitive between players of different abilities.

Warm-up and warm-down

These are essential parts of each training session and competitive situation. They are important in preventing injury and should be closely tailored to the individual sport.

If we start strenuous activity when our muscles and joints are cold, they are likely to suffer damage because they will be unable to cope with the sudden stresses. Gentle exercise for the whole body warms up the muscles and joints and prepares them for more vigorous activity. A combination of gentle jogging and stretching exercises will help to prevent injury.

If at the end of strenuous activity we simply rest, our recovery will take much longer and there is the possibility of dizziness. Light exercise will maintain the blood circulation, prevent pooling in the skeletal muscles, lower blood pressure and so reduce the possibility of dizziness. It will also help the speedy removal of waste products which will prevent muscle soreness and stiffness. Stretching after exercise can also enable you to increase flexibility – when the muscles are warm, they can be stretched further and for a longer period of time.

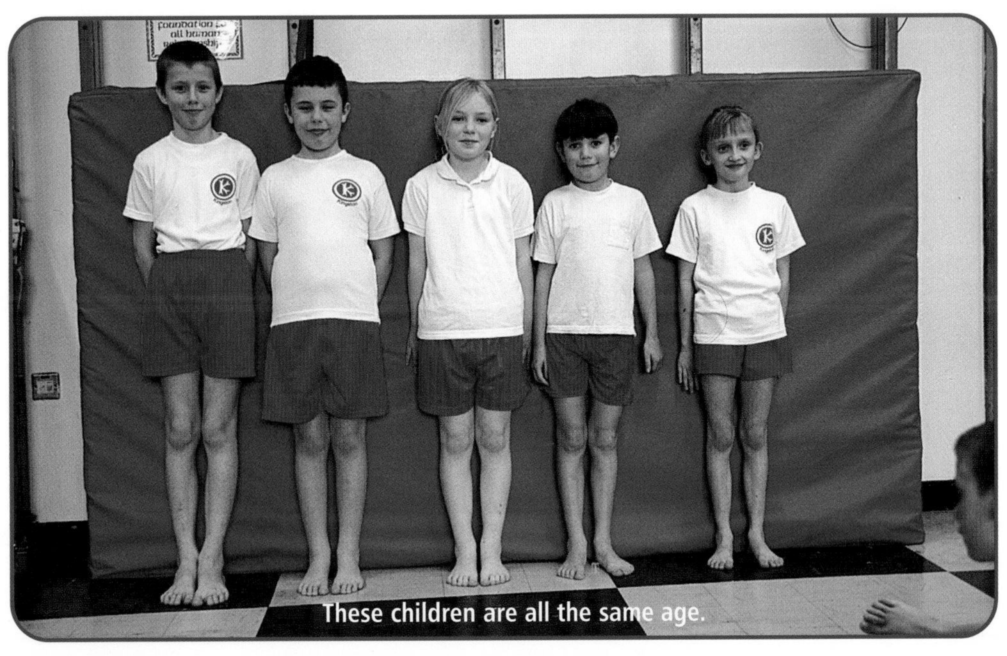
These children are all the same age.

Risk assessment

Taking part in sport always carries some risk of injury. We know that rugby or climbing carry a greater risk of injury than table tennis or swimming. In order to take part in a sport we have to be willing to accept the risk.

However, if we are organising a sporting activity for other people we also have a responsibility for their safety. For this reason organisers of sporting activities must carry out an assessment of all potential risks and ensure that they are minimised before the activity takes place. All those taking part must also be made aware of any specific risks and ensure that they are properly prepared.

We can carry out a risk assessment by asking a number of important questions in different areas. We must then deal with any problems.

Assessing ourselves

The first step is to check that we are well prepared for our activity.

- **Health and fitness**: are we healthy and fit enough to take part in the activity?
- **Techniques and skills**: do we have the ability to compete at this level?
- **Training**: have we completed sufficient training to cope with the demands of the activity?
- **Warm-up**: have we warmed up our body to avoid injury?
- **Clothing, equipment and footwear**: do we have what is needed for the activity and conditions?
- **Jewellery**: have we removed rings and any other item of jewellery that might cause injury to opponents?

- **Rules**: do we have a good understanding of the rules?
- **Etiquette**: do we know the expected behaviour for the activity?
- **Respect**: do we have respect for our opponents?

Assessing risk when organising others

We must be sure we have the right qualifications, knowledge and experience to teach, coach, train or instruct young people in an activity. If we are responsible for young people we must exercise a 'duty of care'. This means that we must take all reasonable precautions to see that they are safe. We must ask the following questions:

- Have we prepared the group members properly?
- Have we planned the activity carefully?
- Have we the right group size?
- Have we ensured fair competition in terms of age, size, weight, sex and skill?
- Are the facilities and equipment safe?
- Will we supervise the activity well?
- Have we taken safety precautions?
- Is First Aid equipment ready?
- Have we explained any emergency procedures?

Assessing the sporting environment

We must be satisfied that the sports facilities, both indoors and outdoors, are in a safe condition.

Indoor areas

- Is the floor surface suitable for the activity?
- Is the floor surface clean, dry and free from dirt?
- Is the area clear of unnecessary portable apparatus?
- Is all fixed apparatus, such as beams, secure?
- Are there any dangerous projections or wall fittings?

Playing fields

- Is the grass clear of litter, especially glass and cans?
- Is the playing surface suitable?
- Are the weather conditions suitable?
- Is the equipment, such as goal posts, in good condition?

Swimming pool

- Are the wet surfaces around the pool clearly indicated?
- Are rules of behaviour prominently displayed?
- Are depth signs clearly visible?
- Are lifeguards on duty?

Outdoor activities

- Are competent instructors present?
- Are the weather conditions suitable?
- Is the appropriate specialist clothing and equipment available?
- Are First Aid facilities available?
- Are emergency procedures known and understood?

Organising a tournament

Choose a sport and plan for the organisation of a tournament.

Describe the basic organisation of the event including the age of teams, the number of teams and the number of pitches/courts or other facilities involved.

Complete a risk assessment and describe the safety precautions you will take. Set it out in the form of a table as shown below:

Hazards	Risk factor (1–5) (1 = low risk; 5 = high risk)	Precautions (actions/instructions)

Sports injuries and their causes

activity

Injuries

Working in groups, look at the following photos of injured sportspeople. See if you can agree on the following:

- What type of injury have they sustained?
- What was the likely cause of their injury?
- How could the injury have been avoided?

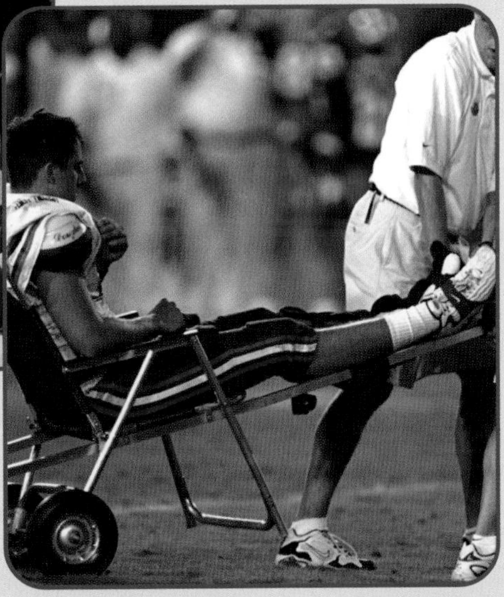

Causes of sports injuries

In order to avoid sports injuries, we need to know what they are and why they happen. A sports injury can be any damage caused to a sportsperson whilst in action. This will include hypothermia brought on by cold weather conditions as well as broken bones and pulled muscles.

Some sports have a greater risk of injury than others – for instance, we are more likely to be injured when playing rugby than when taking part in archery. Knowing the risk can help to reduce it.

Sports injuries can be caused in many different ways. They can be classed as:

- accidental injuries (due to violence or the environment)
- overuse injuries
- chronic injuries.

The force that causes accidental and overuse injuries can be:

- **internal**: that is, from within our bodies
- **external**: that is, from outside our bodies.

Accidental injuries

Accidental injuries are those that surprise us by happening when we least expect them. They can be caused by internal and external forces.

- **Internal forces** are those created when our body works during exercise. When we perform at our highest level, the extra strain on some body parts can cause damage. A sudden stretch or twist can strain or tear muscles, tendons or ligaments. These injuries may be caused by forgetting to warm up, by very sudden powerful movements or by lack of skill. For example, sprinters can tear hamstrings in a race. Footballers often suffer groin strain through stretching for the ball or knee ligament damage through twisting.
- **External forces** come from outside our bodies. Direct contact, or violence, from another player is one external force. Another external force is the environment.

Violence

Injuries caused by violence are due to direct contact between players or equipment. Many sports involve violent contact between opponents. Collisions may result in fractures, dislocations, sprains and bruises. They may also be caused by being hit by equipment such as balls, sticks or rackets. Breaking the rules can lead to violent injury.

The environment

The environment can lead to medical conditions in two different ways:

- An injury may be due to the facilities – for example, you might trip and land heavily on the playing surface or collide with the goalposts
- Alternatively, an injury may be due to weather conditions. Extreme heat can cause dehydration, heat exhaustion and then heatstroke. Extreme cold may lead to hypothermia.

Overuse injuries

Overuse injuries are caused by using a part of the body again and again over a long period of time. These injuries produce pain and inflammation.

Common overuse injuries include:

- 'tennis elbow' or 'golf elbow' – an inflamed elbow joint
- 'shin splints' – pain on the front of the shins
- 'cricketers' shoulder' – damage and inflammation to the front of the shoulder
- blisters and calluses – caused by gripping equipment very tightly during the activity, for example, in rowing.

The only cure for overuse injuries is rest. However, where injuries are caused by incorrect technique, the action must be corrected to prevent the injury recurring.

Chronic injuries

All injuries must be treated immediately and given time to heal. If we put an injury under stress before it is healed it will get worse. If this continues, we will develop a chronic injury, which is difficult to heal. Chronic injuries can lead to permanent damage such as arthritis in the joints.

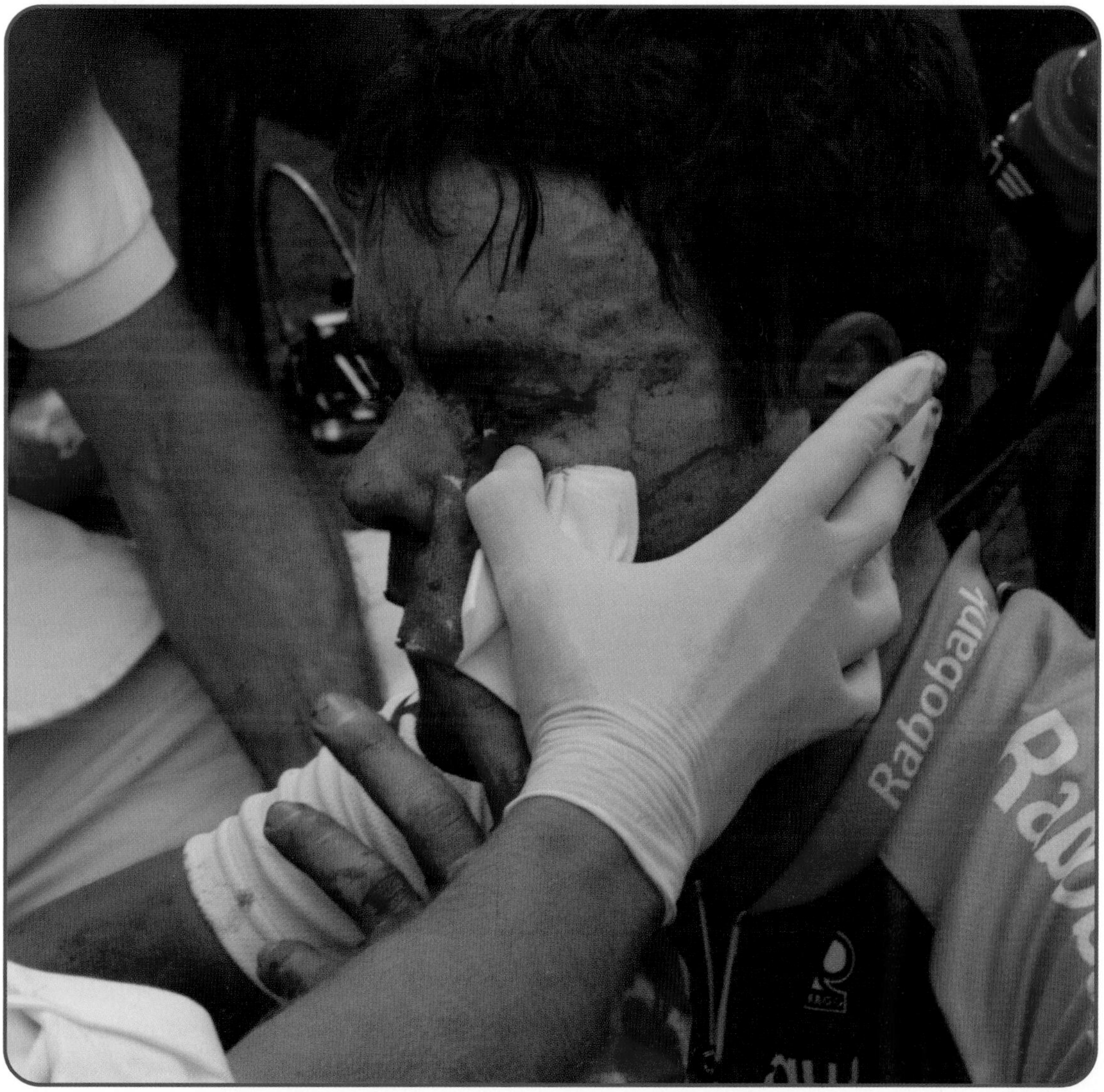

Recognition and treatment of sports injuries

Whenever we have to deal with an injury we are concerned with signs and symptoms. These help us to assess the injury and decide on any action.

- **Signs**: what we can see, feel, hear and smell – for example, swelling, bruising, bleeding, skin colour
- **Symptoms**: what the sufferer feels and describes – for example, pain, discomfort, nausea.

Fractures

A fracture is a break or crack in a bone. There are two types:

- In a simple (closed) fracture the bone stays under the skin.
- In a compound (open) fracture the bone breaks through the skin.

More complicated fractures also involve damage to nerves and muscles. Whenever the skin is broken there is the danger of infection. All fractures are serious and need urgent medical treatment.

Stress fractures

These are small cracks in a bone, often the result of an overuse injury. They can be caused, for example, by too much running on hard surfaces. The signs of a stress fracture are steadily increasing pain in a particular part of a limb, swelling and tenderness. If this occurs the sufferer needs to:

- use ice to reduce inflammation
- get immediate rest
- keep fit by doing other activities
- check running action and footwear for problems
- run on softer surfaces after recovery.

Joint injuries

The joints of our body are often extremely complex and vulnerable to injury. Simple joint injuries may be treated using the **RICE** procedure – that is, Rest, Ice, Compression, Elevation (see page 173). However, if serious damage or dislocation are suspected, the injury should be treated as a break and medical help sought.

Dislocations

A dislocation means that a bone is forced out of its normal position at a joint. The ligaments around the joint may also be damaged. The cause may be a strong wrench to the bone, perhaps in a rugby tackle. Treat all dislocations as fractures (see above). Do not attempt to replace the bone into its socket.

Tennis and golf elbow

These two injuries to the tendons at the joints are both caused by overuse. The tendons become inflamed and should be treated using RICE in the first instance. If the symptoms persist after a lengthy period of rest, then further medical advice should be sought to prevent chronic injury and the development of arthritis.

Cartilage injury

We have two cartilages between the bones of our knee joint which act as shock absorbers. They can be torn when the joint is twisted or pulled in an unusual way, for example, during a tackle in football. Sometimes cartilage injury causes the knee to lock. If this happens, medical advice should be sought.

Twisted ankle

This refers to damage to the ankle received when the joint is forced beyond its normal range of movement. This is a relatively common injury in games such as hockey, football and rugby. The ligaments supporting the joint are torn, causing pain, swelling and loss of movement. Immediate treatment should be RICE.

How do we treat bone and serious joint injuries?

The first step is to identify the problem. The following are all possible indicators of serious bone or joint injury:

- a recent blow or fall
- snapping sound of breaking bone or torn ligament
- difficulty in moving the limb normally
- pain made worse by movement
- tenderness at the site (fracture)
- severe 'sickening' pain (dislocation)
- deformity – that is, the limb has an unusual shape
- swelling, bruising
- signs of shock.

Some injuries are hard to diagnose. A sprained ankle and a broken ankle are very similar. An early sign of a break is that the casualty becomes pale and the skin is clammy. This is a sign of shock that does not often occur when the ankle is only sprained. If in doubt, treat the injury as a fracture.

Action

- Keep the casualty still, steady and comfortable.
- Support the injured part.
- Reassure the casualty.
- Send for medical help.

Soft tissue injuries

Soft tissue injuries include damage to:

- muscles
- ligaments
- tendons
- cartilage.

When soft tissues are injured they become inflamed. Treatment aims to reduce the swelling, prevent further damage and ease the pain. Soft tissue injuries are usually dealt with by using the RICE treatment.

A **sprain** happens when we over-stretch or tear a ligament around a joint. A sprain can be caused by a twist or sudden wrench, for example, a sprained ankle. In this case we must use the RICE treatment. If the injury is severe, we would treat it as a fracture.

A **strain** happens when we stretch or tear a muscle or tendon. This can be caused by a sudden stretch or extra muscular effort. In this case (for example, a pulled muscle), we must use the RICE treatment.

Even minor problems should be attended to quickly and carefully. If ignored, they may become more serious.

Skin damage

- **Cuts**: clean the cut with running water. Dab dry and cover using a dressing. Clean and dry the skin around the cut. Use an adhesive plaster over the dressing. Some lint-free dressings stick directly to the wound. These dressings are designed to remain in place until they fall off naturally.

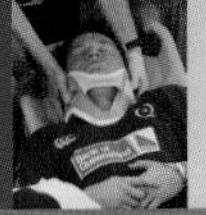

- **Grazes (abrasions)**: the top layer of skin has been scraped off because of friction with a rough surface. Treat it as a cut, but use a specialist non-stick dressing. Be careful to check that the wound is clean.
- **Blisters**: damage to the skin by heat or friction can cause a bubble to form to protect the skin. Do not break the blister. Cover it with a special plaster that stays in place until it falls off naturally. This will ease pain and protect the area from further damage.
- **Bruises**: these are formed by damaged capillaries bleeding under the skin and are the result of an impact. The skin changes colour, the area is painful and can swell. Treat by raising and supporting the bruised part. Put a cold compress (an ice pack) on the affected area.
- **Cramp**: this is sudden and painful muscle contraction caused by strenuous exercise or loss of fluid and salt through sweating. Treat by drinking fluid, stretching and massaging the muscle.
- **Stitch**: a sharp pain in the abdominal area caused by a cramp in the diaphragm. Treat by sitting down and resting. Light massage can also help.

The RICE procedure

The treatment known as **RICE** (Rest, Ice, Compression, Elevation) is a checklist to follow in the case of most soft tissue injuries, including sprains, strains and impact injuries. We should treat such injuries as soon as possible after they occur to prevent them from becoming worse.

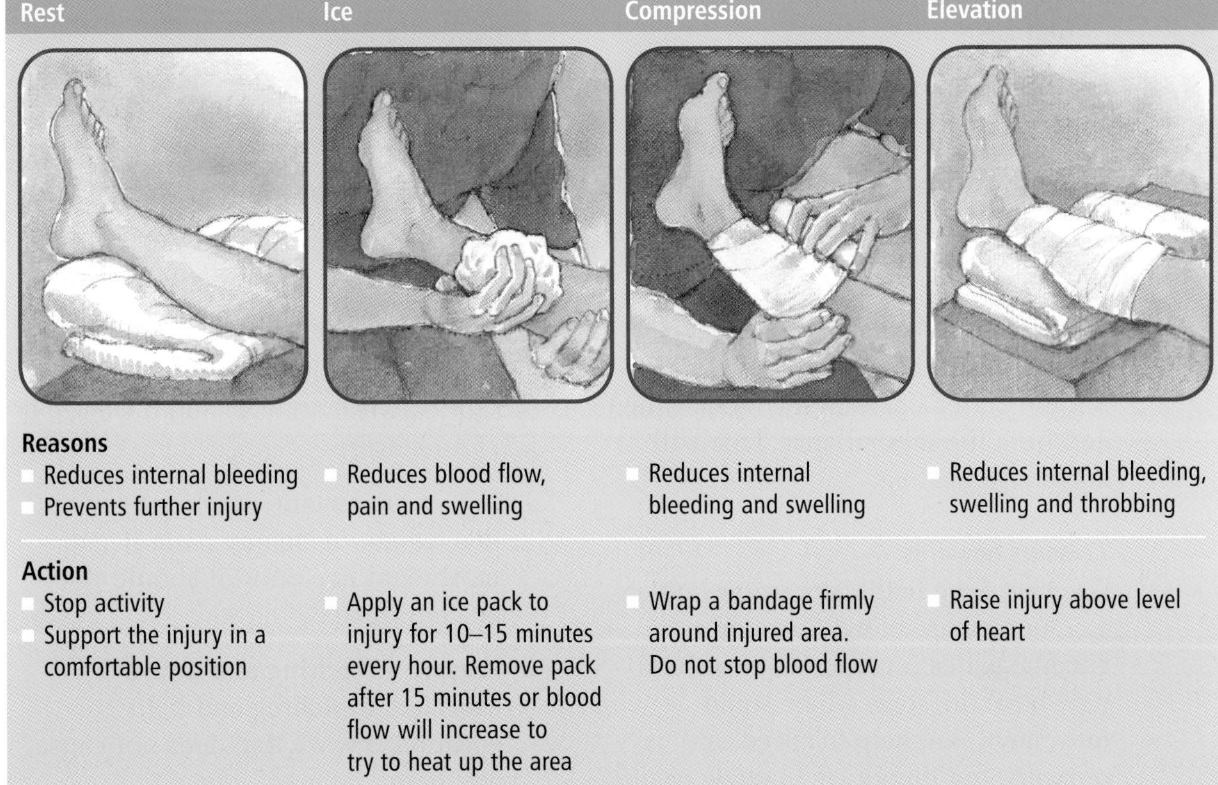

	Rest	Ice	Compression	Elevation
Reasons	Reduces internal bleeding Prevents further injury	Reduces blood flow, pain and swelling	Reduces internal bleeding and swelling	Reduces internal bleeding, swelling and throbbing
Action	Stop activity Support the injury in a comfortable position	Apply an ice pack to injury for 10–15 minutes every hour. Remove pack after 15 minutes or blood flow will increase to try to heat up the area	Wrap a bandage firmly around injured area. Do not stop blood flow	Raise injury above level of heart

Returning to sport

All injuries need time to heal. We can reduce the time before we return to sport by acting quickly when we are first injured. We also need to continue to treat the injury properly throughout our recovery period. If we try to return to play too soon, we can make the injury worse.

There are three stages of treatment for sprains and strains.

The first 48 hours

Ice should be applied for 10–15 minutes every hour during this period.

Remember **HARM** – things to be avoided in the first 48 hours after an injury:

- Do not use **Heat** for 48 hours because it increases internal bleeding.
- Do not drink **Alcohol** because it increases the swelling.
- Do not **Run** because the weight and impact will cause further injury.
- Do not **Massage** the injured area for 48 hours because it increases internal bleeding.

The next 48–72 hours

Apply ice and heat alternately for five-minute periods to increase blood flow to and from the injured area. This will encourage healing.

72 hours onwards

Use heat from baths, hot water bottles, etc., to increase blood flow and encourage healing. Most injuries will now be at the stage where some movement will help to speed up recovery, but do not try to move or play at full strength until you are sure you are able to do so safely.

This phase is called rehabilitation. It can last for between 10 days and 6 weeks. It has four stages:

- **Active movement**: gentle movements that do not cause any pain. If movement is painful it should not be continued.
- **Passive stretching and active exercise**: stretching and light endurance work that does not cause any pain.

- **Active strengthening**: the muscles will have lost some strength during the period of injury. You should first train to improve endurance and only then develop power and speed.
- **Re-education**: if you have no pain or swelling, your muscles and joints will need to be worked through their full range of movement. You can return to full training and then return to play.

Emergency procedures

DRABC (Doctor ABC)

Although you should always get medical help if possible, there are times when you may have to deal with an emergency involving a serious injury. It is important to keep calm and make sure that the first treatment is correct. **DRABC (Doctor ABC)** will help you to focus on the key points. Make sure you follow the points in the right order.

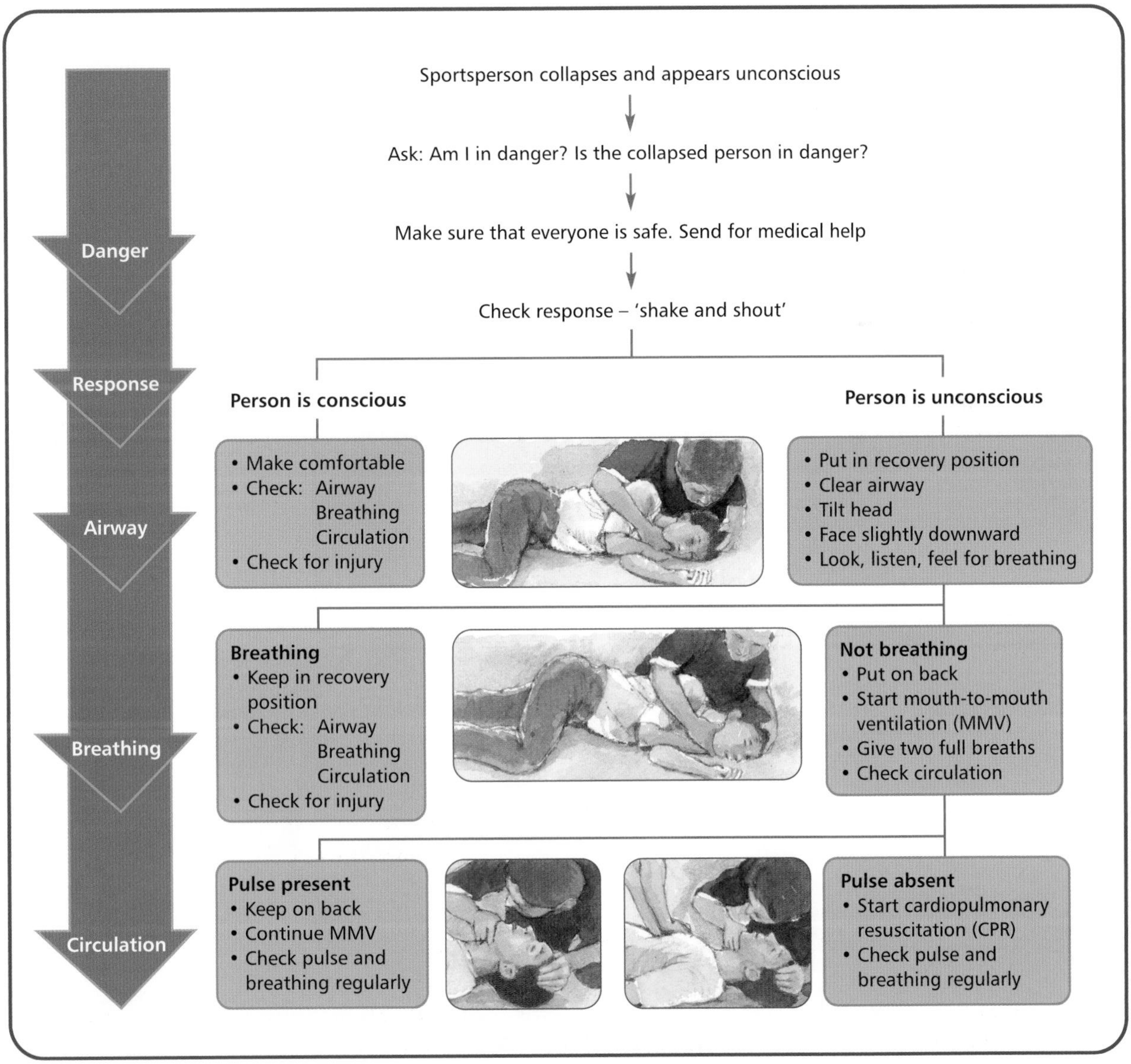

Danger

Sportsperson collapses and appears unconscious

↓

Ask: Am I in danger? Is the collapsed person in danger?

↓

Make sure that everyone is safe. Send for medical help

↓

Response

Check response – 'shake and shout'

Person is conscious

- Make comfortable
- Check: Airway
  Breathing
  Circulation
- Check for injury

Person is unconscious

- Put in recovery position
- Clear airway
- Tilt head
- Face slightly downward
- Look, listen, feel for breathing

Airway

Breathing
- Keep in recovery position
- Check: Airway
  Breathing
  Circulation
- Check for injury

Not breathing
- Put on back
- Start mouth-to-mouth ventilation (MMV)
- Give two full breaths
- Check circulation

Breathing

Pulse present
- Keep on back
- Continue MMV
- Check pulse and breathing regularly

Pulse absent
- Start cardiopulmonary resuscitation (CPR)
- Check pulse and breathing regularly

Circulation

Emergency treatment

When a casualty has stopped breathing we can breathe for them and help restart their breathing by increasing carbon dioxide levels in their blood. We do this by giving **mouth-to-mouth ventilation (MMV)**. If their heart has stopped beating we can try to get it going again by giving **cardiopulmonary resuscitation (CPR)**.

Mouth-to-mouth ventilation (MMV)

We should always try to send for medical help, but we can use MMV whilst waiting for help to arrive.

1 With the casualty lying on his back, open the airway by lifting the chin and tilting the head well back.

2 Clear the mouth and throat of any obstruction.

3 Check for breathing with your face close to the casualty's mouth. Look for chest movement. Listen for sounds of breathing. Feel his breath on your cheek.

4 If he is not breathing, pinch his nose. Take a deep breath. Seal your lips around his mouth. Blow into the mouth, and watch the chest rise. Take your mouth away and watch the chest fall back. Take another breath and repeat.

5 If his chest does not rise, check again for an obstruction in the mouth, check that the airway is open, and that you have a firm seal around the mouth.

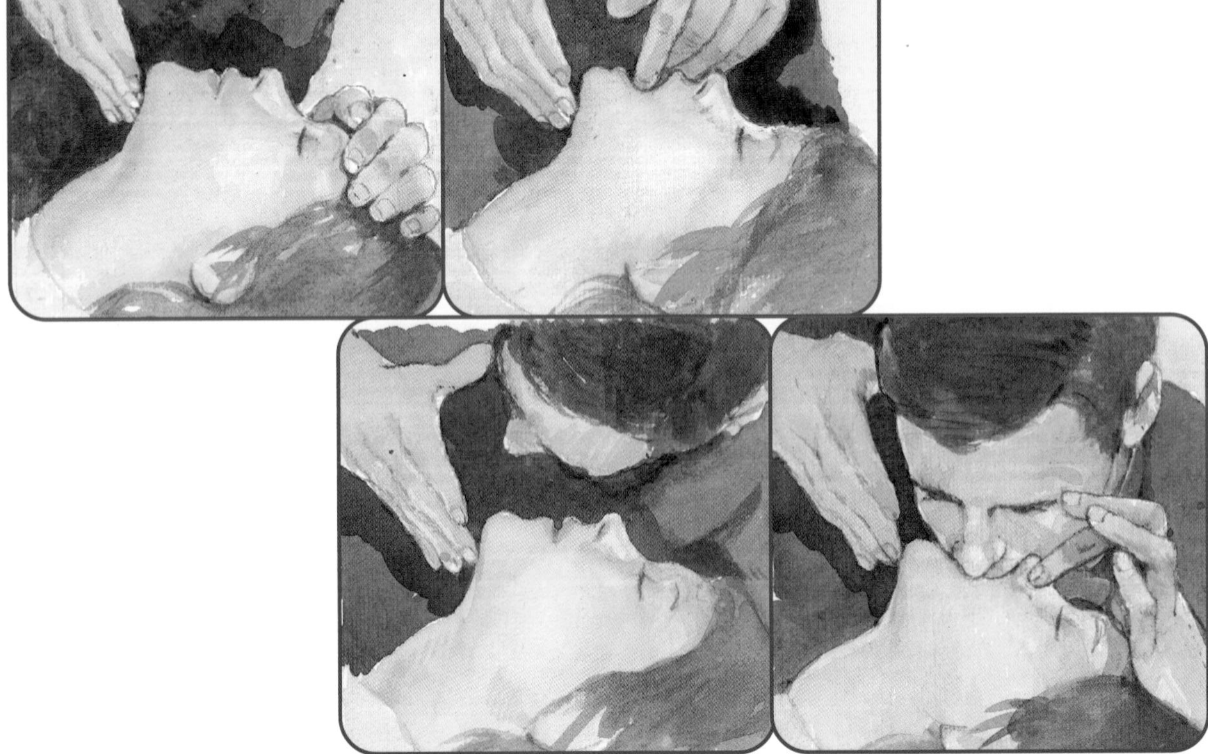

6 Check for a pulse before continuing. If there is no pulse, start chest compressions (see CPR below).

7 If he has a pulse and his chest has risen, continue blowing into his mouth. Use ten breaths a minute and continue until breathing starts. Then put him into the recovery position.

Cardiopulmonary resuscitation (CPR)

If you are certain that a person has no pulse, use chest compressions to get his heart beating again whilst waiting for medical help to arrive.

1 Check for a pulse. If the heart has stopped, you will not be able to feel a pulse. The skin will be pale, the lips blue and the arms and legs will be limp.

2 Place the person on his back and use your fingers to find the point where the ribs meet the breastbone. Put your middle finger over this point and your index finger higher up on his breastbone.

3 Put the heel of your other hand on the breastbone, just above your index finger. This is the spot where pressure should be applied.

4 Move the heel of your other hand over the top of this hand. Interlock your fingers.

5 Lean over him with your arms straight. Press down firmly into the breastbone to a depth of 4–5 cm. Then rock backwards to release the pressure. Keep your hands in place. Repeat at a rate of about 100 compressions a minute.

6 Check his pulse rate regularly. Stop compressions as soon as his pulse returns.

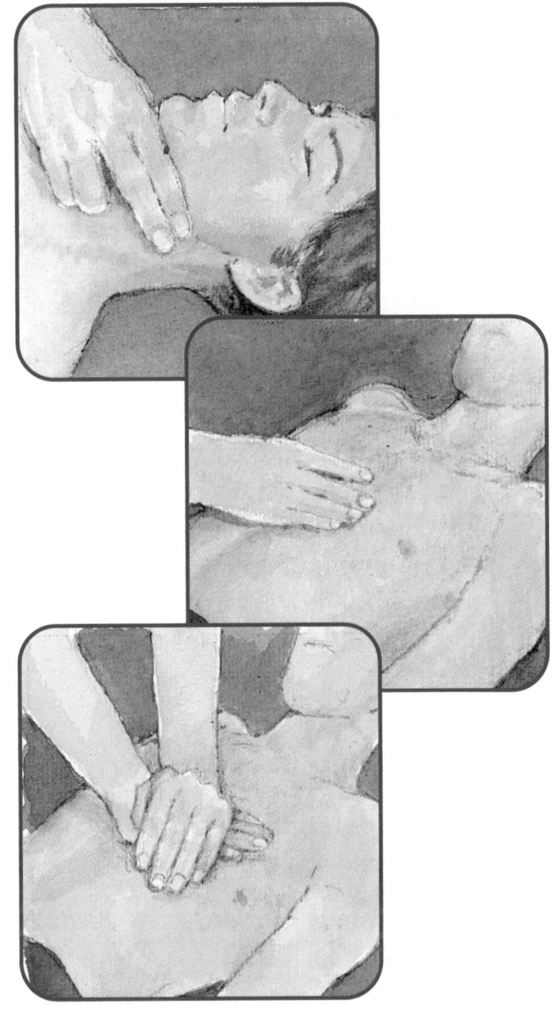

MMV and CPR combined

If you are alone with a person who has no pulse and no breathing, you need to take the following five actions:

1 Open his airway. Give two breaths using MMV.

2 Give 15 chest compressions (CPR).

3 Give two breaths (MMV).

4 Give 15 chest compressions (CPR).

5 Continue until help arrives – keep checking breathing and pulse.

If you have help you can share the work.

Dealing with serious injuries

It is reasonable to expect help when we are injured whilst playing sport, and also to expect that helpers will know what they are doing. Every sports club should have a qualified First Aider at every match and training session. We can all become qualified quite easily and should take the opportunity to do so. The St John Ambulance Brigade and the Red Cross organise First Aid courses. With a little training we may be able to provide life-saving help in an emergency. There are a number of serious injuries and conditions that need prompt action. We should know what to look for and how to act if we face someone who is seriously injured.

The recovery position

Always use the recovery position for an unconscious person who is breathing. You may need to alter the position slightly if the person is injured, but you can roll the body towards you and into the basic recovery position as follows:

- Tilt the head well back. This prevents the tongue blocking the throat.
- Keep the neck and back in a straight line.
- Keep the hip and knee both bent at 90°. This keeps the body safe, stable and comfortable.
- Use the casualty's hand to support the head, which should be slightly lower than the rest of the body. This allows fluids to drain from the mouth.

Remember to:

- Check pulse and breathing regularly.
- Send for medical help.

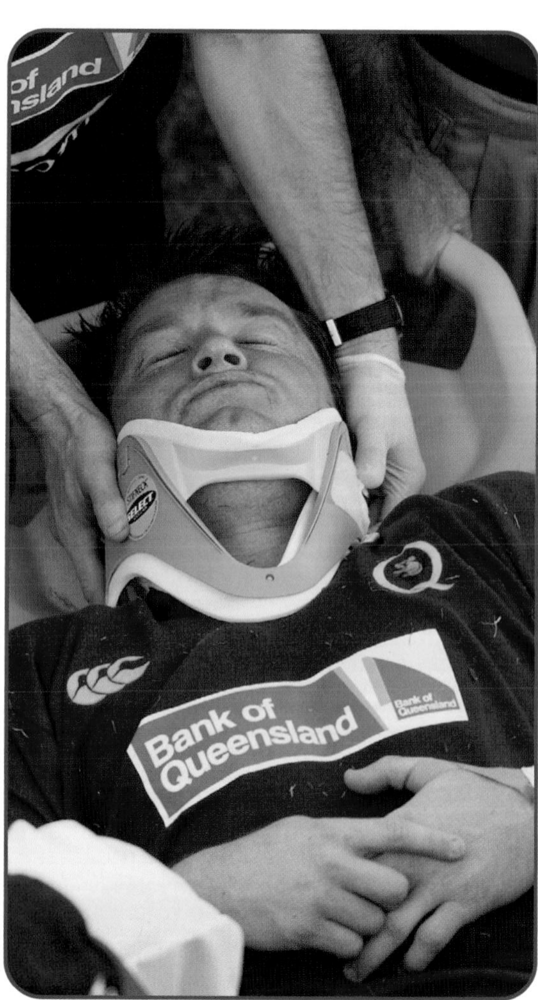

Unconsciousness and concussion

All blows to the head are potentially dangerous. A person may lose consciousness after a violent blow to the head and may suffer from concussion on recovery. Sometimes there is a delay between the injury and losing consciousness. This is a sure sign of concussion.

If you suspect concussion, you should check for dizziness, sickness and headache. People suffering from concussion often cannot remember what has happened to them. Always put someone with concussion in the recovery position and check their breathing and pulse regularly. Never allow anyone who has been knocked unconscious to continue with activity until medical advice has been obtained. In many sports, players who have suffered concussion are barred from playing again for a period of time in order to prevent further injury to the brain.

Dealing with extreme conditions

Extreme sports are becoming very popular. These, and many mainstream sports, take place in very cold or very hot conditions. Such conditions can create very serious problems for sportspeople. Three common but dangerous conditions that we should be able to recognise and treat are **hypothermia**, **heat exhaustion** and **heatstroke**.

Hypothermia

Hypothermia is a condition in which the internal body temperature becomes dangerously low. It can be caused by being outdoors in the cold and wind, or being in very cold water. Signs of hypothermia include:

- shivering
- cold, pale, dry skin
- slow, shallow breathing and slow, weakening pulse
- feeling confused and lacking energy.

If someone is suffering from hypothermia, send for help and then:

- insulate him with extra clothing and cover his head to keep in heat
- move him to a sheltered place and protect him from the ground and weather
- use a survival bag, if you have one
- give him hot drinks if he is conscious
- check his pulse and breathing regularly.

Heat exhaustion

When the temperature around you is the same as your body temperature, your body cannot lose heat by evaporation. If the air is also humid, then sweat will not evaporate from the body and heat exhaustion or heat stroke can occur.

Heat exhaustion develops during activity in hot conditions. It is caused by dehydration – that is, loss of fluid and salt from the body due to excessive sweating.

Signs of heat exhaustion include:

- headaches, light-headedness
- feeling sick
- sweating

- pale, clammy skin
- muscle cramps
- rapid, weakening pulse and breathing.

If someone is suffering from heat exhaustion, send for help and then:

- lie her down in a cool place
- raise and support her legs
- give her plenty of water and sips of weak salty water
- if she is unconscious put her in the recovery position.

Heatstroke

Heatstroke is the result of the body becoming dangerously overheated after being in the heat for a long time. Signs of heatstroke include:

- headaches
- dizziness, restlessness and confusion
- hot, flushed, dry skin
- very high body temperature
- a full, bounding pulse.

If someone is suffering from heatstroke, send for help and then:

- move him to a cool place
- remove outer clothing
- cool his body with wet towels or a cold, wet sheet
- if he is unconscious, put him in the recovery position.

Careful planning and proper training, together with the right clothing and equipment, can help to prevent all the dangerous conditions described above.

QUESTIONS

8 Prevention and treatment of sports injuries

Answer questions 1–4 by choosing statements a, b, c or d. One mark for each question.

1 A sprained ankle occurs when:

- **a** a bone is fractured
- **b** a muscle is torn
- **c** a ligament is overstretched
- **d** a joint is dislocated.

2 RICE stands for:

- **a** Rest, Ice, Confusion, Empathy
- **b** Rest, Ice, Compression, Elevation
- **c** Relax, Injury, Concentration, Excitement
- **d** Rest, Injury, Completely, Elevate.

3 'Balanced' competition means:

- **a** all players must stay on their feet
- **b** each player must be within 10% of standard body weight
- **c** games must be played in two equal halves
- **d** players must compete with others of the same standard, age, gender or weight.

4 A person appears confused, with pale, dry skin and is shivering. He or she is suffering from:

- **a** hypothermia
- **b** hyperthermia
- **c** heatstroke
- **d** shock.

5 **a** Rules encourage good sporting behaviour and protect players from injury. Copy the table below and list two rules of your chosen activity. State how each reduces the risk of injury.

Activity	
Rule 1	How rule reduces risk of injury
Rule 2	How rule reduces risk of injury

(2 marks)

b The table below contains five sporting activities. Complete it by stating a potential risk and an appropriate precaution to reduce risk for each.

Activity	Potential risk	Precaution
Football		
Javelin		
White water canoeing		
Cycling		
Gymnastics		

(8 marks)

QUESTIONS

6 John is a hockey player.

a Give two items of protective clothing that he wears every time he plays.
(2 marks)

b Suggest two potential risks that John faces when playing hockey.
(2 marks)

c Soft tissue injuries often occur in hockey. Explain the RICE procedure which is the recommended treatment.
(4 marks)

d During a recent game a player was knocked unconscious. Name the type of injury that this causes.
(1 mark)

e John applied DrABC when he helped the injured player. Explain each of the five steps he took.
(10 marks)

f Name the position in which John placed the injured player whilst waiting for the ambulance to arrive.
(1 mark)
(Total 34 marks)

Applied anatomy and physiology

9 The circulatory system

Our life depends upon a constant source of oxygen and nutrients in all the cells of the body. Our circulatory system works non-stop, 24 hours a day to deliver these vital supplies. The circulatory system also carries away carbon dioxide and other waste products.

activity

Recording heart rate

The simplest way to see how well our circulatory system is working is to measure our heart rate by taking our pulse. Our pulse is the surge of blood through our arteries which happens every time our heart beats. We must learn how to find and record our pulse accurately and quickly. This will enable us to assess how hard our circulatory system is working at any time.

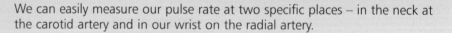

We can easily measure our pulse rate at two specific places – in the neck at the carotid artery and in our wrist on the radial artery.

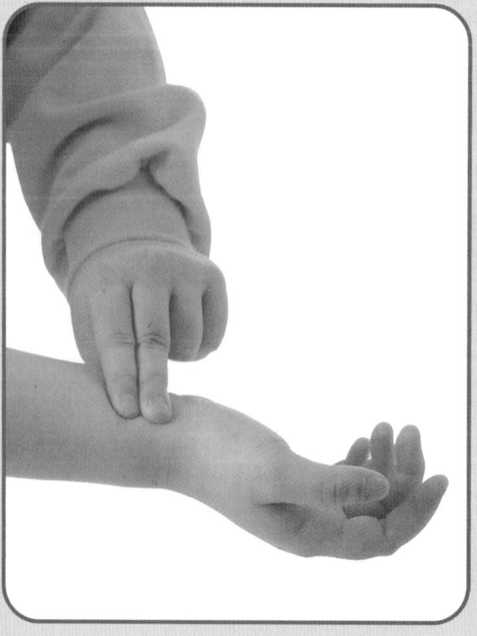

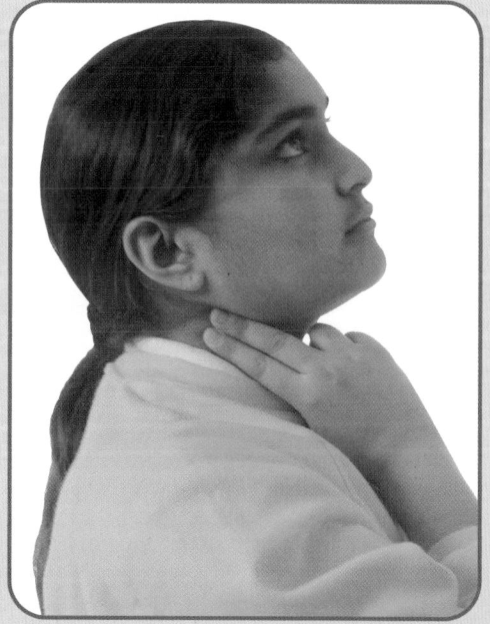

activity

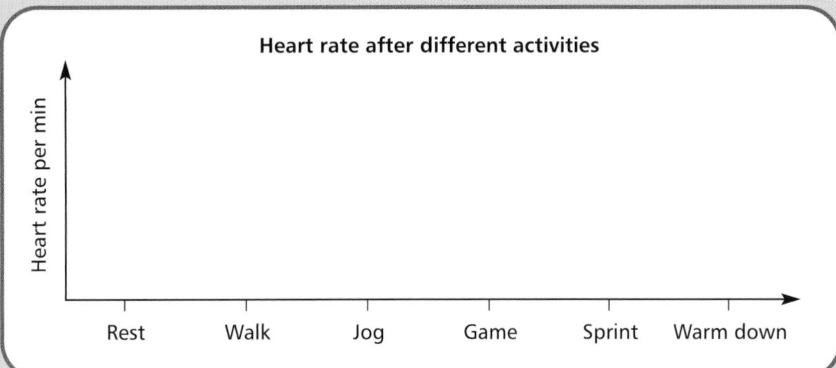

1. Practise counting the number of pulses felt over a time of 15 seconds. You must use your fingers and not your thumb. Try it at both the neck and wrist. Multiply your 15-second count by 4 to get your heart rate in beats per minute. (It should of course be the same at both your neck and wrist!)
2. Practise finding your carotid and radial pulses quickly. This is important when trying to count your pulse after exercise.
3. In pairs, practise counting the pulse of your partner using both the neck and wrist locations, while sitting down at rest.
4. One of you now walks at a brisk pace for one minute. Immediately after walking, the non-active partner measures the other's pulse over the first 15 seconds and records it in beats per minute.
5. Repeat the exercise with the roles reversed.
6. The first partner now jogs for three minutes at a slow pace. Repeat the pulse-taking and swap over.
7. You both now play a game, for instance, basketball, for 10–15 minutes. Repeat the pulse-taking.
8. Your partner sprints for a total of 20 seconds. Repeat the pulse-taking and swap over.
9. You both warm down for three minutes. Repeat the pulse-taking and swap over.
10. Record your results and those of your partner on a graph. Remember, you should not join the points plotted as the data you have collected is not continuous. Explain your results and set them out as shown in the table below.

Time period	Activity	Heart rate (beats per minute)	Explanation
	Rest		
1 minute	Walk		
3 minutes	Jog		
10–15 minutes	Play game (e.g. basketball)		
20 seconds	Sprint		
3 minutes	Warm-down		

KEYWORDS

Arterioles: small blood vessels into which arteries subdivide, taking blood into the capillaries

Artery: Large blood vessel taking oxygenated blood from the heart to the body (exception: the pulmonary artery takes deoxygenated blood from the heart to the lungs)

Blood pressure: force of blood against walls of artery caused by heart pumping blood around the body

Capillaries: microscopic blood vessels which link arteries with veins

Cardiac output: amount of blood ejected from the heart in one minute

Cardiovascular: pertaining to the heart and blood vessels

Circulatory system/cardiovascular system: the heart, circulation of the blood and composition of the blood

Haemoglobin: oxygen-carrying substance in red blood cells

Heartbeat: one complete contraction of the heart

Heart rate: the number of times the heart beats each minute

Pulmonary circulation: carries deoxygenated blood from our heart to our lungs and oxygenated blood back to the heart

Stroke volume: the volume of blood pumped out of the heart by each ventricle during one contraction

Systemic circulation: carries oxygenated blood from the heart to the rest of our body and deoxygenated blood back to the heart

Veins: large blood vessels taking deoxygenated blood from the body to the heart (**exception**: the **pulmonary vein** takes oxygenated blood from the lungs to the heart)

Venules: small blood vessels that take blood from the capillaries to the veins.

Key to Exam Success

For your GCSE you should be able to:

- identify the main parts of the heart and to know how it works
- be able to compare arteries, capillaries and veins
- describe the composition and functions of the blood
- understand how the heart, blood, and blood vessels work together
- know how the circulatory (cardiovascular) system affects training, fitness and performance
- know how the circulatory system links with the respiratory system
- know how training and exercise affects the circulatory system
- apply your knowledge to your Personal Exercise Plan (PEP).

“ KEY THOUGHT ”

‘Our circulation system is a delivery service in perpetual motion.’

The circulatory system in action

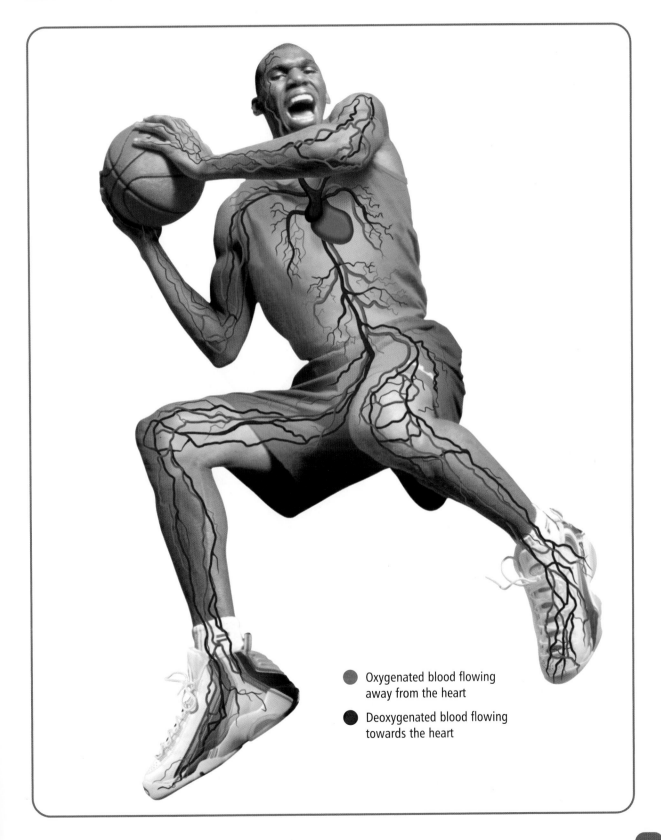

Oxygenated blood flowing away from the heart

Deoxygenated blood flowing towards the heart

Our **circulatory system** (sometimes called our **cardiovascular system**) is made up of our heart, blood and blood vessels.

Our circulation system has two parts, our **pulmonary circulation** and our **systemic circulation**. This is called a double circulatory system because blood is pumped simultaneously to different destinations. Our systemic circulation carries oxygenated blood from the heart to the rest of our body and the oxygen is used by the cells. Deoxygenated blood returns to the heart with waste products, which have to be removed from our body.

The function of the circulatory system is to:

- take oxygen and nutrients to every cell
- remove carbon dioxide and other waste products from every cell
- carry hormones from the hormonal (endocrine) glands to different parts of the body
- maintain temperature and fluid levels
- prevent infection from invading germs.

Our pulmonary circulation carries deoxygenated blood from our heart to our lungs. Here carbon dioxide is exchanged for oxygen. Oxygenated blood is then carried back to the heart.

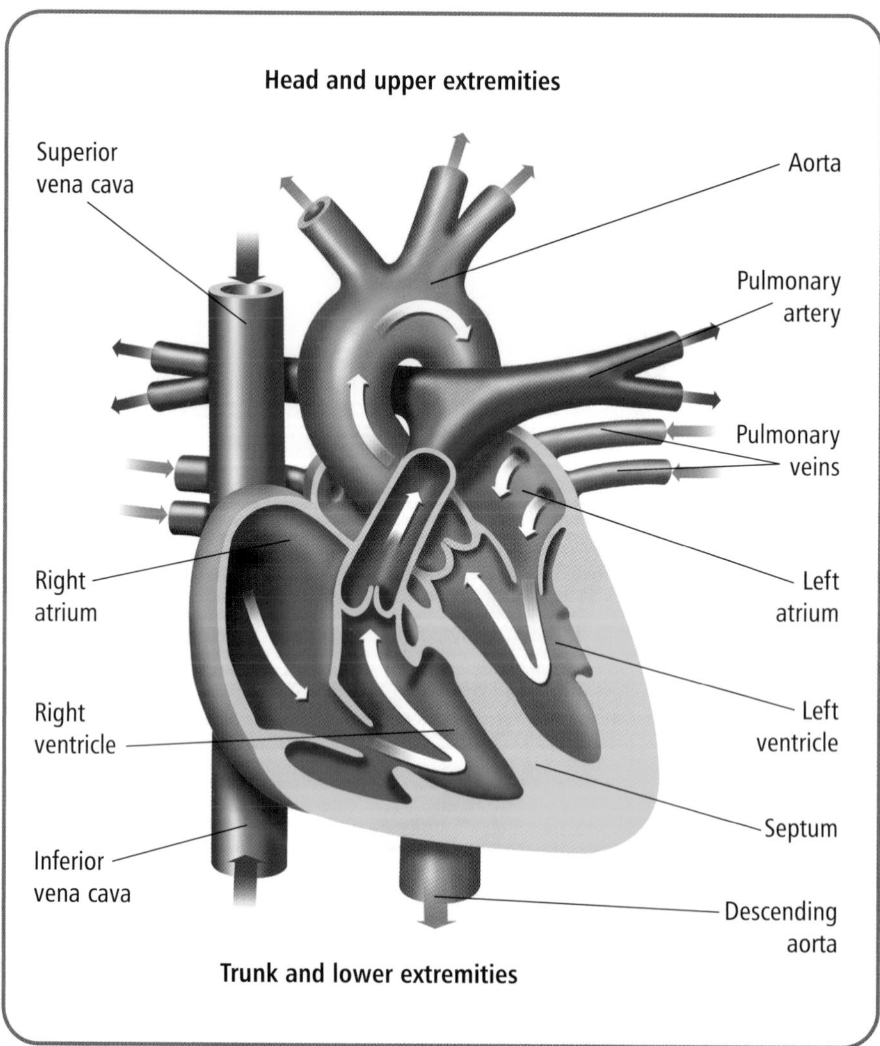

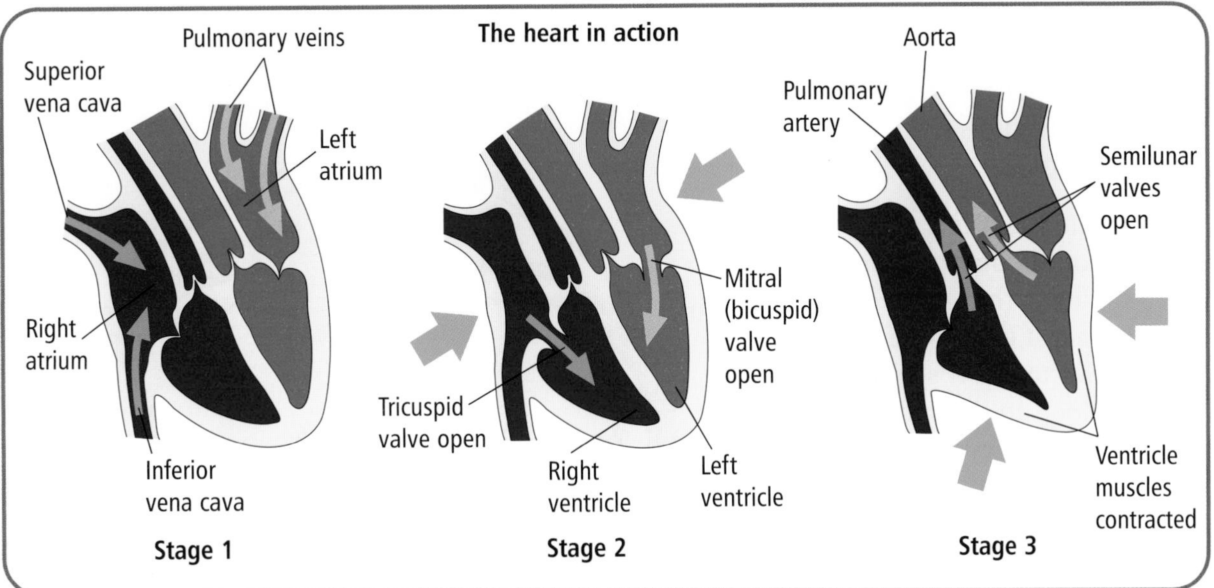

How does our heart work?

Our heart is a muscular pump. It is made up of special cardiac muscle which contracts regularly without tiring. It pumps blood first to the lungs, to exchange carbon dioxide for oxygen. Then blood with the new oxygen is returned to the heart to be pumped out around the body.

The three stages of heart action are shown above.

- Our cardiac cycle is one complete cycle of these three stages.
- Our heartbeat is one complete contraction of the heart.
- Our heart rate (pulse) is the number of heartbeats per minute.

At rest, our heart pumps between 50 and 80 times a minute. It pumps about 4.7 litres of blood around the body. At rest this journey takes about 20 seconds.

Stage 1

- Blood flows into the heart when it is between beats and relaxed.
- Deoxygenated blood from our body enters the right atrium through the two vena cava veins.
- At the same time newly oxygenated blood from our lungs enters the left atrium through the pulmonary veins.

Stage 2

- Our right atrium muscles contract to pump blood through the tricuspid valve into the right ventricle.
- At the same time, our left atrium muscles contract to pump blood through the mitral valve into the left ventricle.

Stage 3

- Our right ventricle muscles contract to pump blood through the semilunar valves into the pulmonary artery to travel to the lungs.
- Our left ventricle muscles contract to pump blood through the semilunar valves into the aorta, to travel around the body again.

How does blood move around the body?

The heart is a double pump. This means that for every beat it carries out two tasks. It sends blood to the lungs to collect oxygen and also sends oxygenated blood around the body. We call this a double circulatory system. For it to work, the heart is divided into two parts by a muscular wall called the septum.

The right-hand side of the heart deals with blood returning from our body through the vena cava. During its journey, our blood has given up much of its oxygen. It has picked up waste products, including carbon dioxide. It is now a dull red colour. The heart pumps this blood to our lungs in our **pulmonary artery**. This is the only artery which carries deoxygenated blood.

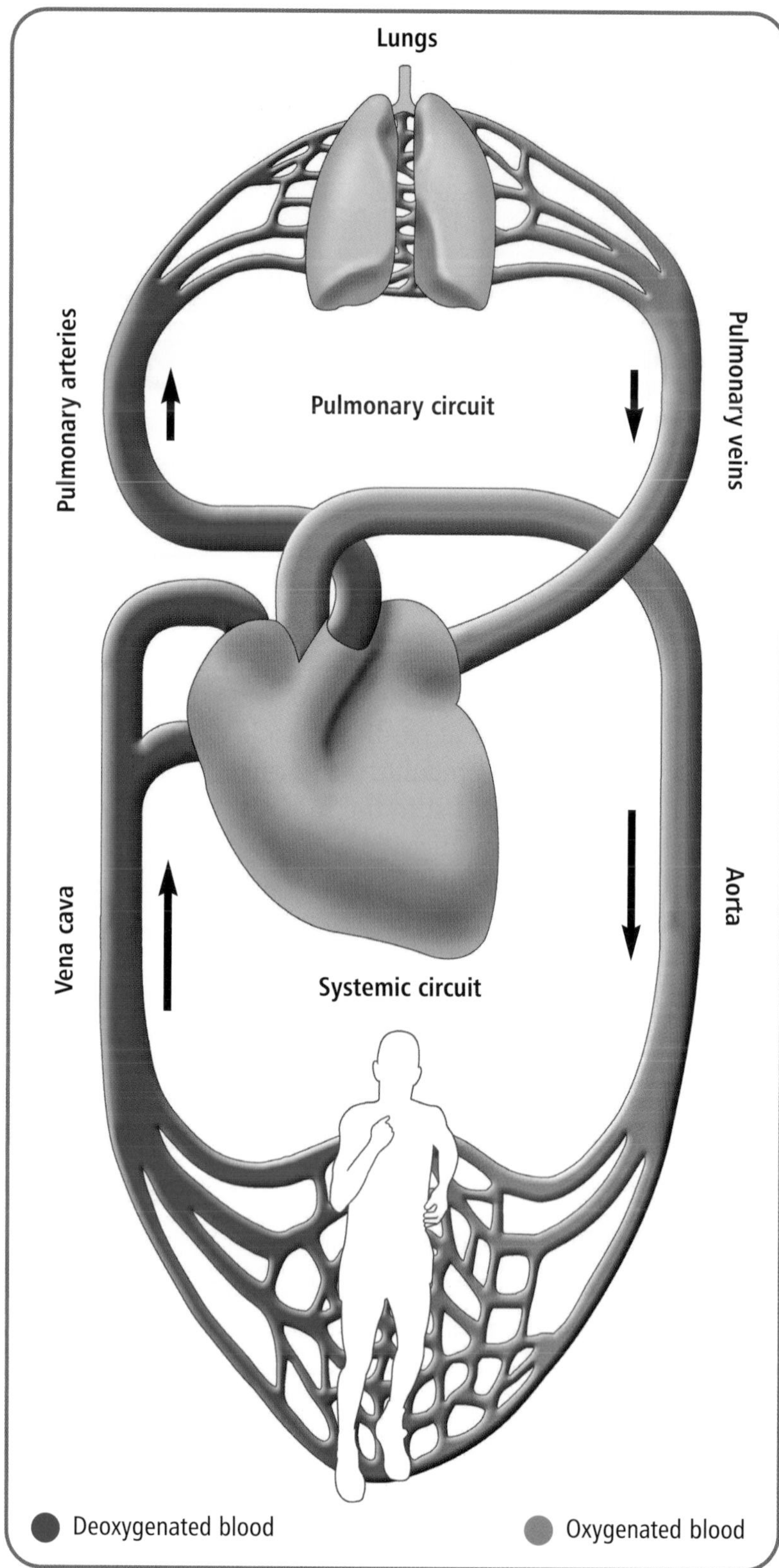

Our blood vessels include **arteries**, **veins**, **venules** and **capillaries**. These carry blood to all parts of the body and back again to the heart.

The left-hand side of the heart deals with the blood returning from our lungs in our **pulmonary veins**. These are the only veins that carry oxygenated blood. In our lungs the blood releases carbon dioxide and other waste products, and is supplied with fresh oxygen. When blood returns to the heart it is bright red. The heart pumps this blood into our largest artery, the aorta, to travel around the body.

The thickness of the walls of the heart vary according to the task which they carry out. The atria are both thin-walled, because they only pump the blood to the ventricles below. Both ventricles have much thicker walls.

The left ventricle has very thick, muscular walls. This is because the blood leaving the heart must be pumped out very powerfully at high pressure to travel the long distance around the body. In contrast, the right ventricle only pumps blood a short distance to the lungs and is therefore not so thick-walled.

Our arteries carry freshly oxygenated blood from the heart. They become smaller and smaller. The smaller arteries are called **arterioles**. They take blood into the tissue where they join up with our smallest vessels – the capillaries. In turn the capillaries join up with venules, which increase in size to become veins. Our veins return deoxygenated blood to our heart.

Our heart and exercise

As we work harder, our muscles need more oxygen and we breathe in and out more deeply and quickly in order to get this oxygen to the lungs. These increased supplies of oxygen are picked up by the blood in our lungs and transported more quickly back to the heart. The double circulatory system ensures that the increased supplies of oxygen collected from the lungs are transported at an increased rate to the working muscles. At the same time, carbon dioxide and other waste products are removed at an increased rate.

The right type of training can increase the size and pumping ability of the heart – that is, the **stroke volume** and **cardiac output** of the heart. Like all muscle, heart muscle responds to training by becoming stronger as its walls thicken. In this way we can increase the amount of blood going to the lungs to pick up oxygen and therefore increase the amount of oxygen going to our working muscles. This helps us to work harder and for longer periods in our sport. During hard physical activity, our heart rate can increase to over 200 beats per minute. The heart of a trained athlete can pump up to 45 litres of blood a minute. Training will reduce the resting heart rate of an athlete considerably.

How well does our heart pump?

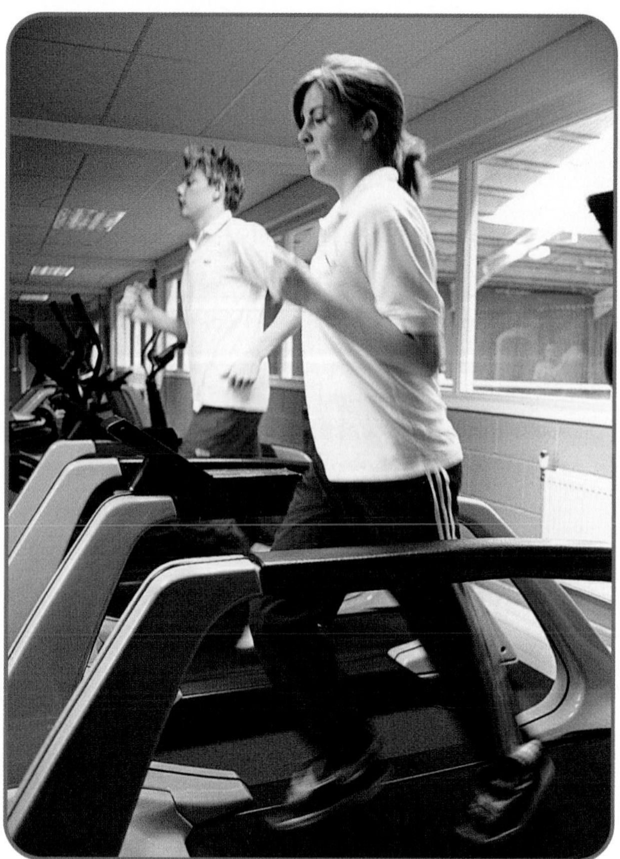

Our heart is made up of cardiac muscle and we cannot control its action voluntarily. Fortunately cardiac muscle never tires. The speed and force of each heartbeat are controlled by our brain. Our brain is affected by what we are doing. If we start running, our brain tells our heart to pump more blood to supply our working leg muscles with more oxygen. Like any other muscle, heart muscle can get stronger when exercised. The amount of blood pumped by the heart depends on heart rate and stroke volume.

Heart rate

Heart rate is 'the number of time the heart beats each minute'. (Edexcel.)

At each heartbeat, blood is pumped out of our heart into the arteries. Our arteries are forced to expand and then contract, which is called our pulse. The number of pulses in one minute is our heart rate. For a normal adult when resting this will be about 70 beats per minute.

A pulse can be felt at points in the body where arteries are near to the skin.

Resting heart rate

Resting heart rates can vary between people, due to factors such as sex, age and health. Endurance sportspeople will have a much lower rate – perhaps as low as 30 beats per minute. This is because their hearts are stronger and are able to pump more blood in fewer beats than a person who is less fit. Their stroke volume is therefore greater.

Resting heart rate can be one way to show fitness level. The speed at which heart rate returns to normal after exercise is called the recovery rate. This rate can also be used to measure fitness.

Stroke volume

Stroke volume is 'the volume of blood pumped out of the heart by each ventricle during one contraction'. (Edexcel.)

Whenever we exercise, stroke volume increases for a number of reasons. Working muscles squeeze blood in our veins, forcing more blood back to the heart. The heart stretches as it fills up with the extra blood and in turn it contracts more strongly. This results in more blood being pumped out of the heart for each beat.

Cardiac output

Cardiac output is 'the amount of blood ejected from the heart in one minute'. (Edexcel.)

It is controlled by both heart rate and stroke volume:

Heart rate x Stroke volume = Cardiac output

In sport we usually want to increase the amount of blood going to the working muscles – that is, our cardiac output. We can do this by increasing stroke volume, heart rate or both.

What is blood pressure?

Blood pressure is the force of the blood against the walls of the blood vessels. It is different in different blood vessels. It depends on how much blood is flowing into the blood vessels and how easily it can flow out.

In our arteries the blood pressure is high because the arteries are narrow and a lot of blood is being forced into them from the heart. Blood flows slowly only in the wider veins, which are a long way from the heart. Here blood pressure is low and so valves are needed to prevent blood from flowing backwards.

How do we measure blood pressure?

We use a special instrument to measure the pressure needed to stop the blood flowing through an artery. It is usually measured in our upper arm and two readings are taken. One reading is our systolic blood pressure, which is the maximum pressure of the blood. The second reading is of our diastolic blood pressure, which is the lowest pressure of our blood, measured between heartbeats. Blood pressure should be taken when we are relaxed and resting. It will therefore be at its lowest.

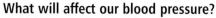

What will affect our blood pressure?

- **Age**: blood pressure increases as we grow older because our arteries are less elastic.
- **Exercise**: blood pressure increases when we exercise but returns to normal after exercise. Regular exercise helps to lower resting blood pressure and prevent cardiovascular disease.
- **Stress**: stress causes hormones to be released into the blood, which increases blood pressure.
- **Smoking**: smoking increases blood pressure because nicotine reduces the efficiency of our capillaries.
- **Diet**: a diet high in fat or salt may lead to increased blood pressure. This is because fatty deposits may block up or harden arteries. Excess salt intake may lead to an imbalance in the body's chemistry.
- **Weight**: being overweight puts an extra strain on the circulatory system and so raises blood pressure.

What does high blood pressure mean?

A person has high blood pressure (called hypertension) if their blood pressure stays high over a long period of time. A high reading would be above 140 (systolic) or 90 (diastolic).

Hypertension may be caused by blockages in the smaller blood vessels, which means that the heart has to work harder to force blood around the body. Arteries taking blood to the heart muscle can also become blocked. Sudden activity can cause a sharp pain (called angina) or even a heart attack.

activity

Recording blood pressure

1 Depending on what equipment is available, practise taking your partner's resting blood pressure when he or she is sitting down. Record both the systolic and diastolic readings. (Remember that the systolic measure records blood pressure as the heart is contracting, whilst the diastolic measure records blood pressure as the heart is relaxing.)
2 One of you now walks at a brisk pace for one minute. The non-active partner measures the other's blood pressure immediately after walking and records it.
3 Repeat the exercise with the roles reversed.
4 The first partner now jogs for three minutes at a slow pace. Repeat the blood-pressure recording and swap over.
5 You both now play a game, for instance, basketball, for 10–15 minutes. Repeat the blood-pressure recording.
6 Your partner sprints for a total of 20 seconds. Repeat the blood-pressure recording and swap over.
7 You both warm down for three minutes. Repeat the blood-pressure recording and swap over.

Using the chart provided, plot your results and those of your partner and display them as a dual bar chart. Remember, you should not join the points plotted as the data you have collected is not continuous. Give reasons to explain your results.

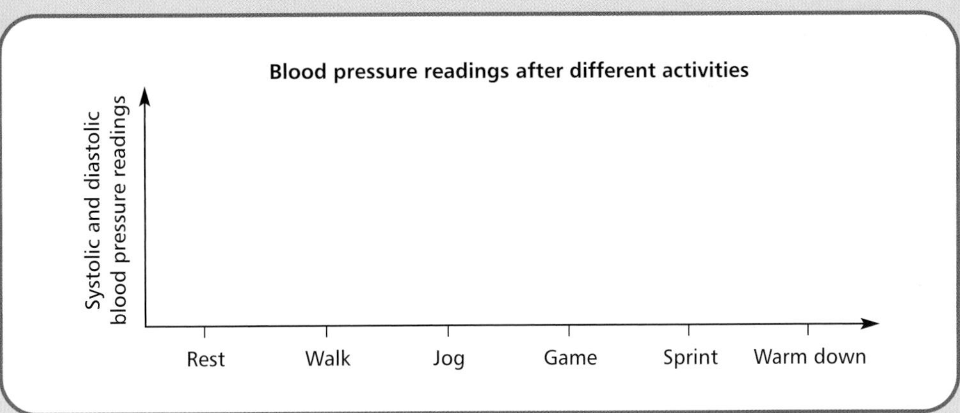

Time period	Activity	Systolic blood pressure	Diastolic blood pressure
	Rest		
1 minute	Walk		
3 minutes	Jog		
10–15 minutes	Play game (e.g. basketball)		
20 seconds	Sprint		
3 minutes	Warm down		

Blood pressure and exercise

During exercise our heart beats faster and pumps out more blood. Our blood pressure rises. This is quite normal. Regular sensible exercise linked with a healthy diet and lifestyle will actually lower our resting blood pressure. Recently some drugs such as erythropoietin (EPO), which has been taken by some cyclists, have reduced blood pressure to dangerously low levels.

What happens to our circulatory system when we exercise?

- The hormone adrenaline is released even before we start to exercise. It prepares the body for action.
- Adrenaline in the bloodstream causes the heart to beat more quickly, so heart rate increases.
- The heart contracts more powerfully. It sends out a greater amount of blood with each contraction. Stroke volume increases.
- Blood circulation speeds up, and greater amounts of oxygen-carrying blood reach the working muscles. Cardiac output increases.
- The pumping action of muscles forces more deoxygenated blood back to the heart more quickly.
- Blood flow to the areas of the body not in urgent need of oxygen, for example our digestive system, is reduced.
- Blood flow to the areas in greatest need of oxygen, for example, our skeletal muscles, is increased.
- Blood vessels to skin areas become enlarged. This allows excess heat from muscles and organs to be lost more easily from the skin.

- During very hard exercise even these blood vessels will be reduced in size. Body temperature will then rise very quickly. It can cause overheating and fatigue.
- The oxygen going to the muscles can be up to three times the resting amount.
- Blood flow can be increased up to 30 times. Therefore, the working muscles can receive up to 90 times the amount of oxygen they receive at rest.

Why are our blood vessels different?

1 Arteries:

- thick-walled
- elastic, expand to carry blood
- small passageway for blood (internal lumen)
- blood under high pressure
- no valves needed, artery walls contract to move blood
- carry blood away from the heart
- carry oxygenated blood (except pulmonary artery).

2 Capillaries:

- microscopic blood vessels linking arterioles and venules
- extremely thin walls, one cell thick
- allow food and oxygen to pass out to our body tissues
- allow carbon dioxide and other waste to pass into blood from our body tissues.

3 Veins:

- thin-walled
- non-elastic
- large passageway for blood (internal lumen)
- blood under low pressure
- have valves to stop blood flowing backwards
- carry blood to the heart
- carry deoxygenated blood (except pulmonary veins).

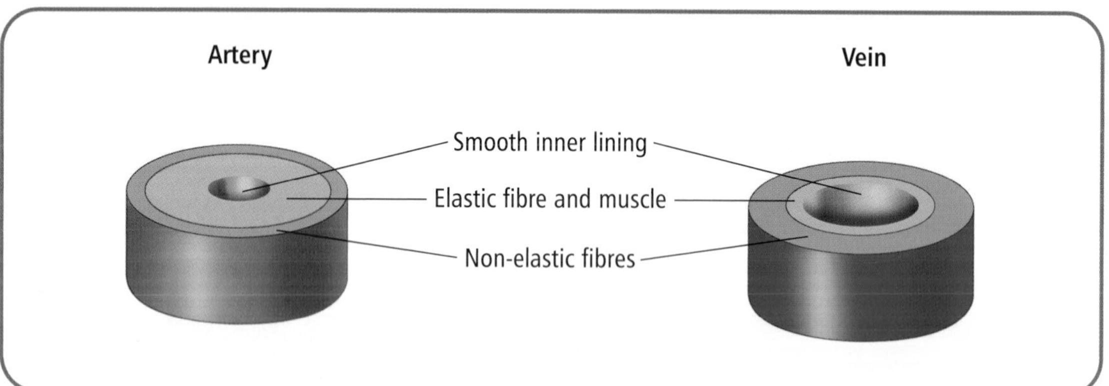

What happens in our capillaries?

Our capillary network is extremely large. It is also very dense in active tissues such as muscles. Arterioles bring oxygen and nutrients to the capillaries. In muscle tissue the oxygen and nutrients squeeze out through the thin capillary walls. This enables the muscles to work. As a muscle contracts it produces waste products, including carbon dioxide, which squeeze back into the capillaries. The capillaries then join up with venules, which lead to veins and back to the heart. Carbon dioxide is then removed by our lungs. Other waste is removed by our kidneys.

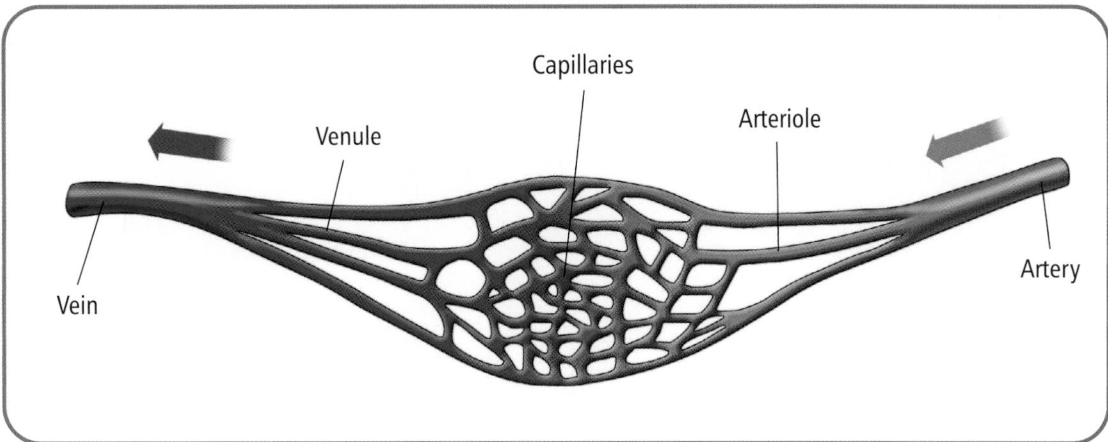

Valves

- Blood returning to our heart is under low pressure.
- Valves are needed to stop the blood flowing backwards.

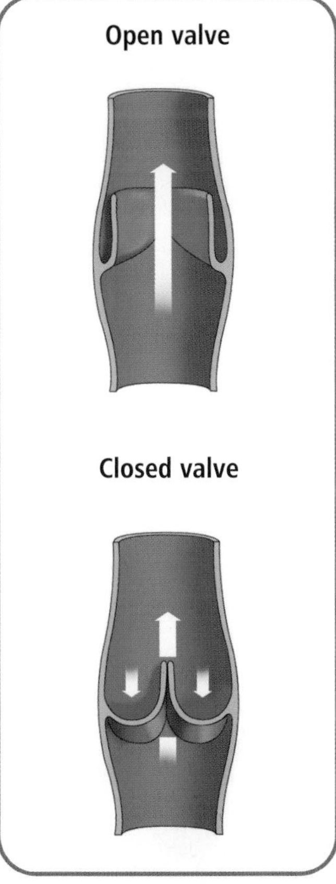

Blood circulation and exercise

The body can alter the flow of blood to different areas. At rest our skeletal muscles need little oxygen, so only 15–20% of our heart's output goes to them. During exercise more blood is directed to these working muscles and away from such areas as the digestive system. As much as 80% of the heart's output may go to our working muscles during strenuous exercise. Training actually increases our body's ability to redistribute blood more efficiently.

Within the working muscles the oxygen reaches actual muscle fibres through the capillary network. As a result of training, this capillary network increases, allowing more oxygen to be delivered to the working muscles. Blood pressure increases during exercise when massive amounts of blood are forced through the arteries. However, regular exercise leads to lower resting blood pressure.

activity

Blood circulation

The following activities are designed to reinforce your understanding of how the double circulatory system works.

Begin by selecting members of your group to represent the following:

Vena cava	Left atrium
Right atrium	Mitral valve
Tricuspid valve	Left ventricle
Right ventricle	Aorta
Semilunar valve	Arteries
Pulmonary artery	Arterioles
Lungs	Venules
Pulmonary veins	Veins.

Each member of the group has a card indicating which part of the circulatory system they represent.

1. You have five minutes to get yourself into the right order in a circle, starting with the vena cava. Now decide whether red, blue or red and blue blood flows through you.
2. A student is chosen to represent a drop of blood, and attempts to circulate through the system. In order to go past each of the various parts of the system they have to correctly answer one or more of the following questions:
   - Are you red or blue blood?
   - Which part of the system have you just come from?
   - Are you carrying oxygen or carbon dioxide?
   - Where are you going next?
3. Repeat Task 2, but with the names of the various parts of the circulatory system hidden. The blood drops have to first name the part of the system which they are visiting before they can proceed.

What makes up our blood?

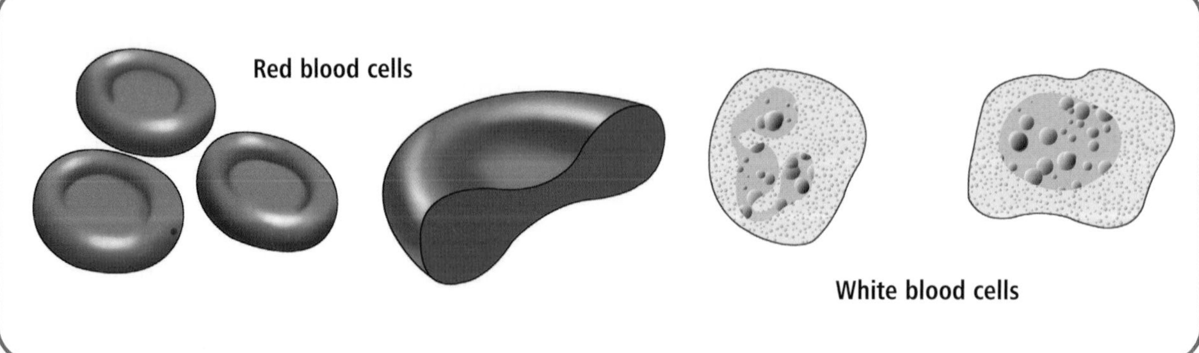

The total volume of blood in the body is different for different people and depends mainly on body size. Men on average have 5–6 litres and women 4–5 litres.

Blood is made up of 55% plasma and 45% formed elements. The formed elements are red blood cells (called erythrocytes), white blood cells (called leukocytes) and platelets (called thrombocytes).

- **Plasma** is a pale yellow, watery liquid which contains dissolved substances: salts and calcium, nutrients including glucose, hormones, carbon dioxide and other waste from our body cells.

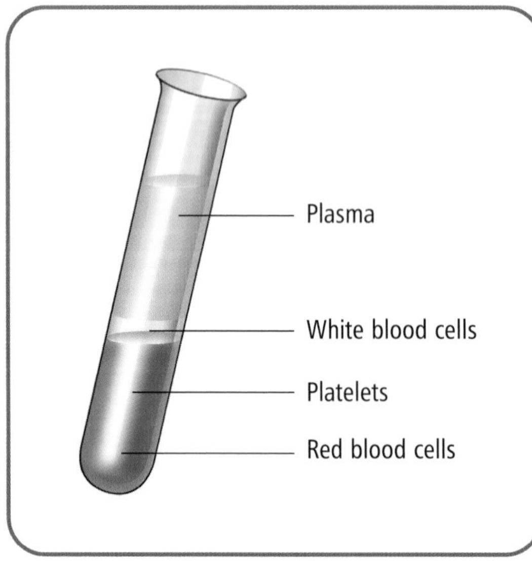

- **Red blood cells** give blood its colour. They contain haemoglobin, which carries oxygen from the lungs to all our body cells, and are made in the marrow of our long bones, sternum, ribs and vertebrae. They are extremely numerous, have no nucleus, last for about 120 days and are replaced in very large numbers.
- **Platelets** are made in our bone marrow. They stick to each other easily and work with fibrinogen to produce clots when a blood vessel is damaged.
- **White blood cells** are three times the size of red blood cells but far fewer in number. They are made in our bone marrow, lymph nodes and spleen and act as a mobile guard system to deal with infection and disease. Some eat up germs, some produce antibodies to destroy germs.

How do our red cells carry oxygen?

Our red blood cells contain an iron-based substance called haemoglobin. When the blood travels to our lungs, the oxygen in the air joins up with the haemoglobin in the blood to form oxyhaemoglobin.

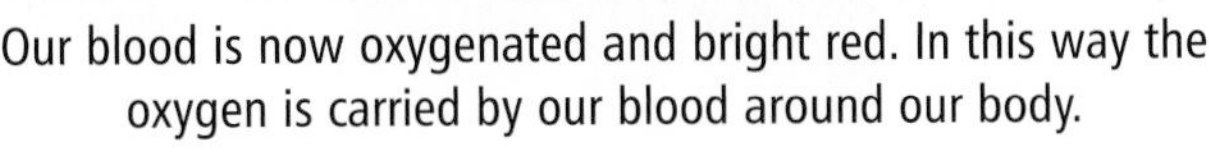

Our blood is now oxygenated and bright red. In this way the oxygen is carried by our blood around our body.
When blood arrives at our capillaries, the oxyhaemoglobin breaks down, setting the oxygen free to pass to our body cells.
Our blood is now deoxygenated and dull red in colour. It is pumped back first to our heart then to our lungs to pick up more oxygen.

What does blood do?

Our blood links all the tissues and organs of the body together. It has four main functions:

Transportation

- carries nutrients from our digestive system to all our body cells
- takes oxygen from our lungs to our working muscles
- removes carbon dioxide from our body in our lungs
- removes waste produces and excess water in our kidneys
- takes hormones to where they are needed.

Protection

- carries white cells to sites of infection
- carries antibodies to destroy germs
- carries platelets to damaged areas to form clots.

Temperature regulation

- carries heat away from working muscles to skin
- carries heat away from centre of body to skin
- maintains temperature within the body.

Maintaining the body's equilibrium

- reduces the effect of lactic acid produced in the working muscles
- regulates fluid balance
- enables hormones and enzymes to work.

Our blood and exercise

Our muscles need a continuous supply of oxygen in order to move our body. This oxygen is carried to the working muscles by the haemoglobin in the red cells in our blood. Regular exercise increases the red cells we produce in our bones. This enables a fit person to work

harder and for longer periods of time than an unfit person.

At high altitude it is more difficult for people to carry sufficient oxygen in their blood to supply their working muscles. As a result people who live at high altitude have more red blood cells and haemoglobin than those who live at lower altitude. This helps them to take in sufficient oxygen in their activities.

Endurance athletes from high-altitude areas usually have an advantage when they compete at lower altitudes since they can carry extra oxygen in their blood. For this reason, sportspeople will train at high altitude to increase the number of red blood cells and to improve their cardiovascular endurance.

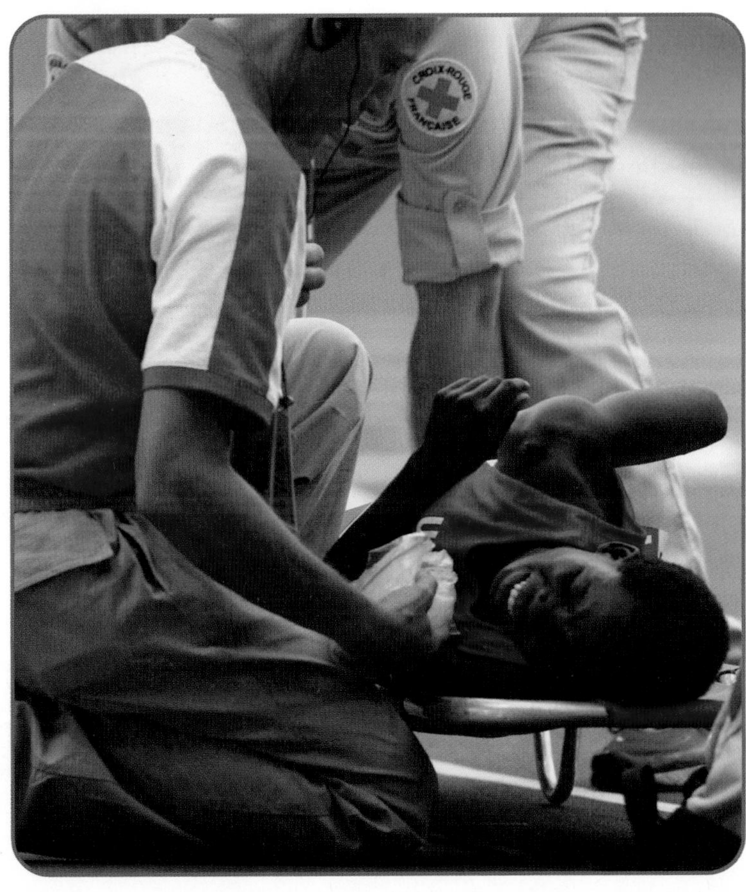

QUESTIONS

9 The circulatory system

Answer questions 1–4 by choosing statements a, b, c or d. One mark for each question.

1 Oxygen is carried in the blood by the:

- **a** platelets
- **b** red blood cells
- **c** white blood cells
- **d** glycogen.

2 Blood is carried from the heart to the lungs in the:

- **a** aorta
- **b** inferior vena cava
- **c** pulmonary vein
- **d** pulmonary artery.

3 Veins:

- **a** are thin-walled
- **b** are elastic
- **c** carry blood under high pressure
- **d** carry blood away from the heart.

4 Cardiac output is:

- **a** the number of times the heart beats per minute
- **b** the amount of blood ejected from the heart in one minute
- **c** the volume of blood in our circulatory system
- **d** the amount of blood pumped by the heart in each beat.

5 **a** Our circulatory system is very important when we exercise.

i It carries out a number of functions. Give three.

(3 marks)

ii Explain what happens to the blood when it reaches the lungs.

(2 marks)

b Give the function of the following three parts of the heart:

i the right ventricle

(1 mark)

ii the left ventricle

(1 mark)

iii the right atrium.

(1 mark)

c Give two factors which affect blood pressure.

(2 marks)

QUESTIONS

6 Andy is about to run in a 1,500-metre race.

a What effect has the hormone adrenaline already had on his body?

(1 mark)

b The race has now started and his heart contracts more powerfully and quickly. Explain why this happens.

(2 marks)

c Andy has now covered the first 1,200 metres and is sweating a lot. Explain why his body has reacted in this way.

(1 mark)

d Define stroke volume and explain why Andy's stroke volume changes during the 1,500-metre race.

(3 marks)

e Describe two different ways in which the change in Andy's stroke volume can be made.

(2 marks)

f Unfortunately Andy had a large meal only an hour before his race. What effect is this likely to have on his performance?

(2 marks)

g Name the four main components of blood.

(4 marks)

h Explain how one of them is vital to Andy's performance.

(3 marks)

i Andy is a trained runner while his friend Bob's only exercise is the occasional game of golf. Explain why Andy's resting pulse rate is likely to be lower than Bob's.

(2 marks)

(Total 34 marks)

10 The respiratory system

Our bodies are made up of millions of cells, all of which use oxygen to break down the nutrients contained in food. This sets free the energy the cells need to work. Our respiratory system takes in oxygen from the air and transfers it to the blood in our lungs. The oxygen travels to the cells in our blood, where it is exchanged for carbon dioxide. Our respiratory system then removes the carbon dioxide.

The respiratory system and sport

The respiratory system is important for health and sporting performance, but more so for some sports than for others. For example, in archery, snooker and shot putt competitions, the efficiency of the respiratory system is not a factor. However in swimming, running, cycling, major team games and most other sports, performance will be affected by the efficiency of the respiratory system. As sportspeople we should avoid activities which reduce the efficiency of our respiratory system such as smoking cigarettes.

activity

Getting oxygen to our working muscles

Matt and Dwayne are 23-year-old middle-distance runners. When they are resting, their breathing rates are both the same: 16 breaths a minute. However, Matt has an advantage over Dwayne as he is able to get much more oxygen to his working muscles and therefore produces much faster times than Dwayne.

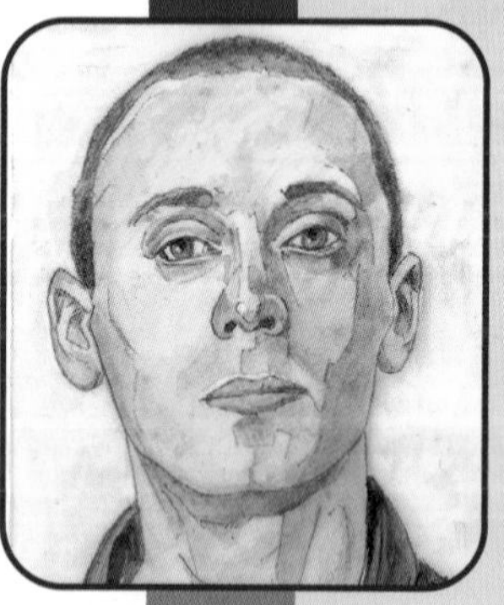

Read the descriptions below and try to think of three reasons to explain the difference in their times. The following questions may help your discussions:

- Body size and lung size are closely linked. Will this have any effect on cardiovascular endurance?
- Can body weight or body type have an effect on cardiovascular endurance?
- What is the importance of ærobic fitness and anærobic fitness for running the 1,500 metres?
- Do you think the time they have given to training and the way they have trained will affect their performances at 1,500 metres?

Matt is 1.6 metres tall, weighs 61 kg and is of ectomorphic body type. He works as a bricklayer and is able to vary his working hours to fit in his training. He is a member of his local athletics club and trains three times a week on the track. He has a very experienced coach who bases his training on high-quality track work involving interval training.

Dwayne is 1.9 metres tall and weighs 85 kg. He is a call-centre operator and works long, regular hours (9 am to 6 pm) five days a week. He is a member of his local athletics club but trains on his own with some advice from his father, a former athlete. His training consists mainly of long runs and a body-building session in the gym once a week.

KEYWORDS

Aerobic activity: activity when enough oxygen is available to supply the needs of the working muscles

Anaerobic activity: activity performed in the absence of sufficient oxygen from our lungs to meet the needs of our working muscles

Expiration: breathing air and waste products out from the lungs

Inspiration: breathing air into the lungs

Lactic acid: waste product of muscular action that builds up if oxygen is not available

Oxygen debt: the amount of oxygen consumed during recovery above what would ordinarily have been consumed during the same period at rest (creating a shortfall of oxygen available)

Oxygen deficit: build-up of lactic acid during activity when insufficient oxygen is available

Tidal volume: the amount of air breathed in or out of the lungs in one breath

Vital capacity: the maximum amount of air that can be forcibly exhaled after breathing in as much as possible.

Key to Exam Success

For your GCSE you should be able:

- to identify the main parts of the respiratory system and to know how it works
- to describe how breathing in and breathing out takes place
- to understand how respiration takes place both in the lungs and at the working muscles
- to understand how the body deals with the waste products of respiration
- to explain the effects of exercise and training on the respiratory system
- to know how the respiratory system links with the circulatory system
- to know how training and exercise affect the respiratory system
- to know how our respiratory system affects our training, fitness and performance
- to apply your knowledge of the respiratory system to your Personal Exercise Plan (PEP).

“ KEY THOUGHT ”

‘Cell respiration is at the centre of all human activity.’

How do we breathe?

- Air enters through the nose and mouth.
- The **nasal passages** contain mucus and hair. They moisten, filter and warm the air.
- The **palate** separates the nasal cavity from the mouth. It allows us to chew and breathe at the same time.
- The **epiglottis** is a flap at the back of the throat. It closes when we swallow to stop food from going down the trachea.
- The air passes through the **larynx**, or voice box, on its way to the **trachea**.
- The **trachea** or windpipe has rings of cartilage to hold it open. It divides into two **bronchi**. Each bronchus branches out into smaller tubes, which in turn become **bronchioles**.
- The bronchioles split up and end in **alveoli**.
- The **alveoli** are thin-walled, spongy air sacs. Most of our lung tissue is made up of large numbers of alveoli. When we breathe these tiny air sacs fill with air and then empty.

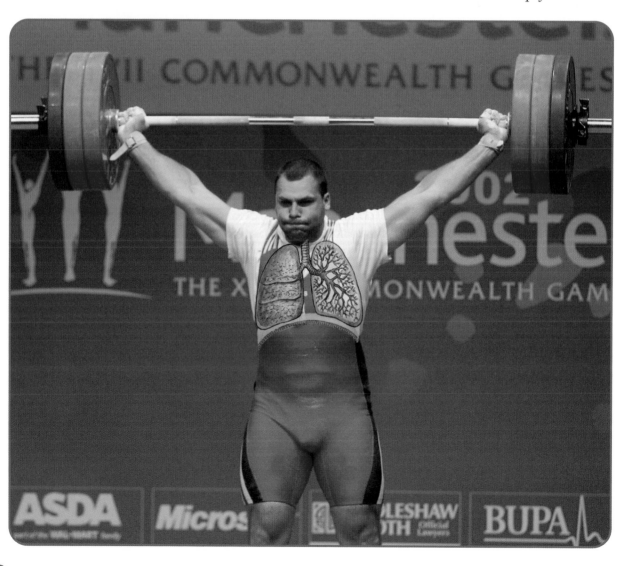

- The **lungs** are two thin-walled elastic sacs lying in our chests, in the thoracic cavity. This is an airtight area with ribs at the back and front and the diaphragm below.
- The **pleural membranes** surround the lungs. They are slippery, double skins which keep the lungs moist. They also lubricate the outside of the lungs. The membranes slide against one another as our lungs expand and contract. This reduces friction with the surrounding ribs and diaphragm.
- The **diaphragm** is a sheet of muscle which separates the thoracic cavity from the rest of the body. It is very important for breathing.
- The **intercostal muscles** are found between the ribs and control rib movement. They are very important for breathing.

What happens when we breathe?

Breathing is the first stage in supplying oxygen to our body cells. Breathing is also called **external** or **pulmonary respiration**.

When breathing in (inspiration):

- Our intercostal muscles contract, lifting the ribs upwards and outwards. Our chest expands.
- Our diaphragm contracts. It pulls down and flattens out the floor of our rib cage. Our chest expands further.
- Our lungs increase in size as our chest expands. This is because their outside surface is stuck to the chest wall.
- The pressure inside our lungs falls as they expand. The higher pressure of air outside means air is now sucked into the lungs through the nose and mouth.

When breathing out (expiration):

- Our intercostal muscles relax. Our ribs move downwards and inwards under their own weight. The chest gets smaller.
- Our diaphragm relaxes. It is pushed back into a domed position by the organs underneath it. Our chest gets even smaller.

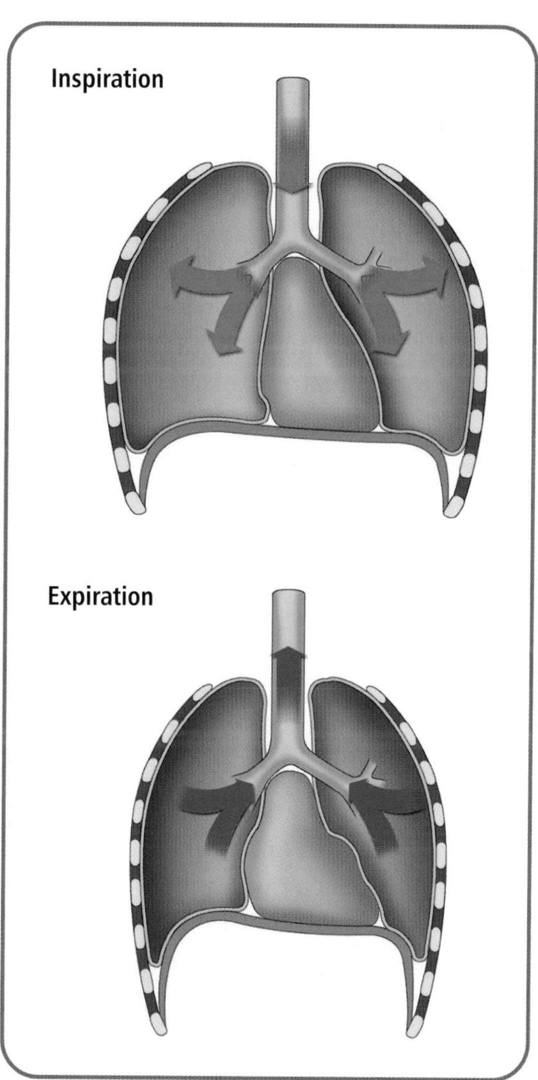

- Our lungs decrease in size as our chest gets smaller. They are squeezed by the ribs and diaphragm.
- The pressure inside our lungs increases as they get smaller. The air pressure outside is now lower than in our lungs. Air is forced out of the lungs through the nose and mouth.

Breathing and sport

When our body is at rest, the movements of the diaphragm alone are enough for breathing. Breathing is automatic. As soon as we start physical activity, we use our intercostal muscles to increase the depth of breathing. As a result of exercise and training, all the muscles involved in breathing (the diaphragm and intercostal muscles) become stronger, allowing us to breathe more deeply and for a longer period of time and to inhale a greater amount of air in each breath. Exercise and training will also increase the capillary network surrounding the alveoli in the lungs. This will improve the process of exchanging oxygen for carbon dioxide. Regular exercise therefore makes our breathing more efficient.

When we are at rest we breathe in and out about 16 times a minute, taking in about 0.5 litres of air in each breath. If we exercise very hard, our breathing rate can increase to 50 times a minute and the amount of air taken in can exceed 2.5 litres in each breath. Therefore the amount of air breathed in can increase from 8 litres to 125 litres a minute.

Some sports performers use nasal strips which they claim help them to breathe better whilst they are playing. However, little evidence has been found to support this claim. Training can certainly improve breathing (see Chapter 5, page 78–95).

How do we get oxygen to our working muscles?

The respiratory system needs two stages to supply oxygen to the working muscles and all the other body cells.

Stage 1: External or pulmonary respiration
This part of the process is what we know as breathing. It includes:

- getting air into and out of the lungs
- exchanging oxygen and carbon dioxide in the lungs
- getting oxygen into the bloodstream.

The individual steps are as follows:

- The air we breathe in passes through our trachea into our bronchi and through our bronchi into our bronchioles. The bronchioles end in tiny air sacs called alveoli. There is direct contact between the walls of the alveoli and the capillaries. The capillaries contain deoxygenated blood that has been brought to the lungs in the pulmonary artery.
- The haemoglobin in the blood of the capillaries takes up oxygen from the alveoli.
- Carbon dioxide is exchanged for the oxygen and is breathed out.
- The oxygenated blood is carried in the pulmonary veins to the left side of the heart.
- The oxygenated blood is then pumped through our aorta to muscles and other body cells.
- After exchanging oxygen for carbon dioxide and other waste products in our cells, the deoxygenated blood returns to the heart in our veins.
- In the alveoli the carbon dioxide is exchanged once again for oxygen and is breathed out.

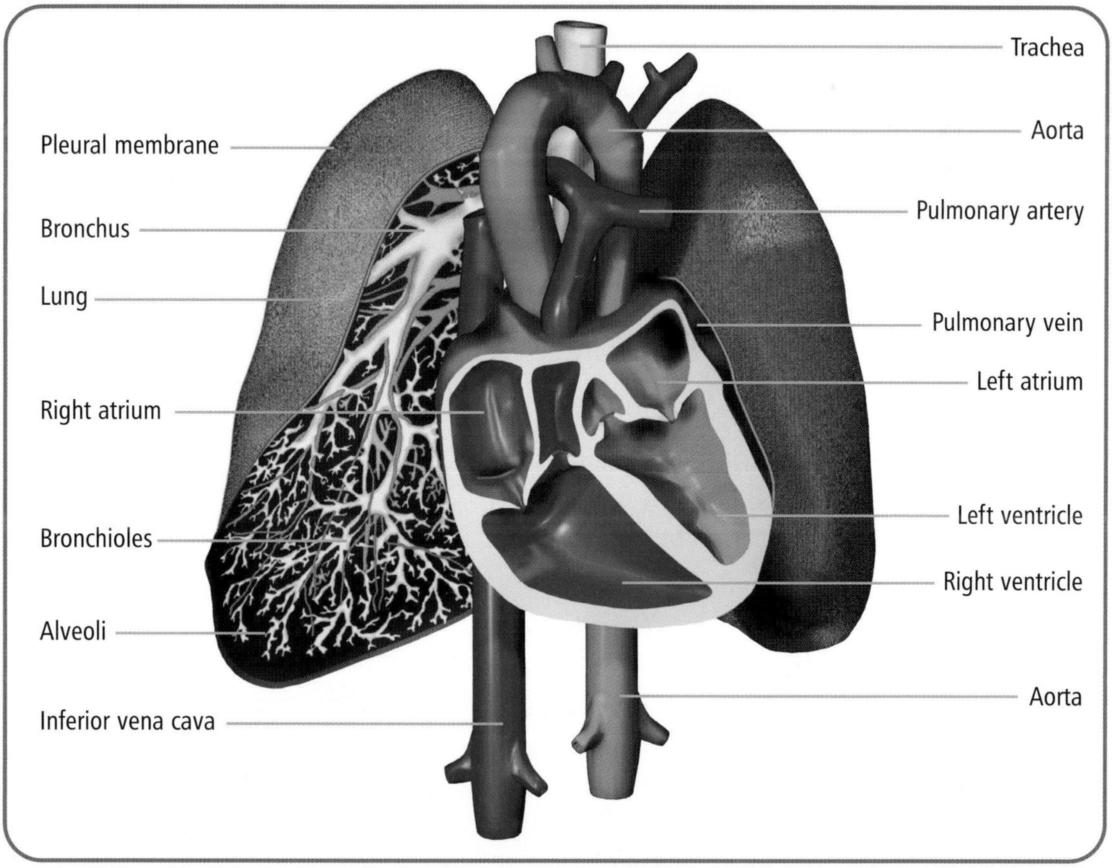

Stage 2: Internal or cell respiration

The respiratory system needs a second stage to supply oxygen to the working muscles and other body cells. This is called internal or cell respiration. It includes:

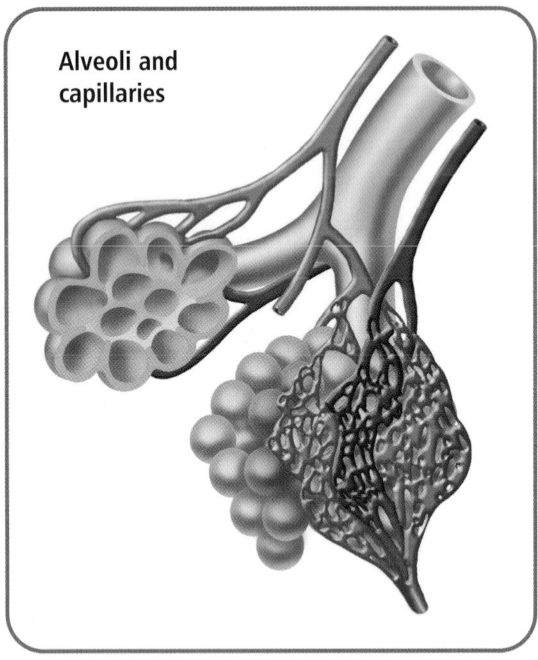

- getting oxygen into the body cells
- exchanging oxygen and carbon dioxide in the cells
- removing carbon dioxide and waste.

The individual steps are as follows:

- The heart pumps the oxygenated blood around the body in the arteries. The oxygen is carried by the haemoglobin in the red blood cells.
- The arteries get smaller and smaller, becoming arterioles. These end in a network of capillaries which cover every part of the body cells. The capillaries are tiny, with walls only one cell thick. It is easy for oxygen and nutrients such as glucose to escape through these walls into the cells.

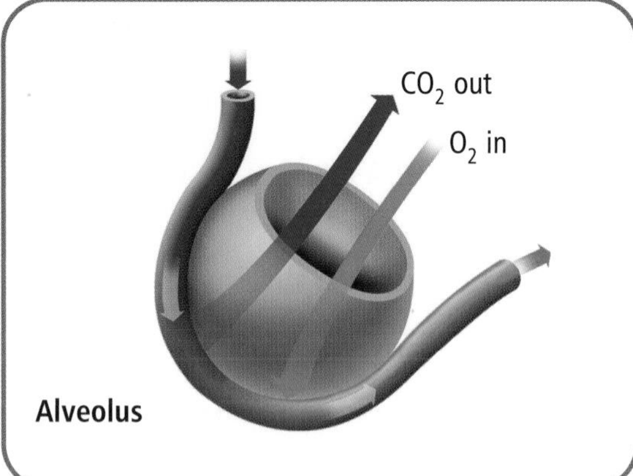

- At the same time carbon dioxide and other waste products such as water move from the cells to the capillaries. The blood has now lost its oxygen.
- The capillaries join up with small veins called venules. These carry deoxygenated blood to the veins.
- Blood returns to the heart in the veins.

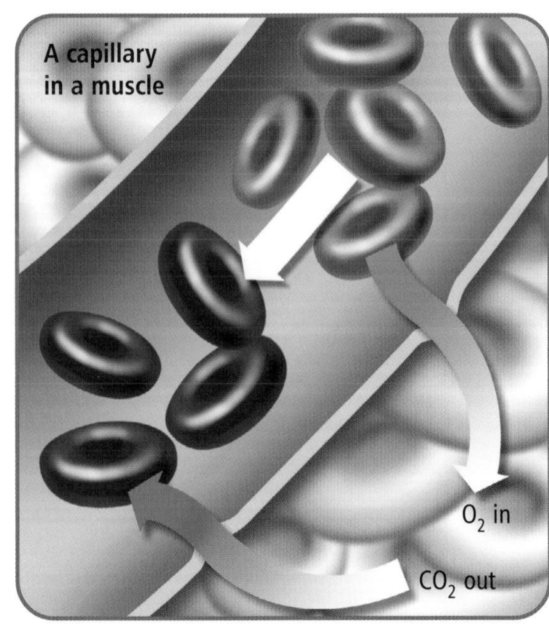

In this process we use oxygen to release the energy from glucose inside our body cells. This can be shown as:

Glucose + Oxygen	=	Energy + Carbon dioxide + Water

This glucose is obtained from glycogen stored in our muscles and liver. The glycogen comes from the carbohydrates in our diet. This is why we need to keep our intake of carbohydrates high while we are training and taking part in sport. If activity continues over a long period of time, as, for example, when running a marathon, then glycogen can also be obtained from fat reserves in our body.

As a result of training more oxygenated blood reaches our working muscles; the exchange of oxygen and carbon dioxide is improved and waste products are removed more quickly. The overall result of training is that internal respiration becomes more efficient, improving our cardiovascular endurance and improving our sporting performance.

Your PEP and the respiratory system

You need to understand the importance of the respiratory system for exercise in order to produce an effective Personal Exercise Plan. When constructing your PEP you will need to bear in mind the importance of the following:

- composition of inhaled and exhaled air
- vital capacity and tidal volume
- aerobic and anaerobic energy systems
- oxygen debt and lactic acid.

Factors affecting respiration

The air we breathe in (called inhaled air) exchanges some of its oxygen for carbon dioxide in our lungs. The air we breathe out (called exhaled air) therefore contains less oxygen and more carbon dioxide. It also has much more water vapour, which is also a waste product from our cells.

The composition of inhaled and exhaled air

Inhaled air	Exhaled air
Nitrogen 79%	Nitrogen 79%
Oxygen 21%	Oxygen 16%
Carbon dioxide 0.04%	Carbon dioxide 4%

Vital capacity and tidal volume

Tidal volume is 'the amount of air breathed in or out of the lungs in one breath'. (Edexcel.) It can vary a lot. When we are resting, only about 0.5 litres of air moves in and out of our lungs with each breath. Not all of this reaches the alveoli; some remains in our nose and throat. If we start an activity, the body will need more oxygen. We achieve this increase in our tidal volume by breathing more deeply, by increasing our rate of breathing, or both.

Vital capacity is 'the maximum amount of air that can be forcibly exhaled after breathing in as much as possible'. (Edexcel.) It is our maximum tidal volume and is usually about 4.8 litres in adults. Both tidal volume and vital capacity can be improved by a training programme, as exercise will strengthen the muscles involved in breathing. Improved vital capacity will increase the oxygen inhaled and will help improve performance.

Aerobic and anaerobic energy systems

The energy we need for taking part in sport can be found by using either of our two energy systems: the **anaerobic** or the **aerobic** system.

In the anaerobic system our body works without sufficient oxygen being supplied to the muscles, while in the aerobic system there is a constant supply of oxygen. In order to improve our aerobic and anaerobic fitness for sport we must train in the aerobic and anaerobic target zones. This means we must keep our heart rates above a certain level during training. Both types of fitness can be improved by a training programme, and games players will need to improve both types of fitness.

Lactic acid and oxygen debt

We can continue to perform strenuous activity for some time, even when we run out of sufficient supplies of oxygen. This is because we can draw on glycogen stores in the body as an alternative energy supply. However, in the absence of oxygen, **lactic acid** is formed in the working muscles. This makes our muscles hurt and eventually we have to stop the activity.

In the recovery period after exercise, we take in extra oxygen which is used to convert the painful lactic acid into simple waste products. The oxygen required to do this is called our **oxygen debt**. By following a training programme we are able to improve the ability of our muscles to use oxygen better and to cope with extra lactic acid. This means we are able to continue with our activity for a long time before fatigue sets in. Through training we are also able to repay our oxygen debt more quickly.

activity

Feel the burn

Feel the effects of lactic acid by straightening and curling your index finger as quickly as possible and for as long as possible. Describe the effects as muscle fatigue begins to occur.

Checking breathing rates during exercise

Your breathing rate tells you how much air, and therefore oxygen, is entering your lungs and will be passed into the blood and taken to the tissues. You can measure this rate by placing one hand across your chest and counting the number of times your chest rises in 15 seconds.

1 Look at the table below.
2 Perform each activity and check your breathing immediately after the time period ends.
3 Complete the table.

Time period	Activity	Breathing rate (beats per minute)
	Rest	
1 minute	Walk	
3 minutes	Jog	
10–15 minutes	Play game (e.g. basketball)	
20 seconds	Sprint	
3 minutes	Warm down	

4 Now plot the results on a graph to show how breathing rates are affected by exercise.
5 What do you notice about the changes in your breathing rate?
6 Can you explain this effect?
7 Calculate the mean breathing rate for your class in each time period.
8 Compare the mean for the class with the breathing rates of individuals.
9 Note and discuss any large differences in breathing rates within your class.
10 How do you explain any differences?

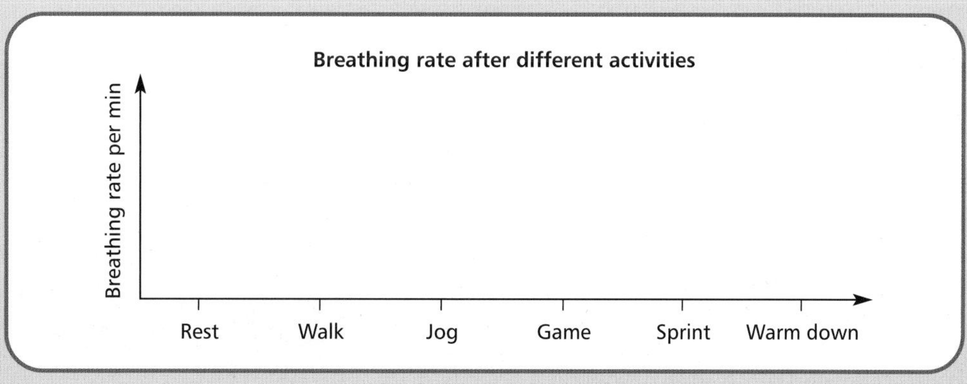

QUESTIONS

10 The respiratory system

Answer questions 1–4 by choosing statements a, b, c or d.
One mark for each question.

1 The thin-walled air sacs in the lungs are called the:

- **a** pleural membranes
- **b** tracheas
- **c** alveoli
- **d** bronchioles.

2 The air breathed in and the air breathed out contains the same amount of:

- **a** nitrogen
- **b** carbon dioxide
- **c** oxygen
- **d** glycogen.

3 Vital capacity is:

- **a** the amount of air breathed in over one minute
- **b** the amount of air taken in or out in one breath
- **c** the amount of air left in the lungs after breathing out
- **d** the largest amount of air breathed out.

4 Lactic acid:

- **a** produces energy
- **b** removes carbon dioxide
- **c** makes our muscles tired
- **d** increases the oxygen available.

5 **a** The intercostal muscles and the diaphragm help in breathing out. What do they each do?

(2 marks)

b **i** What is the percentage of carbon dioxide in expired air?

(1 mark)

ii Why is this much greater than the percentage of carbon dioxide in inspired air.

(2 marks)

c Why is there much less oxygen in expired air than in inspired air?

(2 marks)

d Strenuous exercise will affect tidal volume.

i Define tidal volume.

(1 mark)

ii Explain why tidal volume is affected by strenuous exercise.

(2 marks)

6 Anil is an experienced marathon runner.

a What part do the following play in his breathing?

i trachea
ii alveoli
iii pleural membranes.

(3 marks)

QUESTIONS

b What happens to Anil's breathing rate in a marathon race:

- **i** immediately after the start of the race
- **ii** during the middle of the race
- **iii** when he sprints over the last 100 metres?

(3 marks)

c Explain why Anil's breathing rate changes at each of these times.

(6 marks)

d Which words describe the energy system Anil will be using

- **i** during the middle of the race
- **ii** when he sprints over the last 100 metres?

(2 marks)

e 'Lactic acid production is the enemy of the marathon runner.'

- **i** Why is lactic acid produced?

(1 mark)

- **ii** Why does it reduce aerobic performance?

(1 mark)

- **iii** How can training help to reduce the effect of lactic acid build-up?

(2 marks)

f Give two possible effects of long-term regular training on the respiratory system.

(2 marks)

(Total 34 marks)

11 Bones

Our body is made up of many bones of different shapes and sizes. These are grouped around a number of different joints and, with joints, they make up our skeletal system. The different arrangements of bones and joints in our body allow us a very great variety of body movements. For example, we can perform the very fine movements necessary for darts as well as making a full-blooded tackle in rugby.

Without our skeletal system we would look very different. Our bodies would have no framework, our delicate organs would be unprotected and we would be unable to move.

Although we all have the same number of bones and joints, our skeletal systems vary a great deal due to the wide difference in the size of our bones. This affects our ability in sport. The longer the bone, the greater the range of movement possible and the greater the amount of force produced. Top-class rowers are usually very tall with the necessary long levers to row a boat at speed.

We are all limited in the choice of sport in which we might be successful because of the size of our skeletal system. Height is necessary for success at, for example, basketball, high jump and volleyball. However, if we are of medium height we can still have some success in these sports if we are skilful and determined enough. Gymnasts are usually shorter but still have long limbs. This enables them to produce a burst of power very quickly and also to move their body with great control.

KEYWORDS

Calcium: a mineral vital to healthy bones, found in milk, cheese and yoghurt

Cartilage: a dense, elastic, connective tissue which cushions and connects many bones in the skeleton

Compact bone: a hard, dense substance beneath the periosteum forming the shaft of long bone

Epiphysis: head of the bone

Ossification: the growth and development of bones

Periosteum: tough membrane which surrounds the bone

Skeleton: the bony framework of the body

Cancellous (spongy) bone: a honeycomb substance consisting of hard, light and very strong bone

Vertebræ: the irregular bones which make up the vertebral column.

Key to Exam Success

For your GCSE you should be able to:

- understand the composition of bones and the process of ossification
- understand the functions of the skeleton in relation to exercise
- identify and classify all the common bones of the body
- relate the common bones of the body to exercise and sporting performance
- relate bone shape, size and strength to exercise
- understand the effects of exercise, age, gender and diet on bones
- relate all aspects of bone to sport, exercise, and physical activity.

“ KEY THOUGHT ”

‘Without bones we could not run, jump, throw or even stand up!’

What does our skeleton do?

Our skeleton gives shape to our body, protects our organs, supports our organs, moves our body and produces blood.

Gives shape

Our body needs a framework and the skeleton gives shape to our bodies, enabling us to achieve a good posture.

When playing sport we need a firm basic shape from which to develop the many different body positions required, from a smash in tennis to a tuck in gymnastics. Sports such as golf, speed skating and riding also require a variety of sporting postures.

Protects

Our delicate organs need the protection of a strong structure of bone, particularly to prevent injury in contact sports such as rugby and judo. The cranium protects the brain, the vertebral column protects the spinal cord and the ribcage protects the heart and lungs.

Moves

Different sports require an extremely wide variety of muscle movements and different amounts of force, from the delicate touch required for a badminton drop shot to the power and control of the hammer throw.

Our muscles use our bones to cause movement. The muscles are attached to the skeleton, which is jointed to allow a wide range of movement. Different joints allow different types of movement.

Supports

We change our body position in most sports and in some sports, for example, gymnastics and trampolining, we are often upside down. Our organs need to be able to function in these positions.

The skeleton holds our vital organs in place, the vertebral column playing a central part in supporting much of our body.

Produces blood

In sport, as in life in general, we need white blood cells for protection and red blood cells to provide the working muscles with oxygen. In endurance sports, the ability of the red blood cells to carry oxygen is vital for success. Red and white blood cells are produced in the bone marrow of the ribs, vertebrae and femur.

How do our bones grow?

In the embryo

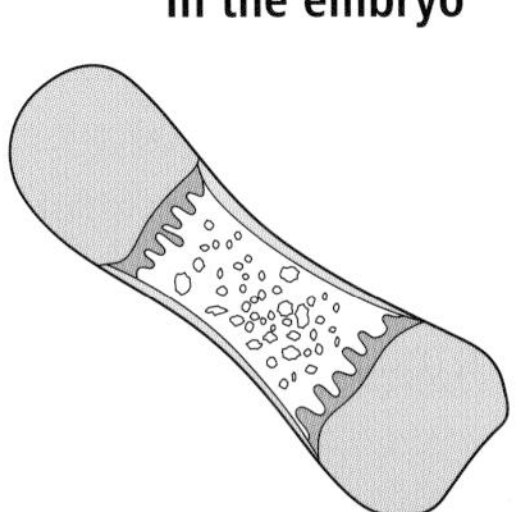

In the embryo (our state before birth) most of the skeleton is made up of **cartilage**. Cartilage is a firm, but elastic material.

Young person

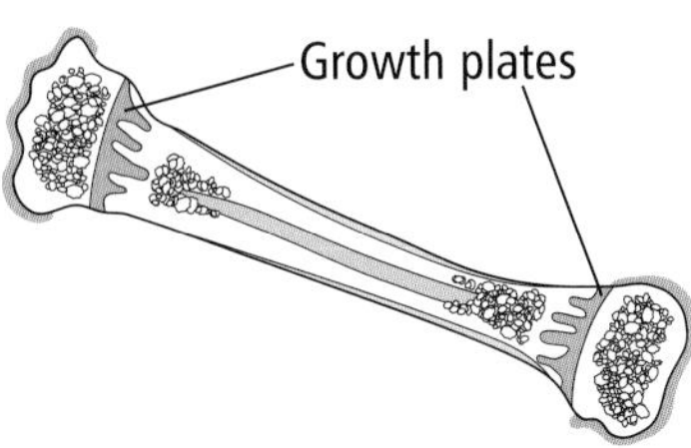

As the embryo grows, cartilage is changed to bone. The development of bone from cartilage is called **ossification**. Ossification also continues through childhood until adulthood. Bones increase in length as the cartilage at growth plates is changed into bone.

Adult

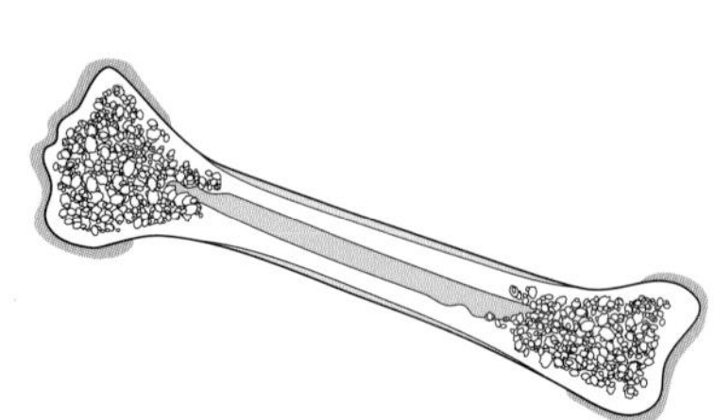

When we are fully grown only a small amount of cartilage remains at the bone ends. The bones have become hard and rigid. Calcium compounds give them hardness. Collagen fibres make them strong and light.

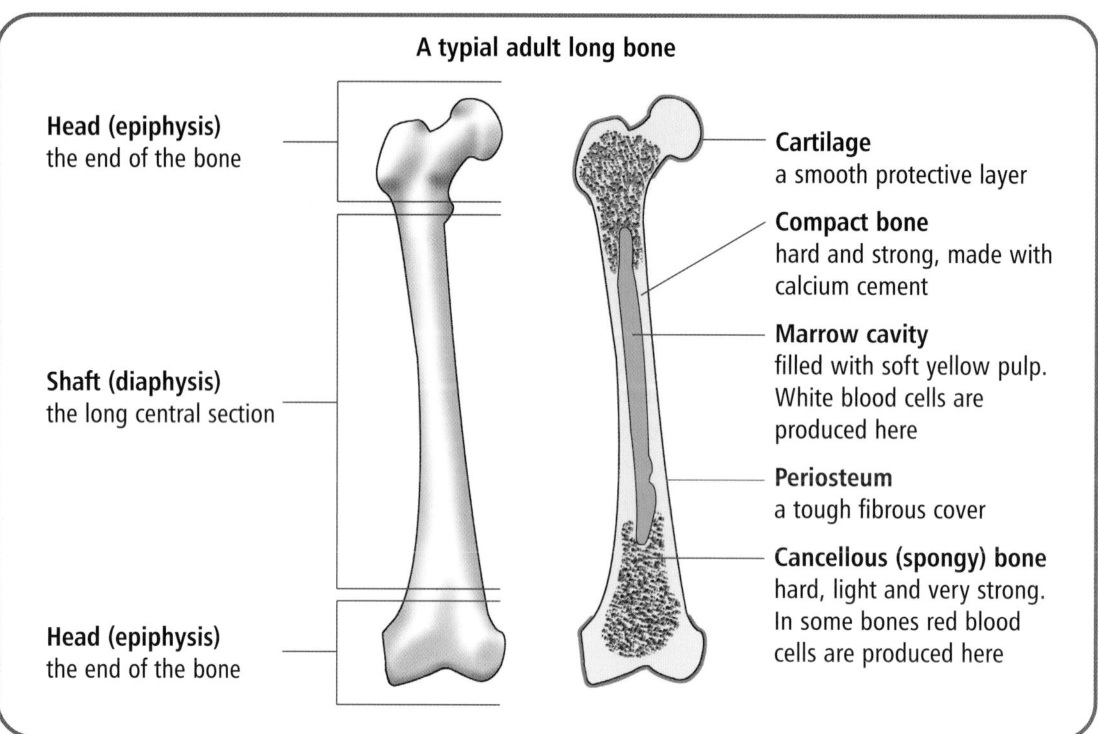

Our bones and sport

As we have seen, our body is made up of many bones of different shapes and sizes. As our muscles contract they pull on the bones and make them move. The longer the bone, the greater the range of movement possible and the greater the amount of force produced. For example, discus-throwers try to apply force to the discus over a very long distance by taking their arm back as far as possible when preparing to throw. Shorter bones move over a smaller distance and so it is easier for them to produce a burst of power, as seen in the tumbling routines of gymnasts who have much shorter limbs than the discus-thrower.

What are the different bone types?

The size and shape of our bones are linked to how we use them.

Long bones

These are the large bones in our legs, arms, fingers and toes. We use them in the main movements of our body.

Short bones

These are the small bones at the joints of our hands and feet. We use them in the fine movements of our body.

Flat bones (or plate)

These are the bones of our cranium, shoulder girdle, ribs and pelvic girdle. We use them to protect the organs of our body. Large muscles are attached to our flat bones.

Irregular bones

These are the bones in our face and vertebral column. We use them to give our body protection and shape.

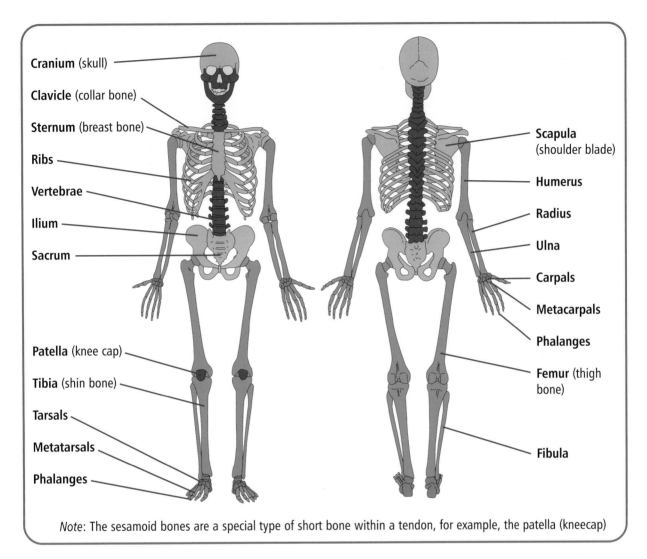

Cranium (skull)
Clavicle (collar bone)
Sternum (breast bone)
Ribs
Vertebrae
Ilium
Sacrum
Patella (knee cap)
Tibia (shin bone)
Tarsals
Metatarsals
Phalanges
Scapula (shoulder blade)
Humerus
Radius
Ulna
Carpals
Metacarpals
Phalanges
Femur (thigh bone)
Fibula

Note: The sesamoid bones are a special type of short bone within a tendon, for example, the patella (kneecap)

Bones in the upper body

The most important bones in the upper body are:

- the shoulder girdle
- the ribs and sternum
- the arms
- the wrist and hand.

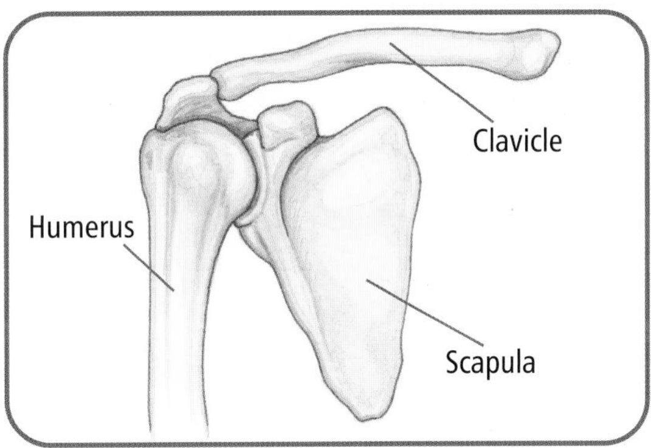

The shoulder girdle
The shoulder girdle consists of two clavicles and two scapulas:

- **Clavicles** are thin, flat, slightly curved bones.
- **Scapulas** are large, flat bones with many muscles attached.

The shoulder girdle is only linked by muscles to our vertebral column. This gives us great flexibility in our arms and shoulders, which is very helpful in sports such as gymnastics and swimming. However, it limits the force we can use.

The ribs and sternum

The sternum is a large, flat bone forming the front of the ribcage which helps to make the ribcage stronger.

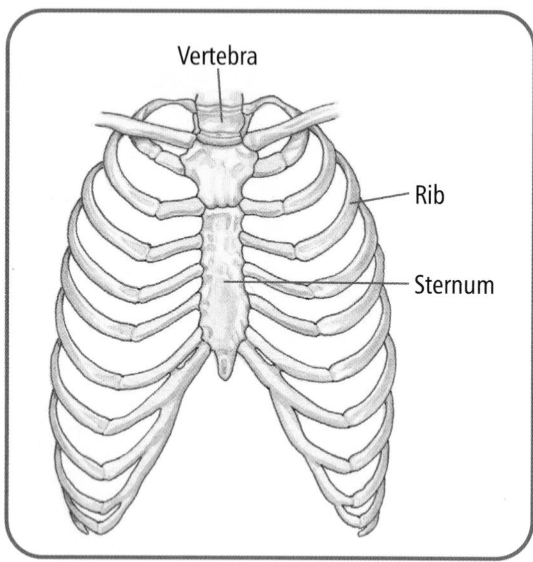

- 12 pairs of ribs are joined to the vertebral column, but only 7 to the sternum.
- 3 pairs are joined to the seventh rib (false ribs) and 2 ribs are unattached (floating ribs).

The ribcage protects our lungs and heart in combat and contact sports. It provides attachment for the intercostal muscles which are vital for deep breathing during strenuous exercise.

The arms

The arms consist of humerus, radius and ulna.

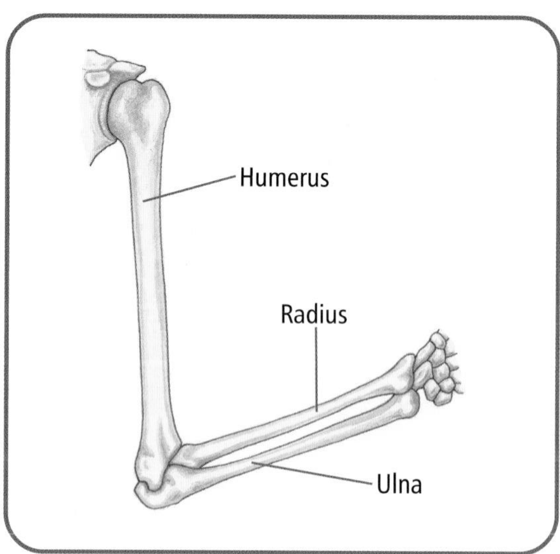

The long bones of the arm enable us to make major movements of the body, applying force over a large range of movement.

The wrist and hand

There are 8 carpal bones in the wrist, and 5 metacarpal bones and 14 phalanges in each hand.

The small bones of the hand enable us to make precise and delicate movements in sport.

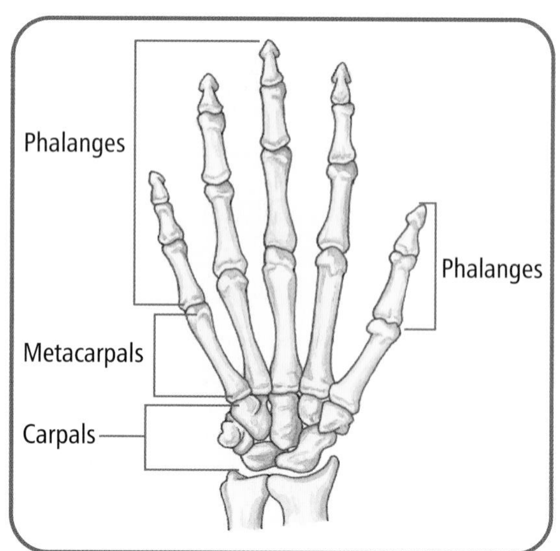

Bones in the lower body

The most important bones in the lower body are:

- the pelvic girdle
- the legs, ankle and foot.

The pelvic girdle

The pelvic girdle is made up of two halves, each formed by three bones (including the ilium), which are fused together on each side. This forms a very stable joint with the vertebral column and passes the weight of the body to the legs. It supports the lower abdomen and provides a strong joint for the femur.

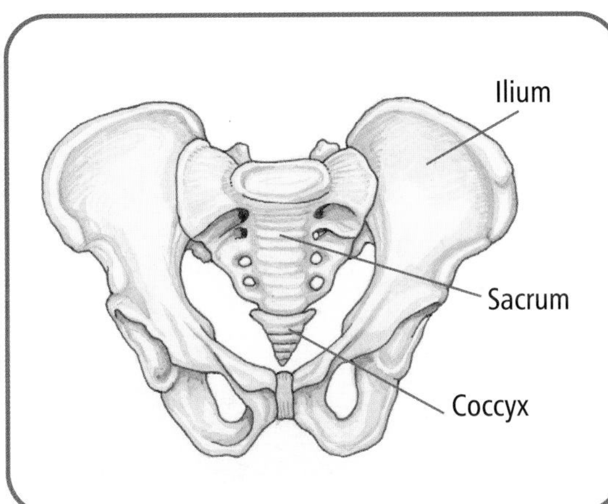

The female pelvis is wider and shallower than the male pelvis. This is to make childbearing easier, but it does make running less efficient.

Legs

The legs consist of the femur, tibia and fibula. These long bones enable us to make major movements of the body, applying force over a large range of movement.

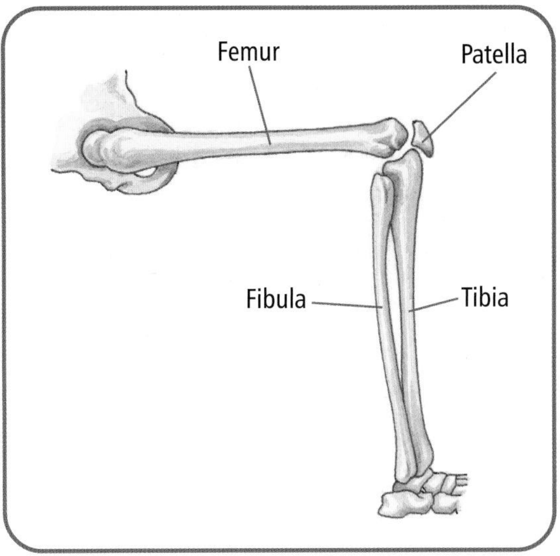

Ankle and foot

There are 7 tarsals in the ankle and 5 metatarsals and 14 phalanges in each foot.

In order to perform most skilful actions, we need our feet to provide a solid base for our body. This is true of a drive in tennis, a shot in hockey or a take-off in the long jump. Even simple running requires a solid base for the thousands of steps which take place. All sportspeople should check the soles of their footwear for signs of abnormal wear.

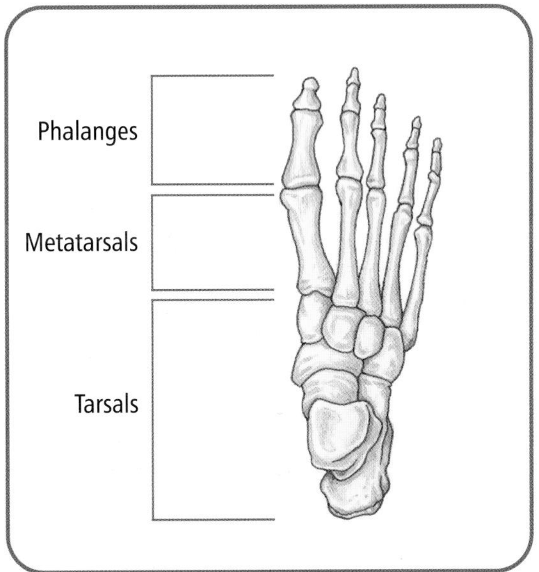

The vertebral column

Our vertebral column is also called the spine or spinal column. It is made up of 33 small, specialised bones called **vertebrae**. The vertebral column is divided into five regions. Each region has its own type of vertebrae which work in their own way.

Vertebral discs

Between each pair of vertebrae is a disc of cartilage. Each disc is a thick circle of tough tissue which acts as a shock absorber for the vertebral column and allows movement between the vertebrae.

Twelve thoracic vertebrae

- Our larger vertebrae.
- Our ribs are attached to them.
- They support the ribcage.
- They allow us some slight movement, bending forward, backward and from side to side.

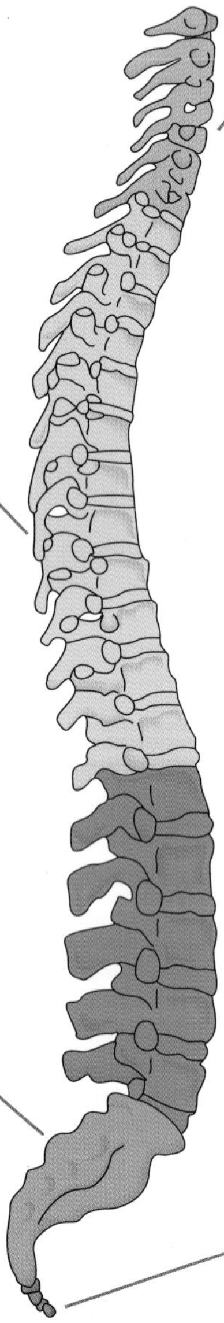

Seven cervical vertebrae

- Our smallest vertebrae.
- The neck muscles are attached to them.
- They support our head and neck.
- The top vertebra, the atlas, fits into the cranium and lets the head nod.
- The second vertebra, the axis, lets the head rotate.

Five lumbar vertebrae

- The largest vertebrae.
- Our back muscles are attached to them.
- They allow much bending forward, backward and from side to side.
- The large range of movement means that this region can be easily injured.

Five sacral vertebrae

- These vertebrae are fused together. They are also fused to the pelvic girdle.
- They make a very strong base, which supports the weight of the body.
- They also pass force from the legs and hips to the upper body.

Four coccyx

- Our other fused vertebrae.
- They have no special use.

Functions of the vertebral column

The vertebral column:

- protects the spinal cord
- supports the upper body
- gives us a wide range of movement
- is important for posture
- passes force to the other body parts.

The vertebral column and sport

Our vertebral column is important to all sporting movements. It has many joints and is both flexible and strong. This allows us to bend and stretch our bodies into very many different positions. We must always learn the correct technique in our sport to help avoid injury to the vertebral column.

This is especially important in weight lifting, bowling in cricket and the throws in athletics. All spinal injuries should be treated very seriously. The injury can become permanent or even be life-threatening.

Our bones and age

Our bones change from cartilage in the embryo to bone in adults. This process of ossification continues through childhood into adulthood. Even when we are fully grown our bones change, adapting to any pressure that is put upon them by making new bone and becoming stronger.

Regular weight-bearing exercise throughout life will keep our bones strong and healthy.

When we get older this process stops and our bones become lighter, losing both density and strength. This increases the risk of broken bones. This condition is called osteoporosis and it affects many older people. Osteoporosis usually affects the whole skeleton but most commonly it causes breaks to bone in the wrist, spine and hip.

If we do not strengthen our bones enough when we are young they may weaken and break easily when we are older. Statistics show that 1 in 3 women and 1 in 12 men in the UK will have osteoporosis after the age of 50.

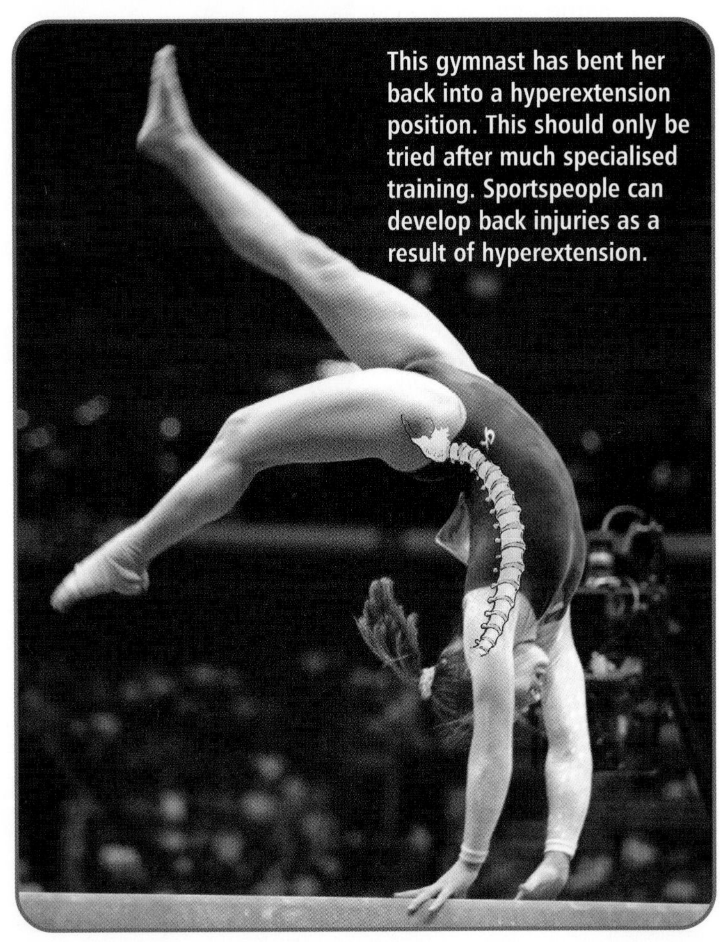

This gymnast has bent her back into a hyperextension position. This should only be tried after much specialised training. Sportspeople can develop back injuries as a result of hyperextension.

Our bones and gender

Before puberty there is little difference between boys and girls in terms of height and weight. They have similar body shapes and similar amounts of bone, muscle and fat. Sporting competition between the sexes is quite fair at this stage.

At puberty boys develop larger bones, which, together with a great increase in muscular development, makes them much bigger and stronger than girls of the same age.

Overall men have larger skeletons and are taller than women. Men also have thicker bones than women and so are, in general, bigger and heavier than women. At puberty the pelvic girdle in girls becomes wider to make childbearing easier. This widening of the pelvic girdle changes the angle of the hip joints and makes their running action mechanically less efficient.

As described above, older women suffer from osteoporosis, when their bones get so weak they break easily. This can be avoided by maintaining regular, gentle exercise.

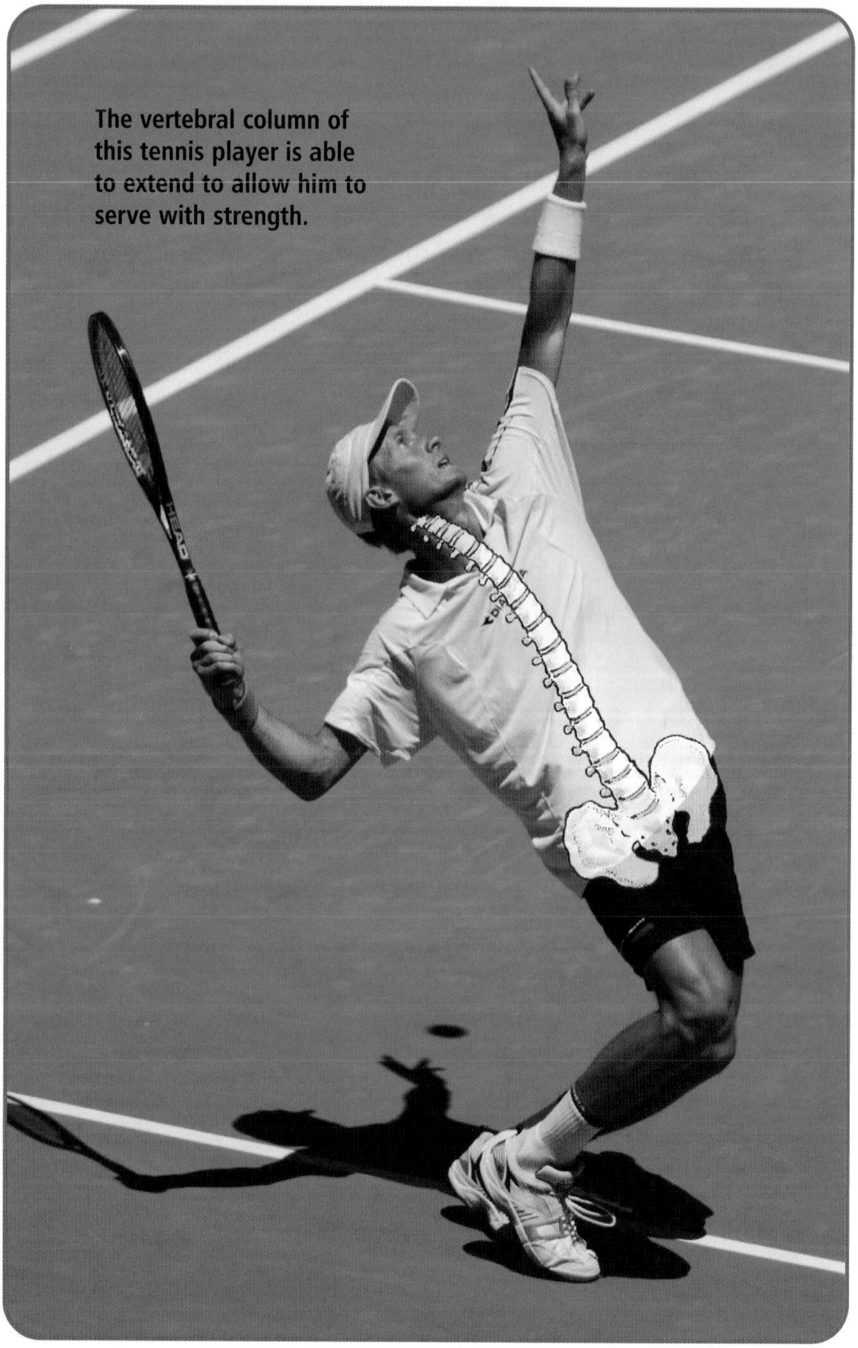

The vertebral column of this tennis player is able to extend to allow him to serve with strength.

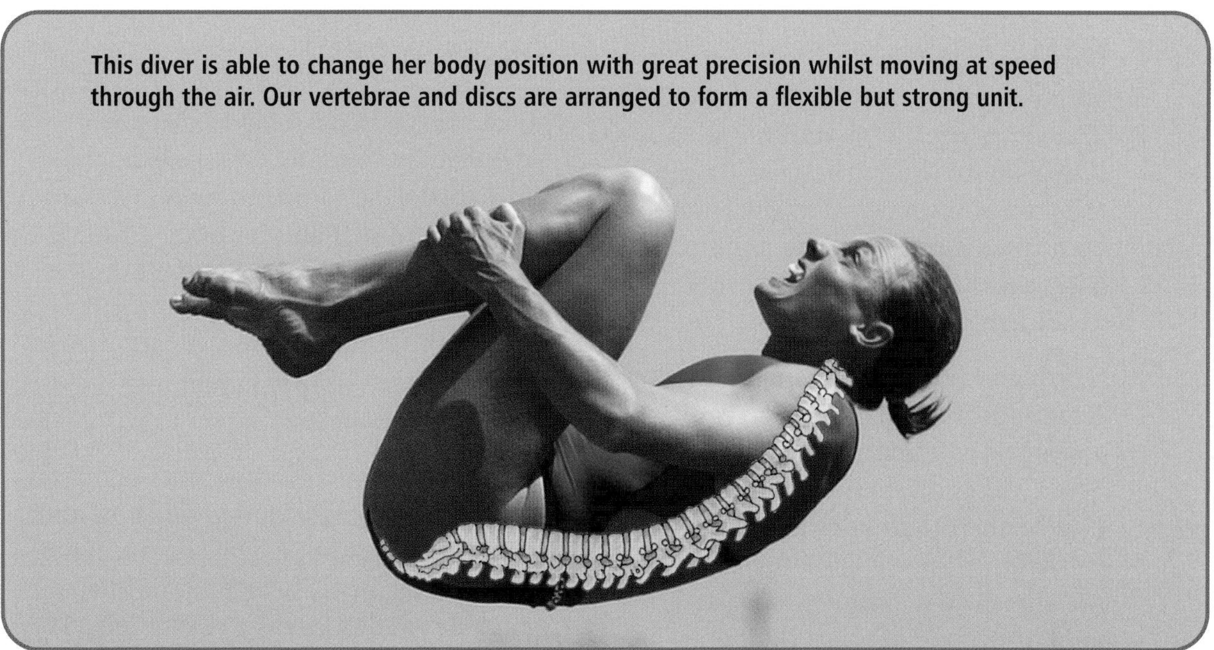

This diver is able to change her body position with great precision whilst moving at speed through the air. Our vertebrae and discs are arranged to form a flexible but strong unit.

It is very important for this rugby player that the weight pushing against his shoulders is passed to his legs through a straight vertebral column. A bent back with his vertebrae out of line could lead to injury.

Our bones and diet

We need a balanced diet for good health. Protein in our diet is important because it deals with the repair, growth and efficient working of all our tissues, including bones. Proteins are found in both animal and plant foods including meat, fish, milk and cereals.

Our bones are living tissue and to remain healthy they need a regular supply of **calcium** in the diet. This can be provided by such foods as milk, cheese and other dairy products. Lack of calcium will result in bone weakness. We also need a sufficient intake of vitamin D, which helps the bones absorb the calcium. It is found in oily fish, liver, butter and eggs.

Our bones and body shape

The size of our skeleton is largely decided by heredity. This means that if our parents are tall and heavy, we are likely to be of a similar body build. If we follow a balanced diet with all the nutrients we need for bone growth, especially calcium, then we are likely to reach our maximum height and maximum bone size.

Our actual body shape will depend not only on the height of our skeleton and the size of our bones, but on a number of other factors. These include the capacity of our bones to carry muscle, our body type (mesomorph, endomorph, ectomorph – see page 60), our diet and our regular exercise patterns.

Whatever size we are in terms of height, we need to maintain our optimum weight for our body type. This will ensure that we do not carry excess fat which will not only be a disadvantage in sport, but may also cause health problems.

Our bones and exercise

Exercise helps the development of the skeleton in young people. Exercise can increase bone width and density and therefore bone strength. It has no effect on bone length.

In particular, regular physical activities which include weight-bearing exercises help to keep our bones in good condition.

Children and young people should not overdo some types of exercise during the growing period in adolescence. For example, lifting heavy weights, taking part in strenuous contact sports and long-distance road running can all damage the growth plates in the bones and lead to abnormal growth.

If muscle strength develops faster than skeletal strength, bones can break up at the attachment point of the tendon on the bone. This happens in Osgood-Schlatters disease at the knee.

Strength training during adolescence must be planned and supervised by a qualified instructor. Injuries to bone need careful treatment to avoid damage to growth areas.

If we are unable to exercise through injury or illness we will lose both bone size and strength.

QUESTIONS

11 Our skeletal system

Answer questions 1–4 by choosing statements a, b, c or d. One mark for each question.

1 In some bones, red blood cells are produced in the:

a marrow cavity
b periosteum
c cancellous (spongy) bone
d compact bone.

2 The two bones of the shoulder girdle are the scapula and the:

a humerus
b clavicle
c sternum
d sacrum.

3 The ribs are attached to the:

a lumbar vertebrae
b sacral vertebrae
c cervical vertebrae
d thoracic vertebrae.

4 The humerus is attached to the:

a scapula
b clavicle
c ribs
d sternum.

5 Claudia is ten years old and a very good gymnast.

a She knows she needs to have plenty of calcium in her diet.

i Explain why she needs calcium in her diet.

(1 mark)

ii Name one food which will provide calcium.

(1 mark)

b Complete this table about different bone types and their functions:

Bone type	Function
Long bone	Large movements
Short bone	i
Flat bone	ii
Irregular bone	iii

(3 marks)

c At Claudia's age it is recommended that certain training is avoided to prevent possible bone damage. Suggest two types of training she should avoid.

(2 marks)

d Explain why either long limbs or short limbs are an advantage for a gymnast.

(3 marks)

QUESTIONS

6 **Tariq is a rugby player who plays in the scrum.**

a Give three functions of the skeleton and explain how each is important for his sport.

(6 marks)

b The vertebral column is both flexible and strong. Explain how Tariq should protect his vertebral column when pushing in the scrum.

(2 marks)

c There are five different types of vertebrae – sacral, lumbar, cervical, coccyx and thoracic. Put them in order from the neck down.

(2 marks)

d Give two reasons why the lumbar vertebrae are very important to sportspeople.

(2 marks)

e Tariq would like to be taller and have stronger bones. Explain any effects that regular training is likely to have on his height and bone strength.

(3 marks)

f Explain the process of ossification with reference to cartilage, growth plates and calcium.

(3 marks)

g As people get older, regular weight-bearing exercise is necessary for bone health. Explain why.

(2 marks)

(Total 34 marks)

12 Joints, tendons and ligaments

Our skeleton has many joints. Our muscles are positioned around these joints. If we want to make a movement, our muscles contract and pull on the bones around the joints. In this way our whole body can get on the move as fast or as slowly as we like. We have over a hundred different joints in our bodies. These joints, together with our muscles, allow us to perform intricate and powerful movement patterns, as seen, for example, in dance and gymnastics.

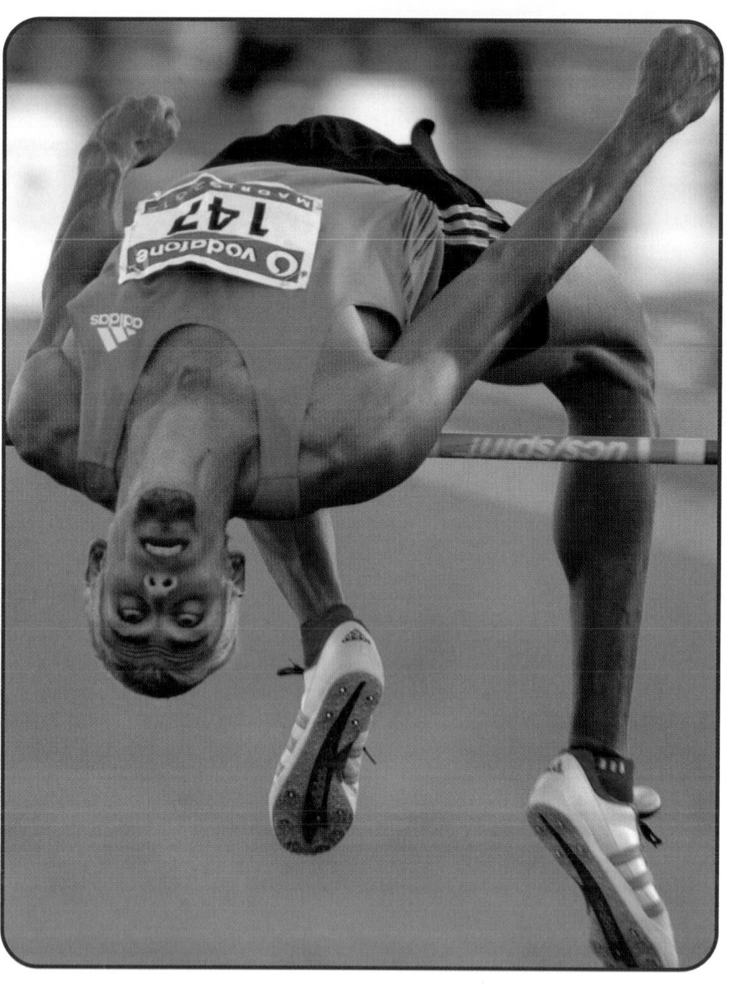

Our body is flexible and this is due to the combination of many of our joints. For example, our vertebral column has 33 small vertebrae, all of which can move a little. The result is that in gymnastics we can bend our back in many different ways, from a forward somersault to a backward walkover. The joints of our upper body allow us to serve in tennis and those of the lower body enable us to high-jump.

In contrast to these powerful movements, the joints in our hands and wrist enable us to spin a ball in cricket, throw a dart and aim an arrow. We are able to adjust our body position constantly in sport and our everyday life by using our muscles and joints together.

activity

Joint observation

Roll up the sleeve of your right arm. Bend your elbow to bring your arm across your chest.

Look at the back of your hand and your forearm near the elbow as you wiggle your fingers. What's going on? See your muscles create movement via some very long tendons. Now move your thumb around and note the muscles creating this movement.

KEYWORDS

Abduction: limb movement away from the middle line of the body

Adduction: limb movement towards the middle line of the body

Cartilage: a dense, elastic, connective tissue which cushions and connects many bones in the skeleton

Extension: straightening the limbs at a joint

Flexion: bending the limbs at a joint

Joint: a place where two or more bones meet

Ligament: a band of tough fibrous tissue which binds bones together at joints

Rotation: a circular movement in which part of the body turns whilst the rest remains still.

Synovial joint: joint containing synovial fluid that allows a wide range of movement.

Tendon: strong cords of fibrous tissue which fix muscles to bone.

Key to Exam Success

For your GCSE you should be able to:

- define the term 'joint' and understand its importance in exercise and sport
- understand the structure of a synovial joint
- recognise ball and socket, hinge and pivot joints and know their value in performance
- describe cartilage and its functions
- understand the importance of joint flexibility in sport and everyday life
- describe the different terms used to explain movement
- understand the importance of tendons and ligaments in movement
- explain how efficient joints with increased flexibility can improve sporting performance.

" KEY THOUGHT "

'Movement is a joint exercise with muscles.'

What are the different types of joint?

A joint is 'a place where two or more bones meet'. (Edexcel.)

The function of joints is to hold our bones together and to allow us to move our limbs and body.

Joints can be divided into three main groups, based on the amount of movement they allow:

- immovable (fibrous) joints

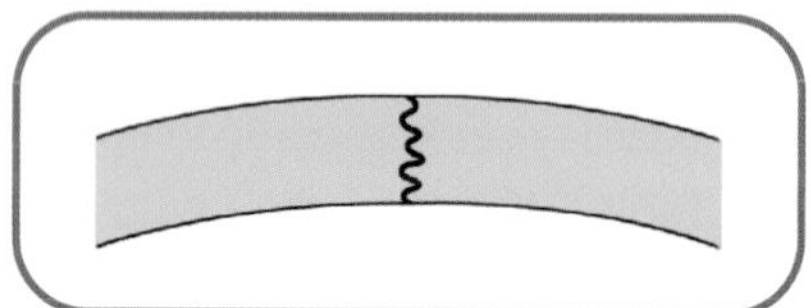

- slightly moveable (cartilaginous) joints

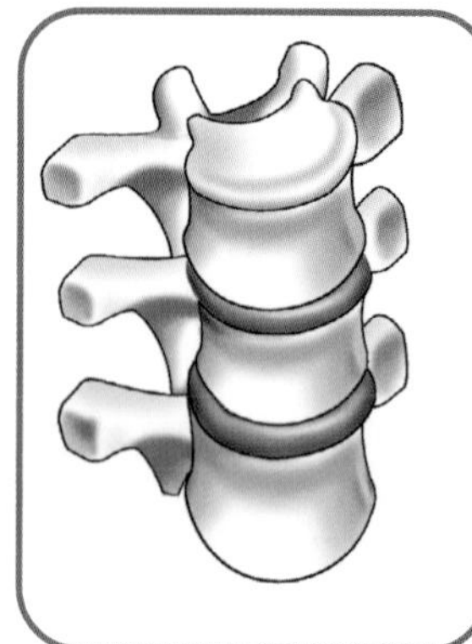

- freely moveable (synovial) joints.

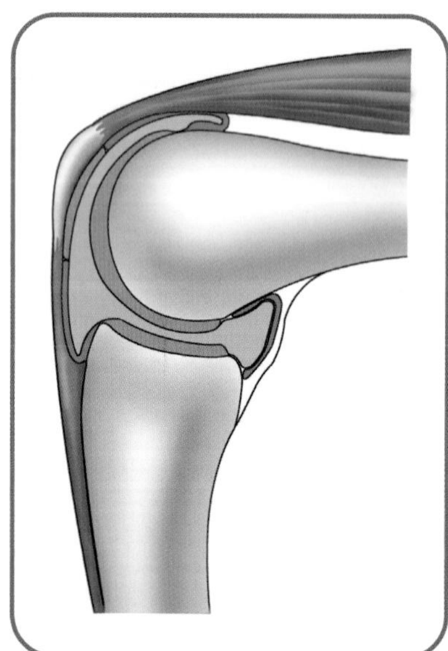

Immovable (fibrous) joints

These are fixed joints with no movement possible between the bones. They have no significance in sport.

Slightly moveable (cartilaginous) joints

- The bones have a pad of cartilage between them.
- Movement is possible between the bones.
- Examples are found in the joints between the ribs and sternum and between the vertebrae.

Note: the knee joint is a synovial joint although there are pads of cartilage within the joint capsule.

What is cartilage?

Cartilage is a tough but flexible tissue found on the ends of bones and as a pad between bones.

Hyaline cartilage is found on the ends of our bones and around the joint socket in all our synovial joints. It is a hard, slippery layer which protects the bones from wear and tear, greatly reducing the friction between the bones during movement. Older people may suffer from osteoarthritis. This causes damage to the layer of hyaline cartilage resulting in severe pain whenever the bones are moved. Modern surgery has made it possible for the heads of the damaged bones to be replaced and the lining of the joint socket to be renewed. This allows the joint to work smoothly again in, for example, the hip joint.

In the vertebral column and knee, the pads of tough cartilage act as shock absorbers, forming a gristly cushion which can be squashed. In the vertebral column the discs of cartilage lie between each pair of vertebrae. Severe back pain is caused if these discs are damaged or slip out of place.

Many sportspeople suffer damage to the cartilage in the knee, especially in games like football. Since the cartilage does not have a blood supply, it will not repair itself easily. If the cartilage is torn it may be removed as this does not badly affect joint flexibility. However, the muscles around the knee will need strengthening to keep the joint stable.

What are ligaments?

Ligaments are bands of tough fibrous tissue which bind our bones together at joints. Some ligaments form a capsule which surrounds the joint and contains synovial fluid. Other ligaments remain outside the capsule, but also hold the joint stable. The ligaments make joints more stable by preventing excessive movement. They also limit the direction of movement. In general, the more ligaments around a joint, the stronger the joint will be.

If a lot of force is put on a ligament, it will stretch, although it can be damaged quite easily. In games like tennis, football and hockey, excessive twisting movements can cause damage to ligaments at the knee and ankle. The hip is a more stable joint because of the strength of the ligaments around it and therefore it is damaged less often. When ligaments are stretched or torn, this is known as a **sprain** (see page 172). The blood supply to ligaments is poor and so sprains heal slowly.

What are tendons?

Tendons are very strong cords of fibrous tissue which attach muscle to bone. They allow us to apply the power of the contracting muscles to the bones at the joint. They are made of tough fibres and are quite small so they can pass over joints and rough bone where the muscle itself would be damaged.

Tendons only stretch a little – much less than ligaments. Although they can be torn or bruised in contact sports, tendons are strong and the muscle itself is more likely to be damaged than the tendon.

Tendons can also be damaged by fierce muscle contraction, as seen sometimes in squash, resulting in damage to the Achilles tendon in the lower leg. Adolescents who overtrain through excessive running on hard surfaces may suffer damage to the tendon below the kneecap, called Osgood-Schlatter's disease.

Both tendons and ligaments respond to the stresses placed upon them. Regular exercise will improve the strength and flexibility of tendons and ligaments and make them less liable to injury during sporting action.

What are freely moveable (synovial) joints?

Synovial joints are complex joints. The amount of movement they allow depends first of all on the shape of the bones within the joint. Movement will also depend on the arrangement of the muscles and their tendons around the joint, together with any ligaments which bind the bones together. Synovial joints are found throughout the body including at the knee, hip and shoulder. They usually permit a wide variety of movement.

How are synovial joints constructed?

- **Hyaline cartilage** covers the head of the bones and the joint socket. It forms a hard, tough, slippery layer which protects bones and reduces friction in the joints.
- **Synovial membrane** forms a layer on the inside of the joint capsule and produces synovial fluid.
- **Synovial fluid** lubricates the joints and allows friction-free movement.
- A **joint capsule** made of fibrous tissue holds the bones together and protects the joint.

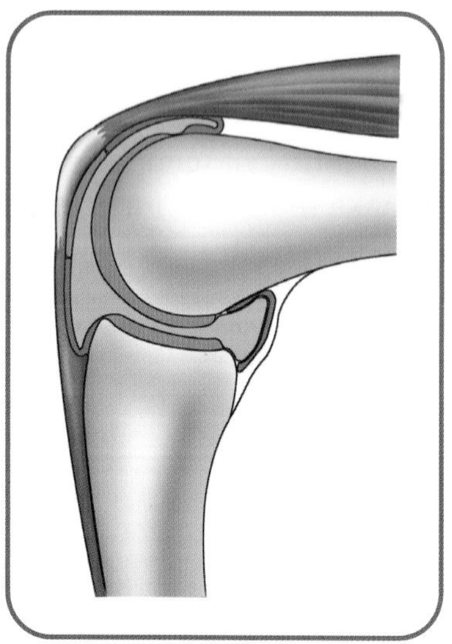

- **Ligaments** hold bones together. Made up of bands of tough fibrous tissue, the ligaments stretch to a limited amount and prevent dislocation.

What are the different types of synovial joint?

Synovial joints have different structures, depending on how they work. This means the shape of the bones varies, as does the arrangement of the ligaments.

There are six basic types of synovial joint, all with different structures. The three most important for sport are:

- ball and socket
- hinge
- pivot.

The other three types are saddle, condyloid and gliding joints.

Ball and socket joint

- Moves freely in all directions
- Ligaments are often used to keep the joint stable
- Examples: hip and shoulder.

Hinge joint

- Movement in one plane only
- Will open until it is straight
- Movement is limited because of the shape of the bones and the position of the ligaments.
- Examples: elbow and knee.

Pivot joint

- Only rotation is possible because the joint has a 'ring on peg' structure
- Example: between the atlas and axis vertebrae in the neck.

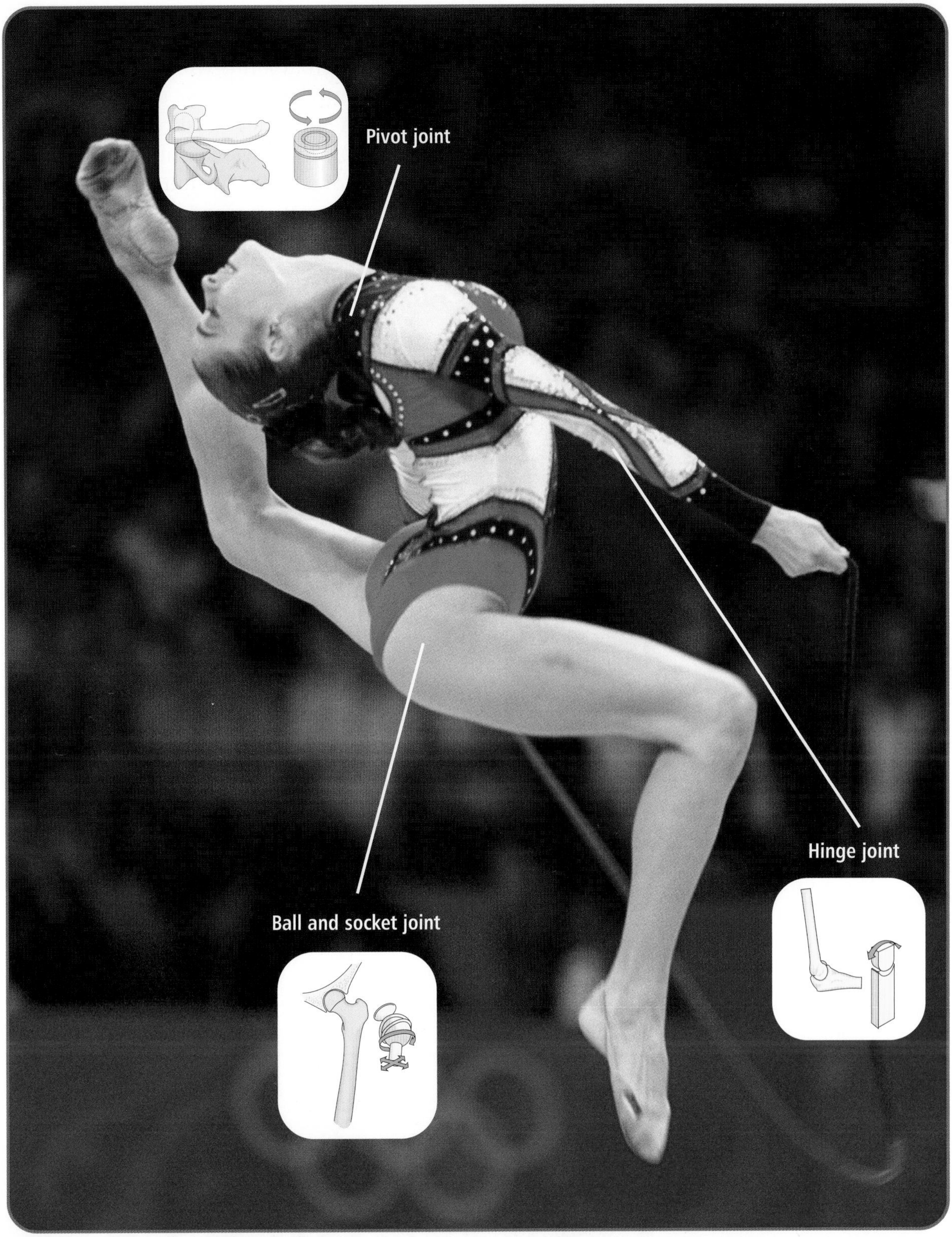

Pivot joint

Hinge joint

Ball and socket joint

Injuries to our joints

Our joints can be damaged by impact or by wear and tear.

Impact injuries

When two players tackle in football, or a netball player lands off balance, damage to the ankle joints is possible. This happens when the force of the impact pushes the bones beyond their normal range of flexibility. As a result the ligaments making up the joint capsule or those around the joint may be torn and/or bruised. When the joint capsule is severely damaged, dislocation of the joint may occur.

Wear and tear

Overuse or abnormal pressure on a joint may cause some of the hyaline cartilage inside the joint to be worn away. Racket players may suffer this damage in their shoulder joint over a long period of time.

Our joints and sport

Our different joints work smoothly together when we make skilled sporting movements. They must be capable of a full range of movement in order to help us perform well. The muscles, tendons and ligaments surrounding each joint must be strong enough to give stability to the joint.

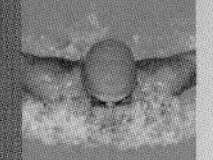

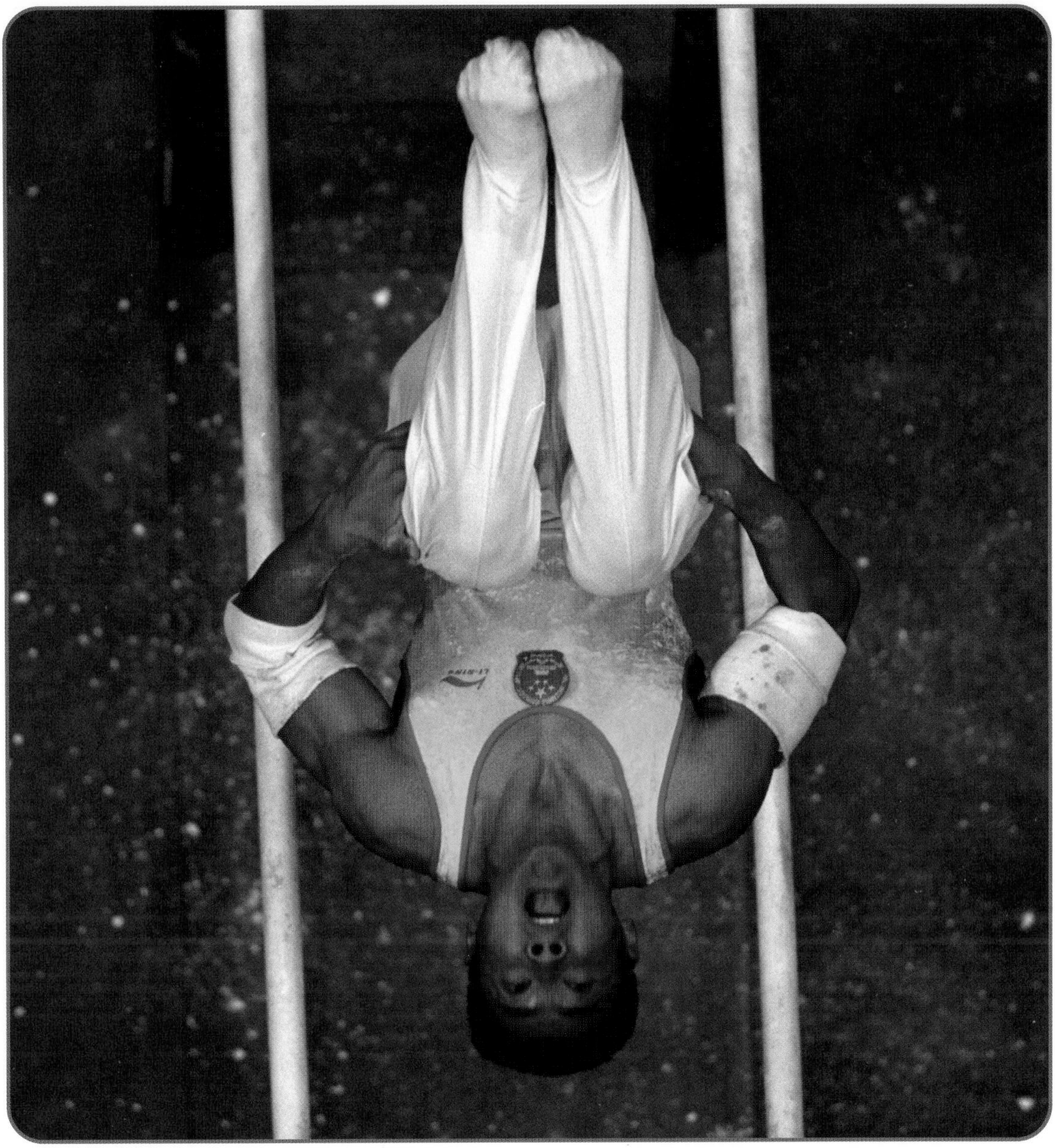

The demands of sport put severe stress on our joints. We must ensure that our joints are in good condition to reduce the chance of injury and to give us the opportunity to improve our sporting performance. We can do this by:

- eating a healthy diet to ensure strong bones, ligaments, tendons and cartilage
- strengthening the muscles around the joints to provide stability
- exercising regularly to prepare our joints for additional strain
- using flexibility exercises to increase the range of movement at the joints
- warming up thoroughly before each activity and warming down afterwards
- training to meet the needs of our particular sport.

activity

Joints and muscles in action

Work with a partner and attempt each of these four movements. Each movement is in two phases, preparation and the action itself:

1. kicking a stationary ball
2. shooting for goal in netball
3. playing a pull shot in cricket
4. performing a straddle jump.

Observe each other as you perform the movements (you might wish to use a video camera). Analyse the movement then copy and complete the table.

Phase	Description	Joint(s) used	Movement
Kicking a stationary ball: preparation	Drawing the leg back	Hip Knee	Extension Flexion
Kicking a stationary ball: action	Kicking the ball	Knee Hip Ankle	
Shooting for goal in netball: preparation			
Shooting for goal in netball: action			
Playing a pull shot in cricket: preparation			
Playing a pull shot in cricket: action			
Performing a straddle jump; preparation			
Performing a straddle jump: action			

What are the main joints we use in sport?

When we play sport we use all the joints of our body at some time. The most important joints for our sporting performance are:

Shoulder joint

- ball and socket joint
- formed by scapula and humerus
- most freely moveable joint in the body
- allows flexion, extension, abduction, adduction, rotation

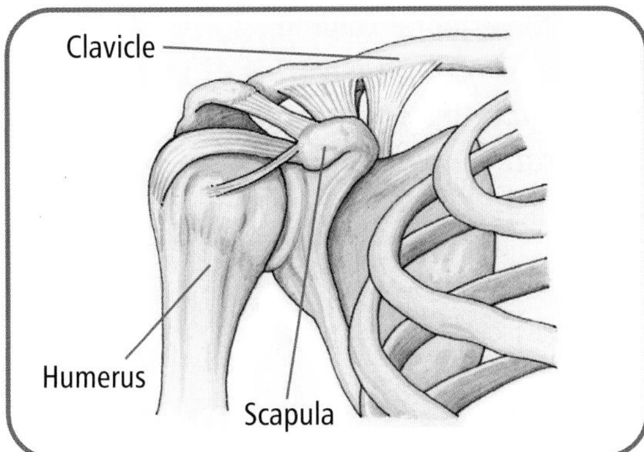

- few reinforcing ligaments
- relatively unstable.

Hip joint

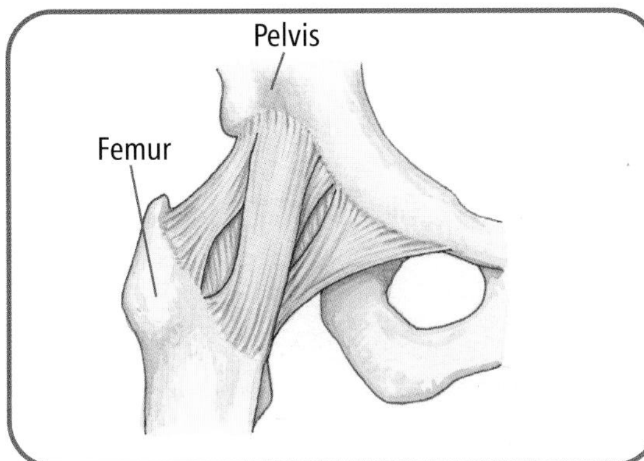

- ball and socket joint
- formed by femur and pelvic girdle
- freely moveable joint
- allows flexion, extension, abduction, adduction, rotation
- adapted for weight-bearing
- movements limited by strong ligaments and deep socket
- very stable.

Knee joint

- hinge joint, but complex
- formed by tibia, femur and patella

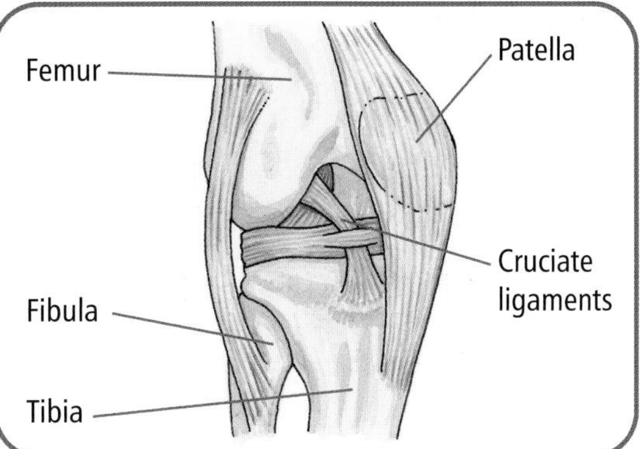

- allows extension, flexion and some rotation
- many ligaments around joint aid stability
- cruciate ligaments within joint to keep bones together
- cartilages for shock absorption
- stability also depends on muscles around knee.

Elbow joint

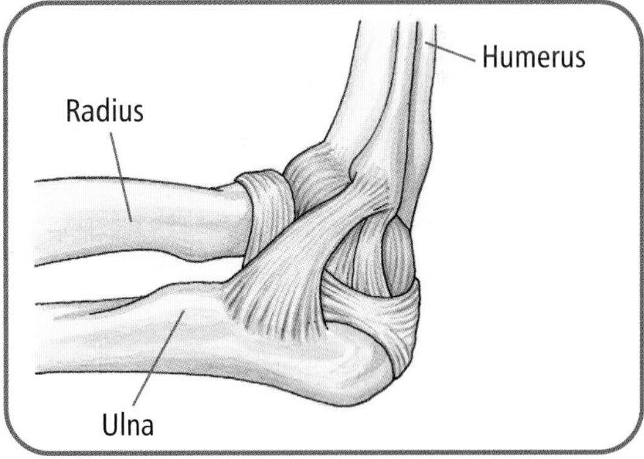

- main joint consists of hinge between ulna and humerus; allows flexion and extension
- secondary joint consists of pivot between ulna and radius; allows rotation
- stable.

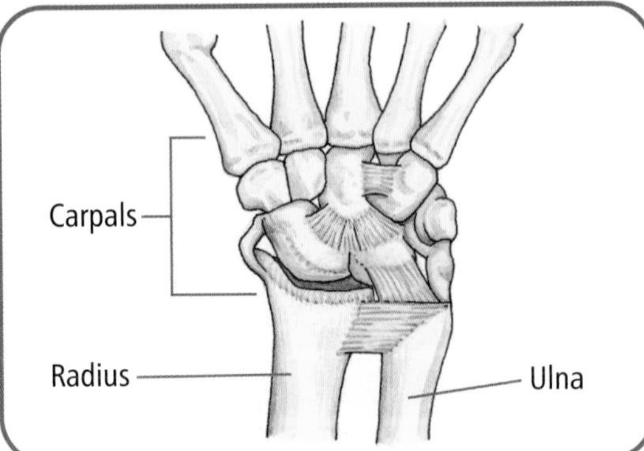

Wrist joint

- complex joint, but mainly hinge
- allows flexion, extension, abduction, adduction and other specialised movements.

Ankle joint

- complex joint, but mainly hinge
- allows flexion, extension and other specialised movements.

Finger joint

- allows flexion, extension, abduction, adduction.

Vertebral column

- complex series of joints which work together to provide a wide range of movement.

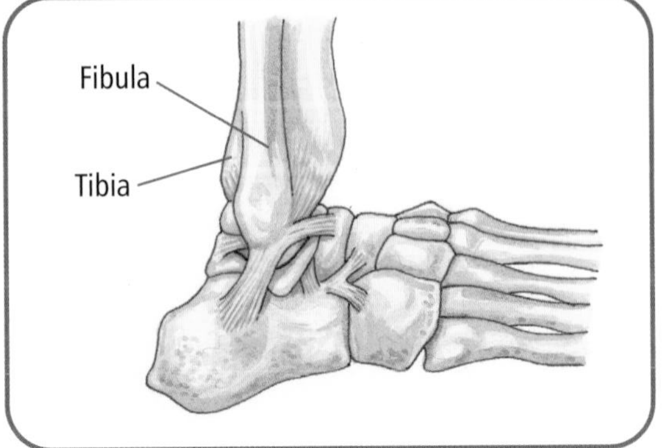

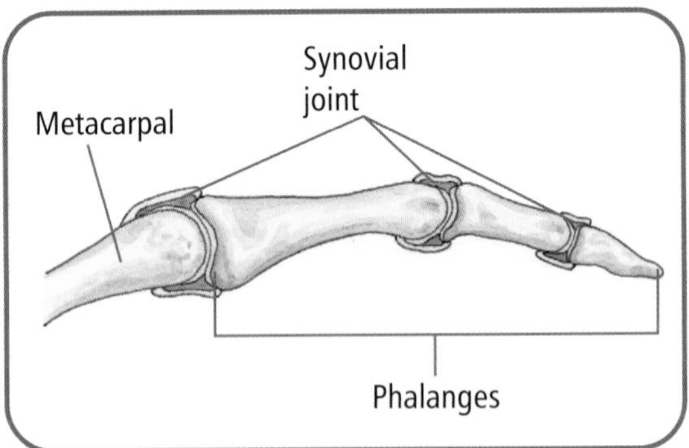

activity

Movements at joints

Look at the pictures of movement on page 247. List the joints used and the type of movement shown, then try to think of examples of other sporting situations where the same, or a similar, action might be performed. Show your results in a table like the one below.

Photo	Joint(s) used	Movement	Further example(s)
A			
B			
C			
D			
E			

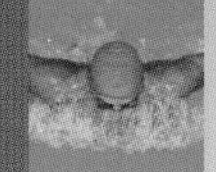

How does our body move?

When we play sport we move our limbs in many different directions. We use special words to describe these movements: extension, flexion, abduction, adduction and rotation.

Abduction: our limbs are moved away from a line down the middle of our body

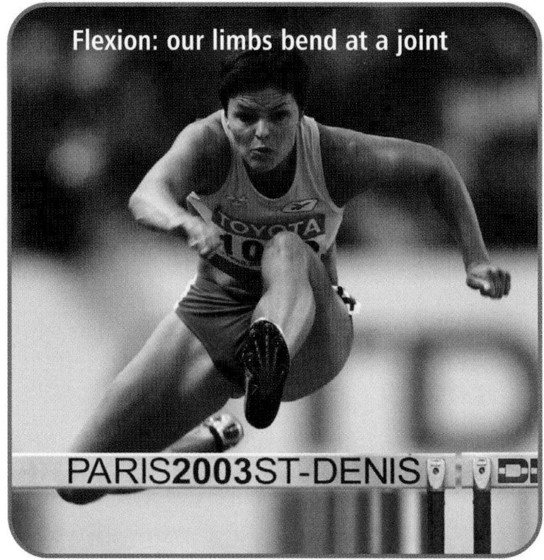

Flexion: our limbs bend at a joint

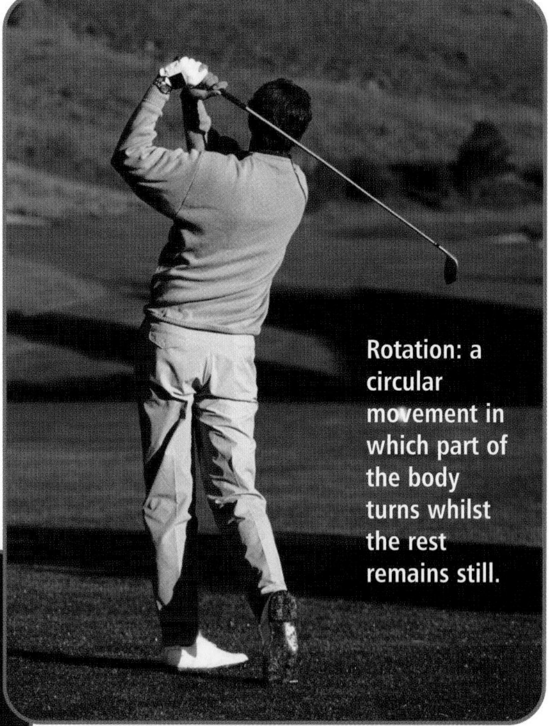
Rotation: a circular movement in which part of the body turns whilst the rest remains still.

Extension: our limbs straighten at a joint

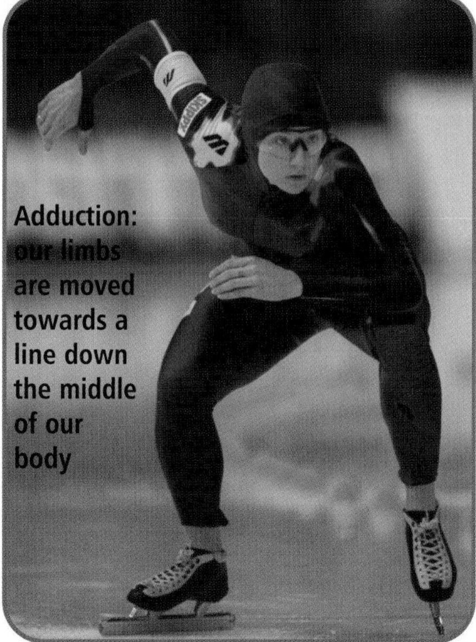
Adduction: our limbs are moved towards a line down the middle of our body

QUESTIONS

12 Joints, tendons and ligaments

Answer questions 1–4 by choosing statements a, b, c or d. One mark for each question.

1 An example of a hinge joint is found in the:

- **a** hip
- **b** knee
- **c** shoulder
- **d** ankle.

2 The movement seen between the atlas and axis vertebrae is called:

- **a** flexion
- **b** extension
- **c** adduction
- **d** rotation.

3 Muscles are attached to bones by:

- **a** tendons
- **b** ligaments
- **c** cartilage
- **d** synovial membrane.

4 The cartilage found between the vertebrae:

- **a** reinforces the joint
- **b** reduces friction
- **c** acts as a shock absorber
- **d** protects the bones.

5 Stuart is a good hurdler. When clearing the hurdle his leading leg is straight.

a Name the type of synovial joint found at the:
- i knee
- ii hip.

(2 marks)

b Name the movement at the hip which:
- i straightens his leg
- ii will return his leg to the ground.

(2 marks)

c When his leg lands, what in his knee will absorb the shock?

(1 mark)

d Explain the importance of each of the following in a synovial joint:
- i synovial membrane
- ii synovial fluid
- iii hyaline cartilage
- iv joint capsule
- v ligaments.

(5 marks)

6 Serena has been attending karate lessons for a year. She does a lot of flexibility exercises.

a Explain why these exercises are important for karate.

(2 marks)

b Describe the movement at her hip joint when she performs the following:

i a sideways kick

(1 mark)

ii her leg returns to a standing position

(1 mark)

iii a forward kick

(1 mark)

iv her leg returns to a standing position.

(1 mark)

QUESTIONS

c What type of synovial joint is found at:

i the shoulder

(1 mark)

ii the elbow

(1 mark)

d Explain why the hip joint is more stable than the shoulder joint.

(2 marks)

e Explain the part played by tendons in Serena's arm when she makes a punch.

(2 marks)

f The knee joint is very important in karate kicks.

i Name the two long bones which form the knee joint.

(2 marks)

ii Name the two movements possible at the hip joint, but not at the knee joint.

(2 marks)

iii What is the function of the cruciate ligaments?

(1 mark)

iv What can be done to improve the stability of the knee joint?

(1 mark)

v Suggest two ways in which Serena can ensure all her joints are kept in good condition.

(2 marks)

(Total 34 marks)

13 Muscles and muscle action

Nearly all the movements of our body are caused by the contraction of our muscles. The speed and power which enables us to jump out of the way of danger also enables us to do well in contact sport. The muscles which control our vision in everyday life also allow us to follow the ball in racket sport. Our heart muscle beats constantly throughout our life to enable us to work, rest and play. Silent muscles within us meet the needs of our body for both energy and nutrients. Above all, our muscles have the special ability to change chemical energy into mechanical energy. This means that if we supply our muscles with food and oxygen they will produce movement. Without movement in sport, we can achieve nothing.

activity

Muscle analysis

Working with a partner, carry out the activities below while your partner identifies which major muscle groups are being used.

Examples of muscle groups include:

- upper back
- lower back
- upper arm
- lower arm
- chest
- shoulder
- stomach.

Begin by lying flat on your back. Then complete each action when instructed to do so by your partner.

Activity	Major muscle groups being used
Move to sit-up position	
Stand up	
Raise hands above head	
Raise one knee and hold for five seconds	
Complete one press-up	
From standing position, jump as high as possible	

KEYWORDS

Abduction: limb movement away from the middle line of the body

Adduction: limb movement towards the middle line of the body

Atrophy: loss of muscle mass due to physical inactivity

Core stability: balanced position in which the body's centre of gravity is over the base of support, ready for movement

Extension: straightening the limbs at a joint

Fast twitch muscle fibres: used in anaerobic activity to provide fast, powerful contractions for a short period

Flexion: bending the limbs at a joint

Hypertrophy: growth of muscles as a result of regular physical activity

Insertion: the end of the muscle which is attached to the bone which moves

Muscle tone: when voluntary muscles are in a state of very slight tension, ready and waiting to be used

Origin: the end of the muscle which is attached to the fixed bone

Posture: the way in which body parts are positioned in relation to one another

Slow twitch muscle fibres: used in aerobic activity to provide contractions over a long period of time

Tendon: strong fibrous tissue that joins muscle to bone.

Key to Exam Success

For your GCSE you should be able to:

- classify and know the importance of the three different types of muscle
- know the position and functions of the main skeletal muscles of the body
- understand why and how muscles work in pairs
- understand the importance for sport of fast and slow twitch muscle fibres
- describe posture and muscle tone
- understand how muscles change when exercised
- know the importance of muscles and muscle action for sport, fitness and training.

"KEY THOUGHT"

'Muscles are the machines of the body.'

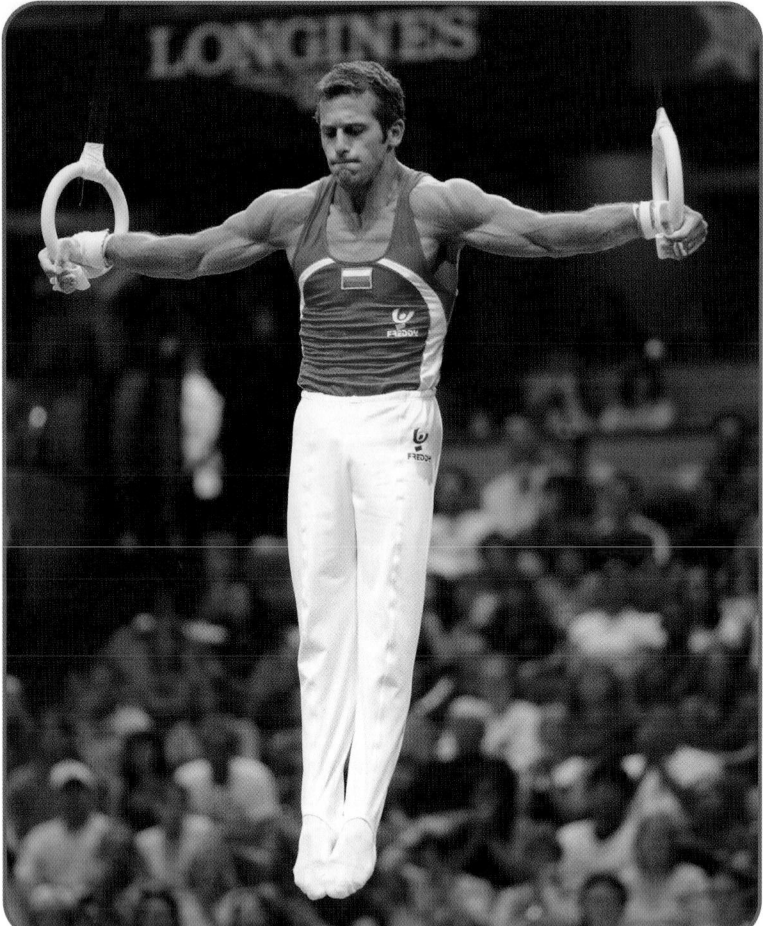

Our muscles in action

All the movements we make happen as a result of the shortening (contracting) and lengthening (extending) of the voluntary muscles which are found around our joints. Our muscles can only pull; they cannot push.

Our muscles:

- enable us to move our body parts
- give us our own individual shape
- protect and keep in place our abdominal organs
- stabilise our joints during movement
- enable us to maintain a good posture
- help in the circulation of our blood
- generate body heat when they contract.

There are over 600 voluntary muscles in the body – 150 in the head and neck. Skeletal muscle accounts for over 40% of our body mass.

Types of muscle

We can divide muscles into three main types, depending on the way they work:

Voluntary muscles

Our voluntary, or skeletal, muscles work as we instruct them. They are under our control. They make our bodies move. We use them for everyday sporting activities such as walking, running and jumping. We also use them for all the specialised movements of sport and training, ranging from somersaults to forward defensive strokes, from press-ups to golf swings. With regular training they will adapt and improve our sporting performance.

Involuntary muscles

Our involuntary, or smooth, muscles work automatically. They are not under our conscious control. They work our internal organs such as the stomach, gut, bladder and blood vessels. We rely on them to provide the nutrients we need for sport and training and to remove waste products from the body. The walls of the blood vessels contract to keep our blood flowing at all times.

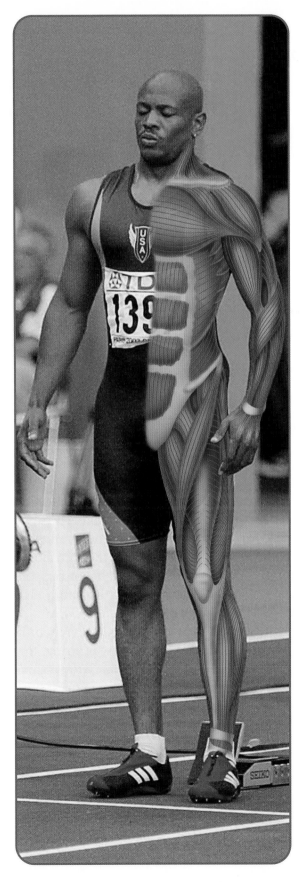

Cardiac muscle

Our cardiac, or heart, muscle is a very special type of involuntary muscle. It is found only in the walls of the heart. It contracts regularly, continuously and without tiring. It works automatically, but is under constant nervous and chemical control. The ability of the heart to adapt to the stresses of training enables us all to improve our cardiovascular fitness to the level required by our sport.

What are muscle fibres?

Our muscles are made up of many tiny thread-like fibres packed together in bundles. These fibres contract and make the muscle shorter. In voluntary muscle the fibres come together at the ends of the muscles into a tough cord-like tendon. Each tendon is attached firmly to the bone. Voluntary muscles are usually long and thin. When they contract they become shorter and thicker.

We have two different types of fibres in our involuntary muscles: fast twitch and slow twitch.

Slow twitch muscle fibres:

- have a very good oxygen supply
- work for a long time without tiring
- are not as strong as fast twitch fibres
- take longer to contract
- are used in all types of exercise
- are used especially in aerobic activities which need cardiovascular fitness, such as long-distance running and cycling.

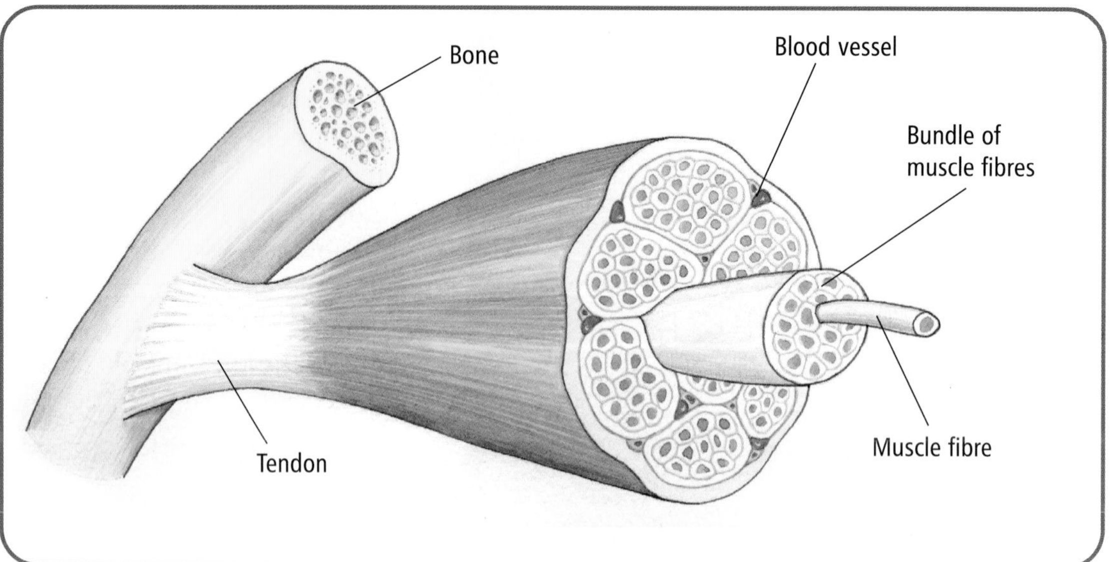

Fast twitch muscle fibres:

- do not have a good oxygen supply
- tire very quickly
- are stronger than slow twitch fibres
- contract very quickly
- are used when we need fast, powerful movements
- are used only in high-intensity exercise
- are used in anaerobic activities which need bursts of strength and power such as sprinting and jumping.

Our muscle fibres and sport

If we jog slowly, only a few of our slow twitch muscle fibres contract to move our legs. When we increase our speed we use more slow twitch fibres. As we run faster, our fast twitch fibres also start to contract to help out. More and more will start to work as we run even faster. At top speed, all of our fast and slow twitch muscle fibres will be working.

In many sports we need to use the different fibres at different times. In hockey, for example, we need to use our fast twitch fibres for quick sprints and our slow twitch fibres for jogging when not involved in the action.

Our muscles are usually an equal mixture of both fast and slow twitch fibres. The exact amount of each depends on what we inherit from our parents, and the mixture can vary widely. A person with more slow twitch fibres is likely to be better at sports needing cardiovascular endurance such as cycling, running and swimming. Someone with more fast twitch fibres is likely to be better at sprinting, throwing and jumping. For many team games we need both short bursts of activity and constant, less demanding activity. Our training programmes for games will therefore contain activities to develop both slow and fast twitch muscle fibres. We can train our muscle fibres to either contract more often (slow twitch) or more powerfully (fast twitch).

Our major muscles

Muscles of the upper body

Note: Movement terms are explained on pages 247 and 251.

Biceps

- Location: front of the upper arm
- Function: flexes the forearm at the elbow
- Examples: drawing a bow in archery, rowing
- Strengthened by: curls of various sorts.

Triceps

- Location: back of the upper arm
- Function: extends the forearm at the elbow; extends the arm at the shoulder
- Examples: smash in badminton, throwing the javelin, press-ups
- Strengthened by: press-ups, triceps curls above the head.

Deltoids

- Location: front and rear of the shoulder
- Function: moves the arm in all directions at the shoulder; adducts (raises) the arm
- Examples: bowling in cricket
- Strengthened by: bent-over rowing, bench presses.

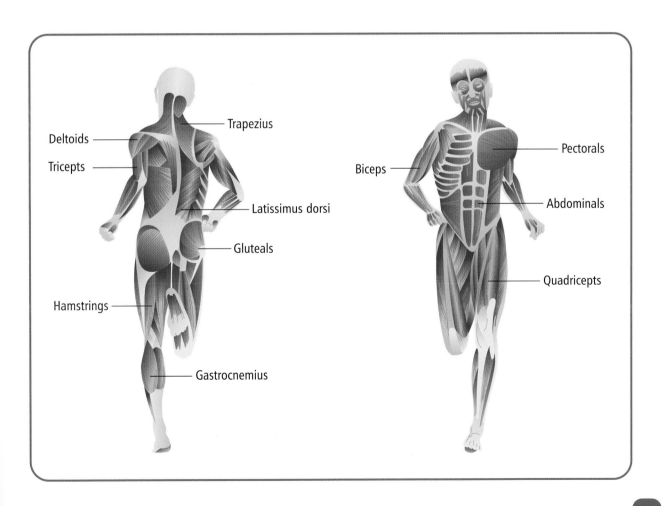

Trapezius

- Location: rear of the shoulders and neck
- Function: helps to raise and control the shoulder girdle; holds back the shoulders; moves head back and sideways
- Examples: holding the head up in a rugby scrum, head back to follow high ball, head back in 'Fosbury Flop'
- Strengthened by: upright rowing.

Latissimus dorsi

- Location: lower back
- Functions: adducts (raises) and extends the arm at the shoulder
- Examples: butterfly stroke, rowing, pulling on the javelin
- Strengthened by: pull-downs.

Abdominals

Four separate muscles.

- Location: front of the abdomen
- Function: rotate, raise and allow the trunk to bend side to side; strengthen the abdominal wall; help with breathing
- Examples: performing upward circles on the bar in gymnastics, pulling the body down in hurdling
- Strengthened by: sit-ups of various sorts.

Pectorals

Consist of pectoralis major and pectoralis minor.

- Location: front of the chest
- Function: adduct (raise) the arm and shoulder; used for deep breathing
- Examples: playing a forehand drive in tennis, putting the shot, front crawl
- Strengthened by: bench presses.

Muscles of the lower body

Hamstrings

Four separate muscles.

- Location: back of upper leg
- Function: extend the hip joint; flex the knee joint
- Examples: drawing the leg back before kicking a ball, jumping activities with knees bent before take-off
- Strengthened by: leg curls.

Quadriceps

Four separate muscles.

- Location: front of upper leg
- Function: flex the hip joint; extend the knee joint
- Examples: taking off in high jump, raising knee in running, kicking a ball
- Strengthened by: squats, leg extensions and leg presses.

Gluteals

Consist of gluteus maximus and two other muscles.

- Location: form the buttocks
- Function: abduct (move away from body) and extend the hip joint
- Examples: stepping up during rock climbing, sidestepping, pulling back leg before kicking a ball
- Strengthened by: squats and leg presses.

Gastrocnemius

- Location: back of the lower leg
- Function: flexes the knee joint and points the toes
- Examples: running, take-off in jumps
- Strengthened by: heel raises.

activity

ICT and muscle analysis

Using a digital camcorder, record a sporting movement – for example, a sprint start – and play it back in slow motion. Using the freeze-frame facility, try to identify exactly how the muscles work. Determine which muscles are the prime movers and the antagonists in the leg action, and which muscles are acting as extensors and which as flexors.

By moving the video on frame by frame, it should be possible to see how the roles of the muscles change. If a printer is available, print out each of the still frames and label the muscles and their actions.

How do our muscles work?

Our voluntary muscles work in two different ways, called **isotonic** and **isometric** muscular contraction.

- In **isotonic** contraction our muscles create movement as they contract. Most sporting actions are of this sort – for example, when our quadriceps pull our knee up as we run, or when our biceps lower us down from a pull-up.
- In **isometric** contraction our muscles stay at the same length when they contract and there is no movement. Our leg, back and shoulder muscles work in this way when we push, but do not move, in a rugby scrum. In many sporting movements the stabilising muscles work isometrically to hold parts of our body steady as other parts move.

How do our muscles work together?

Our voluntary muscles can pull by contracting, but they cannot push. If one muscle contracts across a joint to bring two bones together, another muscle is needed to pull the bones apart again. Therefore muscles always work in pairs. We need a large number of pairs of muscles to work together in different ways for even simple body movements. Our muscles take on different roles depending on the movement we are performing.

They can work as:

- **flexors**, contracting to bend our joints
- **extensors**, contracting to straighten our joints
- **prime movers** (or agonists), contracting in order to start a movement
- **antagonists**, relaxing to allow a movement to take place.

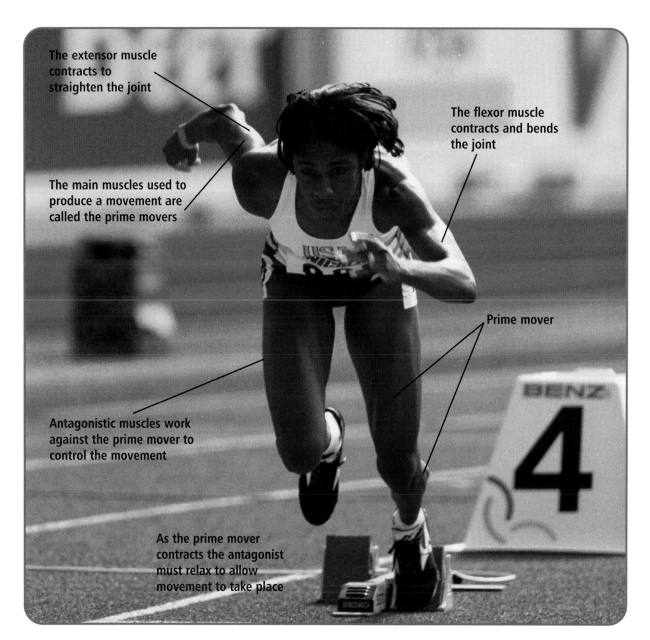

The extensor muscle contracts to straighten the joint

The flexor muscle contracts and bends the joint

The main muscles used to produce a movement are called the prime movers

Prime mover

Antagonistic muscles work against the prime mover to control the movement

As the prime mover contracts the antagonist must relax to allow movement to take place

What am I doing?

From the following description, try to work out what action is being performed.

The body begins in a standing position with the arms by the side. The deltoids contract to raise the arm so that it is parallel to the ground. The muscles of the fingers are flexed to grip an object. The biceps contract slowly and then the triceps contract powerfully and the fingers extend as the object is released.

Write your own movement description and then see if your partner can work out what action is being performed. Be prepared to demonstrate some or all of the action if necessary. You may need to refine your description following discussion.

How are our muscles attached to our bones?

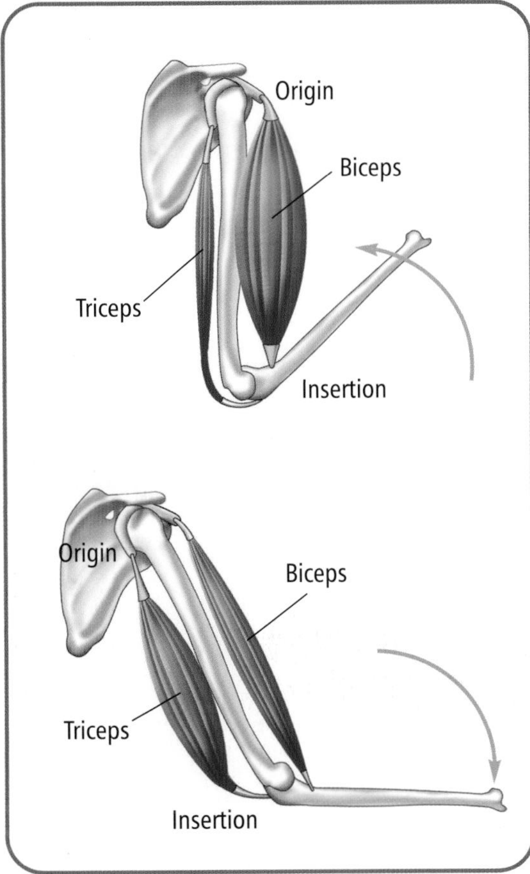

Our voluntary muscles are usually attached to two or more different bones. The muscle fibres end in a strong flexible cord called a **tendon**. The tendon is fixed deeply into the bone and is very strongly attached. Tendons vary in shape and size. Some of our muscles are divided into more than one part. They may end in two or more different tendons, which may be fixed to different bones.

When our muscles make the bones around a joint move, usually one bone stays fixed and the other moves. The end of the muscle that is attached to the fixed bone is called the **origin**. The other end of the muscle is called the **insertion** and is attached to the bone which moves. As the muscle contracts the insertion moves towards the origin.

How do our muscles work in pairs?

Our voluntary muscles are arranged in pairs around our joints to enable us to move. When a prime mover muscle contracts, the antagonist muscle must relax to allow a movement to take place. However, the antagonist muscle will keep some fibres contracting. This is to stop our prime mover moving the joint so hard that the antagonists are damaged. Sometimes this system fails, for example, when sprinters are running flat out. In the upper legs when the knee is raised, the quadriceps are the prime movers and the hamstrings are the antagonists. Sprinters may tear their hamstrings and quickly come to a painful stop.

In isometric muscle action, both of the muscles of the pair at a joint contract at the same time and no movement is seen.

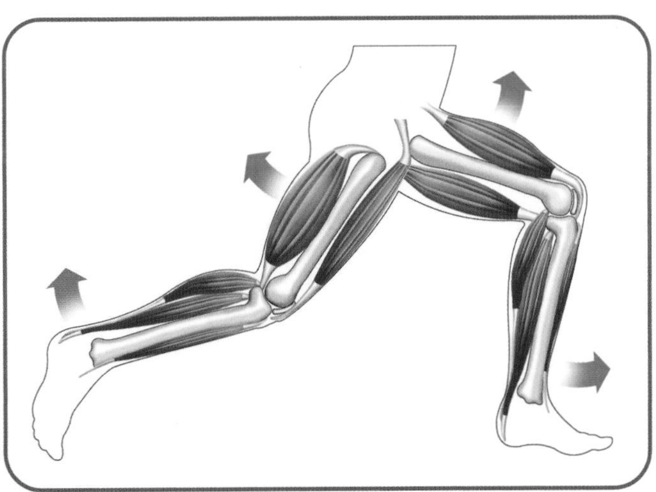

Muscle tone

Muscle tone is produced when voluntary muscles are 'in a state of very slight tension, ready and waiting to be used'. (Edexcel.)

The way our prime movers and antagonists work against each other also gives us muscle tone. At any given time, some muscle fibres will be contracted whilst others are relaxed. This is true even when we are not moving. These contractions tighten the muscles a little, but are not strong enough to cause movement. Different fibres contract at different times in order to prevent tiredness setting in. This continuous slight contraction of our voluntary muscles is very important for good posture and keeps the body ready for instant action. Exercise improves muscle tone.

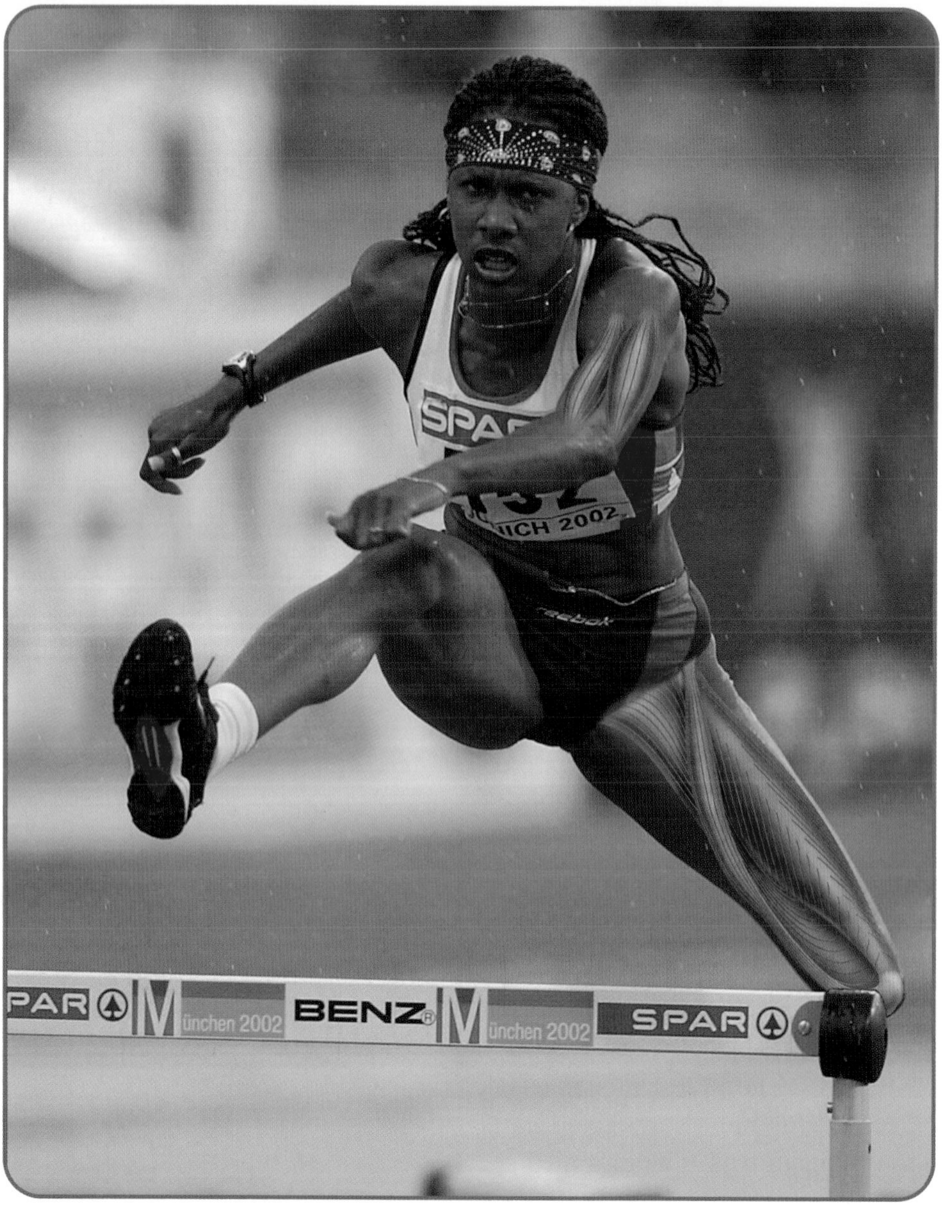

Posture

Our bodies are unstable when we are upright. This is because we have a high centre of gravity and a small base of support.

If we have good posture, we can keep our bodies upright easily by keeping our centre of gravity over our base of support. Most of the weight of the body will be supported by the bones and we will need only a little help from the voluntary muscles to hold us upright. Good muscle tone, particularly in the lower back, leg and abdominal muscles, will help posture.

Bad posture

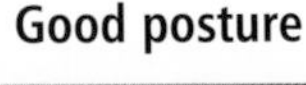

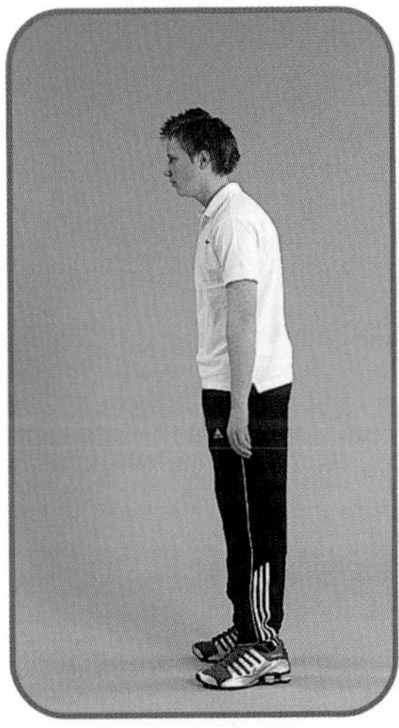

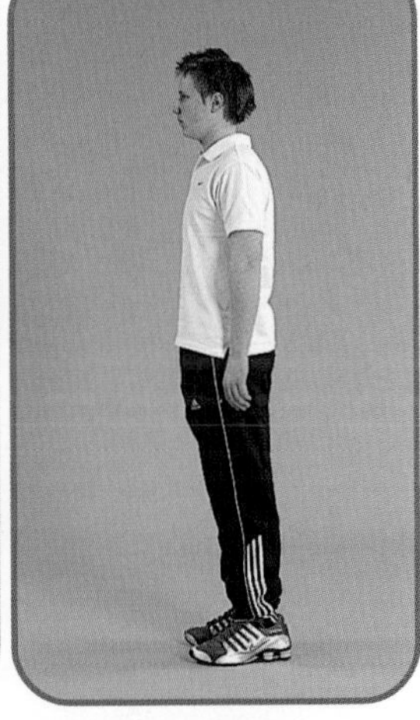

Good posture reduces the strain on our muscles, tendons and ligaments. It allows our body systems to work more easily and makes us less tired. It also plays an important role in creating a positive body shape and self-image and helps us to feel better about ourselves.

When we slouch, the upper back muscles must contract to move the body to the correct posture. If we make a habit of this, the muscles gradually adapt to that position. Poor posture may then become permanent.

How can we have good posture when standing and walking?

- Stand with head up.
- Stretch the back upward.
- Keep shoulders straight and chest high and open.
- Balance weight evenly on both feet.
- Relax the knees.
- Wear sensible shoes.

How can we have good posture when sitting?

- Choose chairs that support the small of the back.
- Sit back in the chair to support the lower back.
- Keep your feet flat on the floor in front of you.
- Try to have your knees higher than your hips.
- Check that working surfaces are at the correct height.
- Have a break every 20 minutes to gently exercise arms and shoulders.

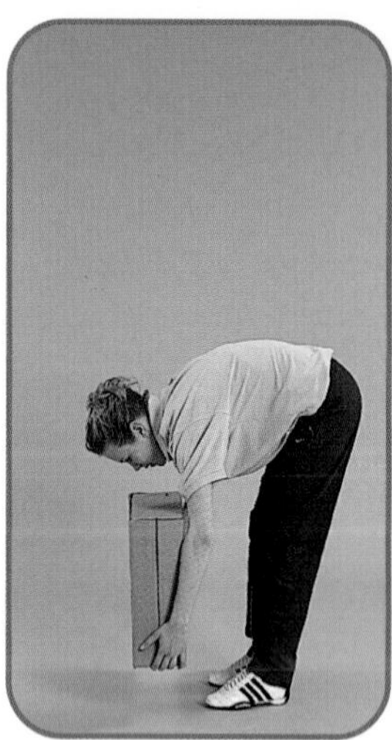

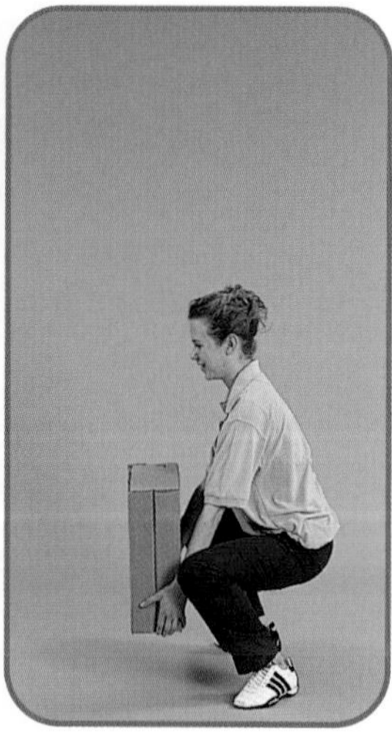

How can we have good posture when lifting?

- Never bend forward without bending the knees.
- Keep your back flat and straight.
- Try to avoid lifting anything above the level of the elbows.
- Keep objects as close to the body as possible.
- Extend legs in order to lift objects.
- Keep head up and eyes looking forward.

Posture in sport

When we play sport we use a wide variety of body positions. We must take up the right body position for the situation we find ourselves in our sport.

To maintain good posture, we need to consider our:

- **starting position** – for example, in movements in golf, discus and fencing (see below)
- **position during the activity**. When performing the movement or action, we must maintain our **core stability**. This means that we are in a comfortable, balanced position and are ready to perform the next sporting movement with power and control. Our centre of gravity is over our base of support. Muscle tone is essential for core stability.

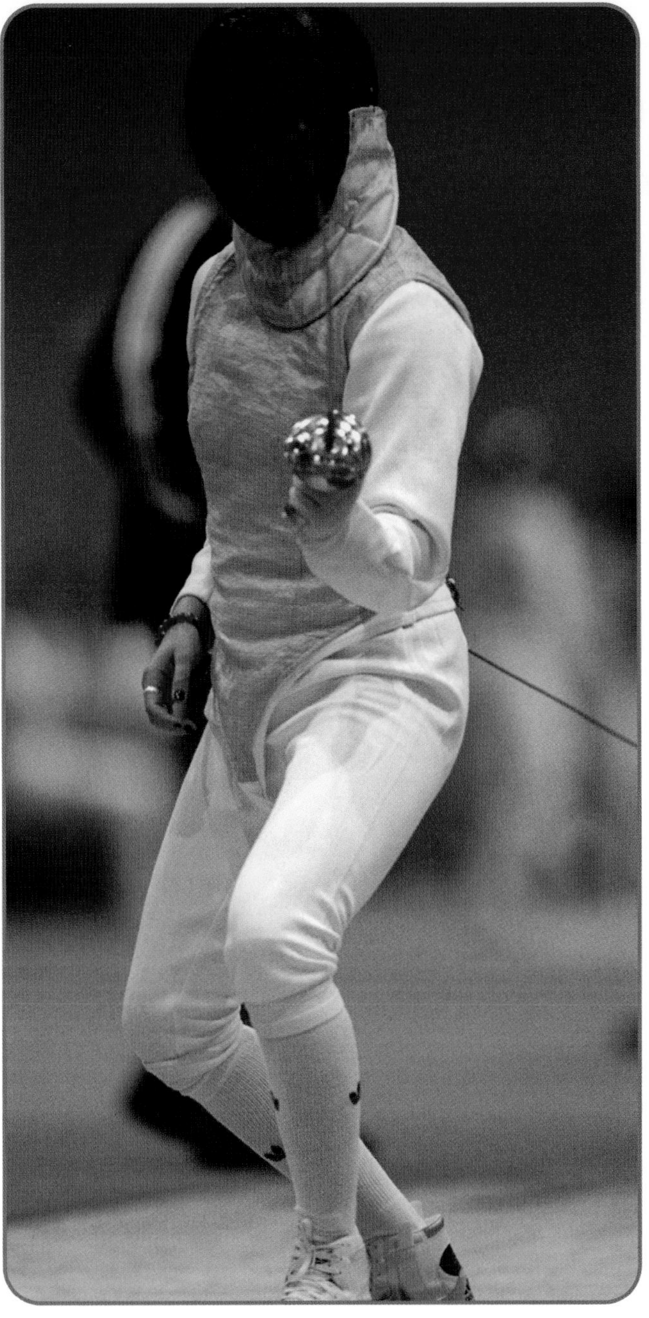

Core stability is essential for all sports. Some sports require a particular posture throughout the activity – for example, when we ski or ride a horse. However, we will still need to adjust our posture to deal with different situations, such as a slalom ski course or jumping fences on horseback.

In sports requiring a great deal of movement and unpredictability, core stability is essential in order to react quickly. For example, in football and netball we need to respond constantly to the position of the ball and other players.

We often take up a special position when preparing to start our sport. For example, for golf we need to stand in a particular way to swing through and hit the ball well. When preparing to putt, we need to position ourselves facing away from the direction of the putt. In fencing, we need to be able to move backwards and forwards very quickly in a sideways-on position.

Muscle training and development

Our voluntary muscles have the ability to adapt in order to cope with the activities for which they are used. If we walk to school everyday, our leg muscles will adapt to this exercise and we will not find it difficult. If we move house and have an extra two kilometres to walk to and from school, at first we may find it tiring. However, after a few weeks our leg muscles will have learned to cope with the additional distance and we will find the walk easy again. This is exactly what happens when we train for sport. We put our muscles under an increased stress and they adapt to the new workload.

We all need a basic amount of muscular strength and cardiovascular fitness to cope with the demands of everyday life. Lifting and carrying involves strength, while walking and moving around requires stamina. As we get older it is important to maintain our fitness for life. Regular weight-bearing exercise can help prevent the weakening of bones and gentle, regular endurance exercise can help maintain cardiovascular fitness.

Muscle hypertrophy and atrophy

Our voluntary muscles become stronger the more they are exercised. If we train and exercise regularly over a long period, we will change our muscles. However, we must always remember that these changes are not permanent. The principle of **reversibility** applies (see page 85), which means that if we stop exercising, our muscles will return to their original state. 'If we don't use it, we lose it'!

Our muscles increase in size, strength and endurance when we follow a regular strength-training programme. This is called muscle **hypertrophy**. When we do not use our muscles regularly, they get smaller and weaker. We call this muscle **atrophy**. This loss of size and strength often happens when we are recovering from an injury. While waiting for a particular injury to heal, we should try to exercise the rest of the body as much as possible. Many joint injuries and weaknesses can be overcome by strengthening the muscles around the joints.

Our muscles adapt very well to an increased workload. If heavy weights are

lifted, new muscle fibres develop and the muscle grows in size and also becomes stronger. This hypertrophy is known as muscle bulk. A sprinter needs large, strong muscles to provide the power required. Sprinters will also have more fast twitch muscle fibres than the average person. With training, these fibres will become able to use the stored energy in short bursts more efficiently.

In contrast, long-distance runners do not need muscle bulk. They use distance training to adapt their muscles to use energy more efficiently, in order to delay fatigue. In fact, carrying the extra weight of large muscles over a distance will be a disadvantage. Distance runners will have more slow twitch fibres than the average person. Through training these fibres will be able to use the stored energy in the muscle more efficiently and for longer.

Our muscles and sport

Sporting action requires muscular strength, muscular endurance, power, cardiovascular fitness and flexibility. Success in sport depends on our voluntary muscles working together to produce skilful movement. The particular muscles we use depend on the sporting activity. For example, in archery we use a limited number of muscles in the upper body to work very closely together for a short period of time. In contrast, for wrestling we use most of the muscles of the body vigorously for a longer period of time. In long-distance cycling we use most of the leg muscles continuously over a long period of time. Sometimes, we use different muscles at different phases of an activity. For example, when throwing the discus we use our leg muscles while turning in the circle and our upper body for the delivery.

Flexibility

Poor flexibility can hamper performance. This may be due to a technique which is not correct and which is therefore less efficient.

It is important that we are able to apply our muscular strength over a full range of joint movement. This allows more power to be developed and relies upon our joints being flexible. For example, in the javelin, we should be able to start the throwing movement from an almost straight arm position.

It is important to combine strength training with flexibility training, so that the muscle can contract more strongly over a full range of joint movement. Strong, flexible joints will also help to prevent muscle injury.

What happens to our muscular system as we exercise?

- There is an increased flow of blood to our working muscles.
- Our muscles take up more of the oxygen from our blood.
- Our muscles contract more often and more quickly.
- More of our muscle fibres contract.
- There is a rise in temperature in our muscles.
- Waste products such as carbon dioxide and lactic acid build up in our muscles. These may lead to tiredness and cramp (muscle fatigue).
- Our stores of muscle glucose are used up.
- Our ability to carry on will be affected.
- Overuse of muscles can lead to soreness and strains.

QUESTIONS

13 Muscles and muscle action

Answer questions 1–4 by choosing statement a, b, c or d. One mark for each question.

1 Muscles are attached to bone by:

- **a** cartilage
- **b** tendons
- **c** ligaments
- **d** synovial membrane.

2 The extensor muscle contracts to:

- **a** straighten the joint
- **b** flex the joint
- **c** rotate the joint
- **d** stabilise the joint.

3 The heart muscle is known as:

- **a** voluntary muscle
- **b** smooth muscle
- **c** skeletal muscle
- **d** cardiac muscle.

4 Increase in muscle size as a result of training is called:

- **a** hypertrophy
- **b** isometric
- **c** atrophy
- **d** isotonic.

5 Copy and complete the table by matching muscles, type of movement and examples from sport. *(10 marks)*

6 Jenny is a keen footballer. She wants to develop a more powerful shot.

a Name three muscles involved in kicking the ball. *(3 marks)*

b Suggest a weight training exercise to develop strength in each of these muscles. *(3 marks)*

c Name two muscles that work as an antagonistic pair when kicking a ball. *(2 marks)*

d **i** Name the type of muscle fibre used when kicking a ball. *(1 mark)*

ii Explain why this type of fibre is used when playing football. *(2 marks)*

e Name the type of muscle contraction taking place when kicking a ball:

i in the kicking leg *(1 mark)*

ii in the standing leg. *(1 mark)*

f Explain why footballers need core stability. *(2 marks)*

g Explain the difference between muscle hypertrophy and muscle atrophy. *(2 marks)*

(Total 31 marks)

Muscle	Type of movement	Example from sport
	Control shoulder girdle	
Biceps		
		Bowling in cricket
	Abduct and extend hip joint	
Gastrocnemius		

INDEX